FROM HITLER TO HOLLYWOOD

FROM HITLER TO HOLLYWOOD

WHEN THE EARTH FELL FROM ITS AXIS AND HOLLYWOOD MADE ITS GREATEST MOVIES

R. MARC KANTROWITZ

FONTHILL

First published in Great Britain in 2026 by
Fonthill
An imprint of
Pen & Sword Books Ltd
Yorkshire – Philadelphia
www.fonthill.media

ISBN 978-1-03614-756-3
ePUB 978-1-03614-758-7
ePDF 978-1-03614-760-0

A CIP catalogue record for this book is available from the British Library.

Typeset by Simon and Sons ITES Services Pvt. Ltd., Chennai, India.
Printed and bound in the UK by CPI Group (UK) Ltd, Croydon, CR0 4YY

MIX
Paper | Supporting responsible forestry
FSC www.fsc.org FSC® C013604

The Publisher's authorised representative in the EU for product safety is
Authorised Rep Compliance Ltd., Ground Floor, 71 Lower Baggot Street, Dublin D02 P593, Ireland.
www.arccompliance.com

For a complete list of Pen & Sword titles please contact

PEN & SWORD BOOKS LIMITED
47 Church Street, Barnsley, South Yorkshire, S70 2AS, England
E-mail: enquiries@pen-and-sword.co.uk
Website: www.pen-and-sword.co.uk
or
PEN AND SWORD BOOKS
1950 Lawrence Road, Havertown, PA 19083, USA
E-mail: uspen-and-sword@casematepublishers.com
Website: www.penandswordbooks.com

To Fred (1945–2024) and Sue

Acknowledgments

In any written project there are always people to thank who helped along the way, some in a large way and others by going out of their way to assist someone they don't even know. In that vein, I'd like to acknowledge the assistance of my wonderful wife Marianne Larson and son Matt Kantrowitz; Amal Bala; Alan Sutton, Jay Slater, Jasper Hadman, Karyn Burnham of Fonthill Media; Margaret Gamm, Director, Special Collections & Archives, University of Iowa Libraries; Matrice Young, Student Life Archivist, Special Collections & Archives, University of Iowa Libraries; Sarah Carrier, North Carolina Research and Instruction Librarian, UNC; Josh Schneider, University Archivist, Special Collections & University Archives, Stanford University; Daryl Faulkner, Account Director, Heritage Werks, Inc., Specialists in Archival Services; Hamilton Meserve, the son of Margaret Hamilton; the folks at the Harbor Theater in Maine; Judith Monachina; R. Michael Cassidy; Frank Mandosa; Kathleen "Windie" Marcaccio; Jeffrey Robbins; Jan Kardys and Barbara Ellis of the Black Hawk Literary Agency; Alex Mena and Soraya Sadeghi. If I have somehow mistakenly omitted anyone, my apologies.

Contents

PROLOGUE

A Year Like No Other

In accepting the 1939 Heisman trophy, awarded to that year's most outstanding college football player, Iowa's Nile Kinnick deviated from the typical sports acceptance speech. Rather than uttering the common themes of sports and hard work, teammates and coaches, he went further, which came as no surprise to those who knew him as class president and member of both Phi Betta Kappa and the national scholastic honor society.

> If you will permit me, I'd like to make a comment which in my mind is indicative, perhaps, of the greater significance of football, and sports emphasis in general in this country, and that is, I thank God I was warring on the gridirons of the Midwest, and not on the battlefields of Europe. I can speak confidently and positively that the players of this country would much more, much rather struggle and fight to win the Heisman award, than the Croix de Guerre.

He was killed on June 2, 1943. His school's football stadium is named for him.

Tom Harmon, from the University of Michigan, came in second that year in the Heisman vote. Also bright, during World War II he flew bombing missions. Two months before Kinnick met his fate, Harmon's plane was shot down. Unlike Nile, he survived the fiery crash. Six months later he was shot down a second time fighting in the Far East. In enemy territory, he was rescued by some friendly locals. He survived the war, played in the NFL, became a sports announcer, and married an actress and model. Their three children prospered and gained fame in their own right.

Two gifted athletes and intelligent men. One died at 24, the other survived, living a long, fruitful, and rewarding life.

As Kinnick and Harmon ran wild on the fields of Iowa and Michigan, America's #1 gangster Al Capone left prison, ravaged mentally and physically by untreated syphilis. As he was leaving both a life of crime as well as life itself, fellow gangster Benjamin Bugsy Siegal was murdering a rival.

Against this backdrop of brutality, far greater atrocities were being committed in Europe as Germany invaded Poland. France and Great Britain responded and World War II started, ultimately killing an unfathomable 60 million people, maybe even more. A few months earlier Bobby Riggs, the future defender of chauvinism in the Battle of the Sexes against Billie Jean King, was winning Wimbledon along with other world-class tennis tournaments. His female counterpart, Alice Marble, matched him success for success. When she left the tennis courts, she remained active, creating and writing about the Wonder Women of Sports, pushing for the desegregation of tennis, teaching youngsters her beloved sport (one of her students was Billie Jean King), singing, and designing clothes. Improbably, indeed shockingly, Marble entered the spy world during the war, travelling to Switzerland where she reconnected with a wealthy former lover, now a banker hiding Nazi treasures. While staying in his castle, she secretly photographed incriminating documents, left, was chased and shot in the back.

During a year of upheaval, "horror." and accomplishment, Hollywood churned out the greatest movies in its history, up to and including today: *The Wizard of Oz*, *Stagecoach*, *Mr. Smith Goes to Washington*, *Goodbye Mr. Chips*, *The Hound of the Baskervilles*, *The Adventures of Huckleberry Finn*, *Of Mice and Men*, *Wuthering Heights*, *Gunga Din*, and perhaps the greatest of them all, based on a book written by Peggy Marsh. The book, originally called *Bugles Rang True*, featured a heroine named Pansy O'Hara who lived in Fontenoy Hall. A few adjustments were made: Peggy reverted to her maiden name Margaret Mitchell; her starlet renamed Scarlett; the location now Tara; and the title, *Gone With the Wind*.

And during the whirlwind of 1939, the World's Fair opened in New York on April 30, 150 years to the day of President George Washington's inauguration in lower Manhattan. A revolutionary endeavor, it provided a glimpse into the future, including RCA's introduction of television to the masses. A multitude of exhibits provided something for everyone, including a scandalous display of barely dressed women that brought in thousands, including the Vice Squad.

There are a handful of years in the century that stick out: 1919, 1927, and 1968; 1939, however, may well head the list. So many momentous events in so many seemingly unrelated areas magically converged in that single historic, magical, and tumultuous year.

As with my prior book, *Old Whiskey and Young Women: American True Crime Tales of Murder, Sex and Scandal*, my goal is to humanize history, to focus on individuals and give them and the times in which they lived a vitality, bringing the readers behind the scenes, revealing life as it was lived; telling what is not known about events that are.

A time machine beckons, its destination: 1939.

R. Marc Kantrowitz

1

The Lead-Up to World War II

The year started out calmly, unlike the weather three months earlier when the "Hurricane of the Century" ravaged the northeast. At its conclusion, between 600 and 800 people had perished and nearly 60,000 houses were destroyed or damaged, resulting in over $300 million (approximately $6.6 billion today) in damages. At one point, winds howled over 160 mph. A local boardwalk was destroyed as waters cascaded through the streets of New York City, ripping 400 boats from their moorings. Nearly all of Nassau County on Long Island lost power. Rhode Island, Connecticut, and Massachusetts as well as Vermont, New Hampshire, and Maine also suffered significant damage. Actress Katherine Hepburn barely fled her Old Saybrook beach house, along with her mother, brother, and servants, as rising waters lifted their home from its foundation and washed it away. She lost nearly all of her belongings including the Oscar she'd won playing Eva Lovelace, a small-town girl with a dream of making it big in show business, in 1933's *Morning Glory*. The home was rebuilt the following year, and the Oscar was miraculously recovered.

As that great storm was destroying part of America, another far greater storm, that of war, was percolating in Europe. The genesis of that tsunami started immediately after the conclusion of the war to end all wars, World War I. There, old nations found themselves, in varying degrees, dissolved, reformed, or reconfigured, as evidenced by a new Austria and Czechoslovakia. Both bordered on Germany and had large numbers of Germans living within their borders. Indeed, Czechoslovakia consisted of nearly 3 million Germans, comprising nearly a quarter of that new nation's population. That substantial enclave came to be known as the Sudetenland.

World War I impoverished nations, including the victors. France and Britain, which in setting the peace terms in 1919's Treaty of Versailles, proposed harsh reparations to ensure that Germany disarm and never again pose a threat to the other nations of Europe. The leaders of France, primarily Prime Minister Georges Clemenceau, were especially intent in their demands. France had been devastated by the war, having lost over a half a million soldiers, which comprised an astonishing 25 percent of men between the ages of 18 and 30. Four hundred thousand civilians also lost their lives. Compounding the vast human loss, its industrialized regions, producing coal and iron ore, had been destroyed. France wanted protection and compensation.

To help accomplish its goals, Germany's industrial rich Rhineland was demilitarized. Further, Germany was not permitted to reunite with pro-German Austria, despite the wishes of both nations. It also ceded land and colonies. As for reparations, the bill came to billions of dollars, a sum so large that even at the time, many thought it excessive, impossible to achieve, and counterproductive.

England, which suffered far less physical destruction, was not as strident as France, opposing revenge and crippling reparations. Prime Minister Lloyd George also looked down the road, sensitive to the balance of power, and wishing to place a check on France's goals and aspirations. A friendly Germany might aid in that endeavor.

America, through President Woodrow Wilson, wanted "peace without victory" and a treaty that was fair and just, and not punitive. To ensure world peace, he proposed a League of Nations, to guide and monitor any hostile moves. As time would prove, he failed on all fronts.

Although compromises were made, France's position essentially held. Ultimately, however, the goals of the treaty were not met. Germany was not permanently militarily compromised. Meanwhile, as many predicted, its population saw the treaty as unjust, unfair, and vindictive.

As a result of losing the war, German Emperor Wilhelm II abdicated. After a period of rebellion and uncertainty, the Weimar Republic came into being, facing a host of serious problems, highlighted by its crushing debt. To pay the reparations, the government printed trillions of dollars, resulting in out-of-control inflation.

As economic hardships continued, in 1922 Germany informed France that it could not make its payments. France, after some reflection, concluded Germany's tale of woe insincere and invaded, along with Belgium, the Ruhr region of Germany, taking control of the area's valuable natural resources and industries. Rather than cooperate, the Ruhr workers refused to work. To lend support, the Weimar Government printed even more money, further weakening the economy and worsening inflation. So bad was the problem, that paper money became nearly worthless. A loaf of bread that cost

200 or so marks in January 1923, when the invasion occurred, soared to the unfathomable 200 billion marks eleven months later. Savings were lost, pensions nullified, crime ballooned, and food shortages abounded.

A year later, in 1924, the crisis abated due to the efforts of the Dawes Committee. Charles G. Dawes, who was born in Marietta, Ohio, in 1865, came from a distinguished family. One relative, Edward Doty, travelled on the *Mayflower* while another, William Dawes, rode with Paul Revere warning that "The British are coming." A successful businessman and banker, Charles also played and wrote music. In 1951, lyrics were added to a tune he wrote in 1912. The song, "It's All in the Game" rose to number one on the Billboard chart and has been recorded by numerous popular artists since, including Dinah Shore, Sammy Kaye, Louis Armstrong, Nat King Cole, Bing Crosby, Donny and Marie Osmond, Van Morrison, Merle Haggard, and Keith Jarrett.

Dawes headed a committee tasked with addressing the economic crisis battering Germany. Its work proved successful. The German bank was reorganized, reparation payments readjusted, and the Ruhr area returned. To help Germany pay its debt, American banks lent vast sums of money and a degree of normalcy returned. Soon the Germans were the leading steel producers in all of Europe.

With his notable work completed, Dawes received and shared the Nobel Peace Prize in 1925. He was also selected to run as vice president with Calvin Coolidge. The ticket won. Soon Dawes found himself at odds with President Coolidge, who vetoed a farm bill championed by his own vice president. When he left office in March of 1929, Dawes's view of politics was aptly summed up by his observation that "I should hate to think that the Senate was as tired of me at the beginning of my service as I am of the Senate at the end." The only vice president in our history to have a #1 hit song, Dawes was also only one of two song composers (the other being Bob Dylan) to win a Noble Prize.

When the 1929 stock market crash annihilated the American economy, Germany also suffered significant collateral damage. With American banks no longer able to provide money, the German economy nosedived. Businesses and industry imploded as unemployment skyrocketed. Six million workers found themselves out of work. As can be expected in such dire straits, social unrest resulted.

Germany after World War I was no stranger to strife. Shortly after the Weimar Government, led by its President Friedrich Ebert and his Social Democratic Party, came into power on November 9, 1918, communist revolutionaries—dubbed the Spartacists—staged a rebellion, starting on January 5, 1919. Apparently, the communists found fault with, or simply disbelieved, the Weimar Government's call for the equality of its citizenry, allowing for free elections by voters aged 20 and older, and guaranteeing freedoms of speech and religion. Hoping to replicate the Russian Revolution, the communist movement lacked coordination and a consolidated leadership. Notwithstanding hundreds of thousands of people protesting and buildings being taken over, the revolt failed when Ebert called upon 3,000 paramilitary troops—anti-communist called the Freikorps—to stamp out the revolt. It ended on January 12 with calm restored and the two main communist leaders, Karl Liebknecht and Rosa Luxemburg, taken into custody and killed, joining approximately two hundred other people who lost their lives during the week. With this ending, the communists and Social Democrats emerged mortal enemies.

At the same time, in 1920, the Nazi Party came into existence. Called the National Socialist German Workers' Party, one year later Adolf Hitler took control. By the end of 1922, it had 20,000 members. A year later it staged its own uprising, the Beer Hall Putsch on November 8 and 9, 1923.

Adolf Hitler, who had fought in the Great War and, like many, remained bitter at its conclusion. Feeling that its army battled bravely and achieved success, the war was lost due to the betrayal of the "November Criminals," composed of communists, inept civilian leaders, and Jews, who had stabbed Germany in the back. German general and war hero Erich Ludendorf, and Ernst Rohm, who was described as a "fanatical, simple-minded swashbuckler" who threw himself into danger, joined Hitler in these beliefs. Rohm revealed his essence in writing that "War and unrest appeal to me more than the orderly life of your respectable [citizen]."

Given the turmoil and agitation in the country, Hitler moved to take advantage of it, hoping to seize control and overthrow first the local government of Munich, the capital of Bavaria, and then move onto Berlin and the nation as a whole.

Beer Halls throughout Germany were popular meeting areas, where the locals gathered to socialize, imbibe, and discuss the local events and issues. Using over 600 supporters, Hitler surrounded one such large Beer Hall—the Burgerbraukeller—where a state official was giving a speech in front of 3,000 spectators. Inside Hitler and his henchman, including Ludendorff and Rohm, grabbed the town leaders and announced that the government was hereby deposed, replaced by new leadership under the guidance of World War I general, Erich Ludendorff. Electrifying the crowd, Hitler bellowed that his actions were not aimed at the police or army but against "the Berlin Jew government and the November criminals of 1918 ... Either the German revolution begins tonight or we will all be dead by dawn."

While some buildings and hostages were seized, the rebellion lacked, as with the communist one before it, coordination and control. Ludendorff, seeking to rally a crowd of now 2,000 followers, led them to the Defense Ministry where government forces awaited. Gunfire ensued. Sixteen Nazis died, as did four state police officers. One of the Nazis killed had been walking arm in arm with Hitler when the fatal shots rang out. The rebels fled, as did Hitler, who was caught two days later and charged with treason, along with others.

The trial, in which he slightly modified his views to limit his true intentions and offend fewer people, lasted from the end of February to April 1. Closely covered throughout Germany and the world, it provided Hitler a vast stage upon which to perform. He took full advantage. It also helped that the trial judges were sympathetic to Hitler, who accepted responsibility for the putsch, claiming his actions were for the aggrieved and suffering German people. Ludendorff was acquitted while Rohm was found guilty and given a fifteen-month suspended sentence. Hitler, also found guilty, received a five-year prison sentence to be served at a jail known for its favorable conditions. He was paroled after nine months. While in, he wrote *Mein Kampf*, dedicating it to his sixteen fallen companions.

Originally titled *Four and a Half Years of Struggle Against Lies, Stupidity and Cowardice*, he was persuaded to change the title, which he did, to *Mein Kampf*, or *My Struggle*. In it, he outlined his background and political views, centered around the Jewish peril conspiring to rule the world and using as their agents, the communists, Social Democrats, and German government. The parliamentary system had to be destroyed. "The nationalization of our masses will succeed only when, aside from all the positive struggle for the soul of our people, their international prisoners are exterminated." If at the outset of the war "twelve or fifteen thousand of these Hebrew corrupters of the nation had been subjected to poison gas ... then the sacrifices of millions at the front would not have been in vain." He also spoke of "Lebensraum," or "living space," in the form of taking the lands of "Russia and her vassal border states."

With his national profile expanding, he radically altered his outlook and views on gaining power. Rather than calling for a violent revolution and fighting from the outside, power was best seized by working within the system. And to do so, to employ the most effective tool for reaching and convincing the populace, he settled upon a vigorous and incessant campaign of propaganda and lies. To lead that charge, he turned to a—if not *the*—master of such deception and deceit, the unattractive, clubfooted lothario Joseph Goebbels, who seduced countless women, including many actresses and society ladies. While ignore parents hoped he'd enter the priesthood, he instead gained a doctorate in philosophy in 1921, wrote fourteen books over the coming two decades, and turned to Hitler and hate.

In the coming years, Hitler toured the nation, giving fiery, nationalistic speeches at various rallies. He also utilized all other means of communication—radio, newspapers, and posters. His message was simple and to the point; essentially: Make Germany Great Again, and stampede all who stood in the way—Jews, communists, and the central government. Thugs brought terror and brute force to those hesitant to go along. Financial support came from big business and rich industrialists.

Hitler's greatest stimulant arrived in the form of the fearsome 1929 stock market crash, plunging the world into crippling depression, sending millions to the unemployment and food lines. In times of despair, disruption, and fear, people turned to one telling them what they wanted to hear. An energetic and passionate Hitler offered an alternative to the constant misery, especially to the millions who were unemployed, who made up a sizable portion of the entire population.

In 1932, the Nazis won more votes than any other party. The communists remained powerful, also advocating violence, but focusing more on destroying the Weimar Government and the Social Democrats than on Hitler, whose abilities they minimized. The starchy Weimar leaders, caught in the middle of two mighty gales, could not calm the storm. Reasoning, falsely, that Hitler could be controlled and used to keep the communists in check, he was invited into the government and named Chancellor, a position below President Hindenburg, who had convincingly trounced Hitler in the presidential race just eight months before. When Hitler was sworn into office on January 30, 1933, little did the Social Democrats and the Weimar Republic leadership know that its days and democracy were on their collective deathbeds; so too the communists and everyone else who spoke up in opposition.

Within a month of Hitler assuming office, on February 27, 1933, a fire broke out in the historic Reichstag, where the parliament met. Significant portions of the building were destroyed, the damage estimated to be over $1 million dollars (over $23 million dollars today). Caught on the scene was Marinus van der Lubbe, a 24-year-old Dutch communist, who had come to Germany that same year to support the communist movement. He and four other communists were caught and ultimately brought to trial. Van der Lubbe was found guilty and put to death. In a show that justice could win out, the others were found not guilty.

Hitler pounced on the inferno and created one of his own, blaming the communists and promising to crush them. So opportune was the arson that some believed Hitler to be responsible. One day later, President Hindenburg invoked Article 48 of the Constitution and called for the implementation of a law for the "Protection of the People and the State," that abolished the basic democratic freedoms—of speech, press, privacy, and assembly—of the very people it sought to protect. Once signed into law, 4,000 or so enemies of the state were arrested. Many were communist soon-to-be-ex members of parliament.

The assault on a dying democracy continued. On March 24, the Enabling Act was passed that granted Hitler the "temporary" power to act as he best thought, without consent from either the parliament or courts. Using a mixture of his classic alternating strategies of seemingly negotiating, intimidating, and/or lying, he laid forth his case in stark terms. "It was for you, gentlemen of the Reichstag to decide between war and peace." Making promises he had no intention of keeping, he secured his goal. Within months, all non-Nazi parties were banned. Even dissent within the party was ruthlessly addressed.

Early on, Hitler established paramilitary groups, the SS and SA (who were also known as Stormtroopers or Brownshirts), to do his bidding, whether it be to protect him or to attack and intimidate his rivals. SS members generally came from the middle class, while the more violent and hard-drinking SA found its base among the unemployed and working class. Despite Hitler gaining power from working within the system, the SA—now under the leadership of an ambitious Ernst Rohm—wished to continue the revolution, implementing sweeping radical changes that threatened the wealthy businessman and industrialists. He also wished to continue openly and violently assaulting any rivals, including the communists and Jews, two groups sufficiently beaten down and controlled by Hitler now that he was in power. As for the military, Rohm desired, if not demanded, that his 2–3 million strong SA absorb the Versailles Treaty mandated and limited armed forces, consisting of 100,000 soldiers, a position obviously vigorously opposed by the generals. Meanwhile, the SS, fearing a strong, growing, and dangerous rival, compiled a list of the many problems presented by Rohm, including, falsely, that France was paying Rohm to overthrow Hitler. To that list they added that Rohm, and much of his staff, were openly gay, running counter to the image Hitler wished to project.

With so many powerful people and organizations warning Hitler of the threat posed by Rohm, Hitler uncharacteristically dithered. He and Rohm went back a long way and were intimate friends. Rohm never held Hitler in the god-like esteem others did, calling him Adolf or his nickname Adi, rather than Mein Führer, when conversing.

On the evening of June 29, 1934, in Munich, the SA unexpectedly stormed the streets, striking out at all perceived foes. An enraged Hitler flew into the city the next evening and accosted the local police chief, berating him for failing to keep order. Whisked away with other members of the SA, Hitler had them assassinated. Hitler then, with the SS and other police officers in tow, departed for Bad Wiessee, a town where Hitler earlier ordered Rohm to appear with his staff for a meeting. Arriving at the hotel where the group was staying, Hitler placed his one-time strong supporter, along with Rohm's generals and senior officers, under arrest. Meanwhile SS troops rounded up other SA members, including one officer who was in bed with an 18-year-old male troop leader. Hitler ordered them all killed.

Two senior SS officers visited Rohm in his cell. Handing him a pistol with one bullet, they told him he had ten minutes to kill himself. Returning after the allotted time, they found Rohm shirtless, with his chest puffed out and defiant, telling them "If I am to be killed, let Adolf do it himself." He was shot where he stood.

Other political opponents were also taken into custody and murdered, including Bavarian Commissioner Gustav Ritter von Kahr, who had put down the 1923 Beer Hall Putsch. It is uncertain how many people were killed during The Night of Long Knives (a phrase taken from a popular German song). Some say as few as 200 died,while others opine it closer to a thousand.

Clearly though, while some were appalled at the bloodletting, most found it justified in protecting Germany from a violent assault by a bunch of thugs, restoring order in the streets, and cracking down on moral turpitude. With Hitler acting outside of the law in assuming the roles of judge, jury, and executioner, only a single person stood between him and absolute authority, the still popular and powerful 86-year-old president, Paul Hindenburg.

Hindenburg died on August 2, 1934. On that day, army personnel took an oath of "unconditional obedience" not to the nation or their office, but to Adolf Hitler. Democracy was now dead in Germany and led by one who told a non-listening world of his ambitious, brutal, and deadly intentions.

Hitler wanted a strong, if not overpowering, Germany, and he set about accomplishing his agenda. Under the goal of developing his nation's sagging economy, he invested heavily in the military. An added benefit of such spending came employment and jobs. Straying close, if not overtly breaching, the lines and parameters set by the Versailles Treaty, he crossed that line when he openly expanded the Luftwaffe—the German air force—and reinstituted conscription. While secret training had been going on for a few years, in 1936 a unit of German army and air force, called the Condor Legion, dispatched to Spain to aid fascist leader Francisco Franco's

Nationalists in its civil war. Not only was the experience vital in executing the coming world war, but it showed the world that the Versailles Treaty, like democracy in Germany, was no more.

On March 7, 1936, under the guise of restoring Germany to its "rightful" boundaries, Hitler remilitarized western Germany's Rhineland by sending in its military, which was forbidden by the Versailles Treaty. France, which was preoccupied with political instability, did nothing; nor Britain's favorably-disposed-to-Germany King Edward VIII, who thought the prohibition unjust. Edward was only king a short time, abdicating in December 1936 due to his desire to marry the twice-divorced American Wallis Simpson, which breached British protocol. Perhaps indicative of how some English felt toward Germany, in October 1937 the former king and now Duke of Windsor, and his wife, the Duchess of Windsor, ill-advisedly visited Germany for two weeks. Throughout their visit, they were given a grand and royal treatment, to which they occasionally reciprocated by giving the Nazi salute. At the end of their German-funded tour, they met a friendly and receptive Hitler, who, in a show of superiority, kept the two waiting. Hitler later opined to others how beneficial to Germany it would have been had the duke remained king. As Goebbels wrote in his diary, "the duke is wonderful—a nice, sympathetic fellow who is open and clear and with a healthy understanding of people ... It's a shame he is no longer king. With him we would have entered into an alliance." Mrs. Simpson, conversely, described the German minister of propaganda as "a tiny, wispy gnome with an enormous skull." The famed photographer Alfred Eisenstadt shared a somewhat similar impression. After snapping a picture of Goebbels in 1933, Eisenstadt described him as the meanest person he had ever seen. Perhaps Goebbels reaction was due to having a Jew take his picture. As for ignore wife Magda, on whom Goebbels was often cheating, Mrs. Simpson thought her "the prettiest woman I saw in Germany."

Magda Goebbels was born out of wedlock in 1901. Her mother, Auguste Behrend, later married and divorced Magda's "father." In 1908, she remarried, this time to Richard Friedlander, a wealthy Jewish businessman, who adopted Magda. Some believe that in fact Friedlander was her real father. Regardless, Behrend ultimately divorced Friedlander.

Magda attended a prestigious college in Berlin in 1919. Around that time she had an affair with Victor Haim (also known as Haim Arlosoroff), a socialist Zionist who preached peace with the Arabs. Magda attended Jewish functions with him and reportedly even wore a Jewish Star of David. After the relationship soured, Magda married Gunther Quandt, who brought two sons into the marriage. Magda gave birth to a son with him and helped raise three other children from a deceased friend. Despite raising six children and having a far too busy husband consumed with expanding his business empire, Magda found time to have an affair which led to her divorce.

In 1930, Magda met antisemite extraordinaire Joseph Goebbels and joined the Nazi Party. They married in 1931 and went on to have six children from 1932 to 1940, all of whom she and her husband murdered prior to committing suicide as World War II came to an end in 1945. The two had affairs throughout the marriage, one of which seriously threatened their union. In 1937, Joseph engaged in an intense liaison with a very attractive Czech actress, Lida Baarová, and seriously considered leaving his wife. When Magda learned of the tryst she complained to Hitler, with whom she shared a close and warm relationship. Hitler ordered Goebbels to end the affair and to put his house in order, at which point he and Magda arrived at an accommodation. When that faltered Magda had an affair with Karl Hanke, a high-ranking minster under, and close associate of, Goebbels. Once again, Hitler intervened and ordered the couple to reconcile.

In 1938, the Anschluss—the annexation of Austria into Germany—came, without a bullet being fired. By threats, bravado, and justifications that Austria was part of Germany, the Austrian leaders, with no support from the outside world, agreed to the fait accompli. Many Austrians, who were of German heritage, hardily consented.

With Hitler doing precisely what he had earlier loudly proclaimed he would do, and the world essentially doing little other than sadly recognizing that war was becoming more and more likely, he continued his conquests, demanding the return of the heavily fortified Sudetenland, which bordered on Germany and was part of Czechoslovakia. Hitler thundered that the Germans in that country were being threatened and needed protection; he also argued that, like Austria, the German population had a right to self-determination and return to the motherland. Goebbels sprang into high gear, lying about the threats posed and the need for action. As Hitler had been appeased before, he had no reason to believe it would be any different now.

With so brazen a move, war now appeared to be imminent, especially given France's military pact with Czechoslovakia. British Prime Minister Neville Chamberlain and his French counterpart Edouard Daladier rushed to Germany, hat in hand, in an attempt to avert the conflict. Chamberlain privately pushed Daladier to renounce his security pact with the Czechs.

Upon Chamberlain's leaving England, he announced his goal, "My objective is peace in Europe. I trust this trip is the way to that peace." To that end, he told Hitler and the others, that they were prepared to fully accept Germany's demand to annex all of Sudetenland. Hitler, having gotten all that he wanted, took further advantage and asked for more. As he later told his generals, "Our enemies are men below average, not men of action, not masters. They are little worms. I saw them at Munich."

Hitler rejected Chamberlain's offer and announced he wanted all of Czechoslovakia, with most of its territories going to Germany, with Poland and Hungary getting some of the lands over which they had a claim. To dramatize his demand, he set up a ruse. At the appointed time, an aide rushed in and interrupted the meeting with the dire, and wholly made up, news that more Germans in the disputed land had been attacked and killed. Upon hearing this, Hitler, drawing upon his most over-the-top and bombastic abilities, rose in shocked outrage, "I will avenge every one of them! The Czechs must be destroyed!"

A shaken Chamberlain left the meeting. Later that night, fearing that he had overplayed his hand, Hitler called Chamberlain accepting the earlier offer, as both a "concession" on Hitler's part and a "gift" to Chamberlain. As for further concessions and gifts, Hitler announced that this was it, with Germany harboring no further claims upon the lands of Czechoslovakia and willing to agree to the borders between the two nations. Lastly, a smiling Hitler willingly agreed to a peace treaty between Germany and England.

Meanwhile, the leaders of Czechoslovakia, who had not been invited to the conference that directly affected its future, prepared for war. Its army was modern, well-equipped, and powerful with a strongly fortified border. The Russians added that it would aid the Czechs so long as it was free to cross Polish and Romanian territory. Both countries refused.

The British and French informed the Czechs that they had two options: either going it alone against Germany or capitulate. Having no real choice, the Czechs gave up. On September 30, 1938, the Munich Agreement was signed and the Sudetenland and its fortifications and rich natural resources were handed over to Germany.

War had been averted. The world was relieved. Prime Minister Daladier of France, under no illusions about Hitler's vast ambitions, recognized the mood of his nation, the military, and the memory of the devastation of World War I, and did not think it wise to go to war over Czechoslovakia. Reading the French people correctly, he received a joyous reception. Chamberlain also returned to England a hero. "My good friends ... [I have] returned from Germany bringing peace with honour. I believe it is peace for our time."

Not everyone joined in the glee. Stalin, seeing how effortlessly France reneged on its treaty with the Czechs, and of how German demands were so easily agreed upon, feared equal acquiescence in the future should Hitler decide to move further east. The Czechs obviously seethed as they lost people and territory and 70 percent of its steel, iron, and electrical industries in an agreement that precluded them; for them it was "About us, without us."

Publicly unknown at the time were the views of some high-ranking members of the German military, who believed that Germany would lose a war against Czechoslovakia, France, and England. If Hitler gave the order to attack, which would have been issued if he had not gotten what he wanted, they were prepared to move against and arrest him. In a secret overture to the British government, which was apprised of Hitler's invasion plans, a request was made that Chamberlain publicly declare support for the Czechs. The British cabinet refused to do so. With no German military action ordered, the coup never came to fruition.

Poland and Hungary which had also made territorial demands, quickly seized upon the now vastly weakened country with no outside support, leading, in Winston Churchill's view, of "vultures upon the carcass of Czechoslovakia." Within one day of the Czechs agreeing to the Munich Agreement, Poland issued an ultimatum demanding Czech territory. Hungary quickly followed. The Czechs had no option but to acquiesce.

Even before the Munich Agreement was signed, Churchill, on August 13, 1938, observed the goings-on between the European powers and wrote: "England has been offered a choice between war and shame. She has chosen shame and will get war."

The war started in 1939.

2

Hollywood

One of the very few positive, if not only, effects of the rise of Nazism in Germany was the emigration of so many of its talented artists. A boatload landed in the United States and found employment in Hollywood. So talented was the group that they were coined "Hitler's gift to America." Once here, they joined over 30,000 fellow employees in the movie industry. It could not have been better timed, for in 1939 Hollywood produced its greatest movies ever. And like Joe DiMaggio's fifty-six game hitting streak, its record will likely never be beaten.

Not only were so many great movies released in 1939, quality-wise, but their sheer number was also breathtaking. In a feat almost unimaginable today, a movie a day came out. Every day a new movie. To a public hungry for entertainment, spending a staggering amount of money, during the depression no less, to see their favorite movies featuring their favorite stars. Today, an actor or actress might make a movie every year or two or three. In 1939, actors worked all of the time. One of the reigning queens, #2 on the American Film Institute (AFI) List of the Top Female Actresses, Bette Davis, starred in four movies that year. Few actresses in their entire careers have worked in so many well-received movies as Davis did in that single twelve-month period. So talented a performer was she that she was nominated for Best Actress in 1938 (*Jezebel*), 1939 (*Dark Victory*), 1940 (*The Letter*), 1941 (*The Little Foxes*), 1942 (*Now, Voyager*) and 1944 (*Mr. Skeffington*). She won only for *Jezebel*.

Meanwhile, the far lesser-known, but exquisitely talented, actor Thomas Mitchell, who played Scarlett O'Hara's father in *Gone With the Wind*, starred in four other movies in 1939, including two others in AFI's Top 100 Films, *Mr. Smith Goes to Washington*, starring Jimmy Stewart, and

Stagecoach, which made John Wayne a star and won Mitchell an Oscar. The two other movies in which he appeared also received Academy Award nominations—*The Hunchback of Notre Dame* and *Only Angels Have Wings*. Despite these heavyweight films, he may be best remembered as the bumbling Uncle Billy in *It's a Wonderful Life* which he made with Jimmy Stewart seven years later.

In the end, various factors came together to create magic in that very special year. Generally, the movies being made were positive in nature as Americans were slowly regaining their confidence as the nation gradually emerged from the worst economic disaster in its history. Further, the most talented directors of the era, indeed arguably ever, were pushing the envelope, tackling subjects hitherto avoided. Studio heads, many of whom were far from pleasant people, possessed a keen sense of what the public wanted and built well-oiled factories to satisfy those needs, churning out films at dizzying rates. Many of the actors and actresses were more than performers, being the brightest of stars in the truest sense of the word, rocketed skyward by overly competent, if not overly zealous, publicity departments that stressed the positive, even if it were not true, and buried the dirt, of which there was tons. Long term and iron-clad contracts tightly bound the stars and kept them under the omnipresent pressing thumbs and demands of their studios and its bosses.

The major studios at the time were Metro-Goldwyn-Mayer, better known by their initials, MGM, Warner Bros., Paramount, Universal, Columbia, RKO, 20th Century, and United Artists. At times, then as now, some of the studio heads were synonymous and equal to the very studios they commanded. Louis B. Mayer at MGM, the Warner Brothers—Harry, Albert, Sam, and its driving force Jack—at, where else, Warner Bros., and Daryl Zanuck at 20th Century. While each had their particular styles, all had ground swelling successes, as well as some notable flops.

Perhaps the most noteworthy was Louis Burt Mayer, who ruled with an iron fist at MGM. Basic facts today are perhaps more readily discernable than those a hundred years ago. Thus, Mayer was born in Russia as either Eliezer or Lazar Mayer on either July 4 or July 12, in either 1882, 1883, 1884, or 1885, depending on Canadian census forms, his marriage certificate, or his US immigration papers. Given, like many immigrants, his desire to be everything American, he may have falsely claimed his birth date to be the same as that of the great country to which he emigrated.

After living briefly on Long Island, his family moved to Canada, where they barely scratched out a living, his father working as a junk dealer. Mayer joined him after dropping out of school at a young age. In 1904 he moved to

Boston, where he remained in the junk business, along with other endeavors, to feed himself and his new bride, Margaret Shenberg, who appears to have been born in Pennsylvania on October 3, 1883.

Saving what little money he had, he purchased a run-down theater in Haverhill, Massachusetts, and renovated it in 1907. Crowds came in, money was made, and soon he owned five theaters. Seeing that Hollywood, not Boston, was the epicenter, along with New York, of the movie business, he relocated there and opened his own production company. Six years later, in 1924, his company merged with Metro Pictures, owned by Marcus Loew, and Goldwyn Pictures, owned by Samuel Goldwyn, and a super nova was born.

In 1939, MGM released mega movies such as *The Wizard of Oz*, *Boys Town*, and *Gone With the Wind*. In another one of their hits, the comedy *Ninotchka*, Greta Garbo, #5 on AFI's Top 25 Female Stars, stepped out of her dramatic character—movies in which she either drowned, crashed, was shot, threw herself under a train, or died of a deadly disease. So typecast was the star that the poster for the movie trumpeted the thought-to-be-highly improbable, "Garbo Laughs." Ten years earlier, when she had moved from silent films to talkies, her first being *Anna Christie*, promotions included "Garbo Talks."

The German-born Ernst Lubitsch directed the film, which entails three bumbling Russians, Iranoff, Buljanoff, and Kopalski, travelling to Paris to sell jewelry confiscated during the Russian Revolution. A debonair man-about-town, Count Leon d'Algout, played by Melvyn Douglas, gets involved to thwart the scheme. When the Russian government discovers their mischief, they send agent Nina Ivanovna "Ninotchka" Yakushova to straighten out the mess and return with the three stooges. When she arrives, she is led to her lovely and large hotel suite. Upon entering she asks, "Which part of the room is mine?" Later in a restaurant, she orders raw beets and carrots, to which she is told, "Madame, this is a restaurant, not a meadow."

Soon the count falls for Ninotchka, who has developed strong feelings for him and the West as she slowly transforms from drab to fashionable. When she asks him, "Must you flirt?" he responds, "Well, I don't have to, but I find it natural."

She completes her mission, however, and sadly returns with the three to gray, boring, and rigid Russia. While there, she receives a letter from the count that is so heavily censored that the only legible parts are its opening—"Ninotchka, my darling"—and closing—"Yours, Leon".

As time passes, she is again assigned, by Commissar Razinin, played by the famed horror film actor Bela Lugosi, to fix the next mess that Iranoff,

Buljanoff, and Kopalski make when they arrived in Constantinople to sell furs. When she reluctantly arrives there, the three tell her they have opened a restaurant and aren't going back. When she asks who put them up to this, they point to the balcony which holds the lovestruck Count Leon. He asks her to stay with him and she agrees. The happy film ends with Kopalski carrying a sign, protesting that Iranoff and Buljanoff are being unfair to him by not having his name on the restaurant.

Common and serious problems for Mayer and his fellow moviemakers existed both on and off screen. First, the Motion Picture Production Code had to be addressed. Second, their stars had to be closely monitored to ensure that some of their more randy lifestyles remained under wraps and far from public view. For MGM, that often-difficult task fell to its fixers, Eddie Mannix and Howard Strickling, who had to address unwanted pregnancies, arrange illegal abortions, straighten out drunken and drug debacles, and keep the homosexuality of many of its stars hidden. And with Greta Garbo, rather open in her relationships with other women, that was no easy task. Not only were same-sex liaisons taboo at the time, but also ran counter to the Production Code.

By 1939, Hollywood was still a young and essentially new town. Initially an agricultural area, in the 1880s real estate tycoon Harvey Henderson Wilcox and his wife Daeida decided to leave their Kansas home and relocate to a sun-drenched but essentially barren area, buying 160 or so acres. Daeida had a friend from the Midwest who called her estate Hollywood. Daeida liked and appropriated the name for their newfound California domain. Wilcox subdivided the area and in 1887 submitted a grid map of Hollywood to the Los Angeles County Recorder.

By 1900, only 500 or so people lived there, dwarfed by the 100,000 people residing 6 miles away in Los Angeles. Like many emerging towns, it slowly grew, with a post office, newspaper, hotel, churches, city hall, library, and a few small markets. Meanwhile, a nearby group of oil drillers, including Burton Green, grew rich and decided to also develop part of the surrounding area. When it came to naming it, Green recalled his fondness for time spent in Beverly Farms, Massachusetts, and thought of naming it that. Reminded that the area was hilly, he settled on calling it Beverly Hills. The area was restricted to whites only with the added exclusion of all Jews.

Slowly, filmmakers from the East Coast started migrating to Hollywood, given its hospitable weather and wide, empty, and cheap expanses. Green, in developing the area, helped build the now famed Beverly Hills Hotel, which opened in 1912, housing those making movies. Liking the area, many of those individuals purchased nearby properties and built homes, if not mansions like "Pickfair," the palatial residence of megastars Mary Pickford and Douglas Fairbanks.

In 1913, wishing to film a Western, *The Squaw Man*, on location far from the inhospitable and cold East Coast, the Goldwyn-Lasky group with Cecil B. DeMille took the long train trip to its planned shooting site in Falstaff, Arizona. Quickly, however, they found the area not conducive to their needs, it being too hot, too rainy, and in the middle of a range war between the locals. Hopping back on the train, they travelled further west to Hollywood, where they found nirvana with excellent weather and proximity to mountains, desert, and ocean. DeMille, in his directorial debut, joined his co-director Oscar C. Apfel, and made one of the earliest feature-length movies. At 74 minutes, it was released in 1914.

With the growing influx of executives, actors, directors, carpenters, electricians, plumbers, extras, and the sundry others all needed to make the then silent movies, the natives, small in number and liking the quiet, slowly found their world exploding before their eyes. The small boarding houses and hotels exhibited their disdain, if not outright bigotry, by limiting who could rent a room. Signs sternly warned that Jews, actors, and dogs were not welcome. It could be easily assumed that Blacks and other minorities also fell within the prohibition. House sales were also so limited. Even DeMille could not find something to rent and resorted to posing as a movie-hating salesman to convince the landlord to let him one.

With studios slowly settling in Hollywood, their product came to be devoured by an entertainment-starved America with its masses overwhelming the over 17,000 movie houses throughout the nation. In Boston, the Exeter Theater held nearly 1,400 people, in Los Angles the Palace sat nearly 2,000 while New York's Strand housed a thousand more. While the typical yearly salary for many laborers throughout the land was miniscule, some studios and its owners, overwhelmingly Jewish and mainly from eastern Europe, were hauling in $20,000 a week.

Some of that vast amount of money trickled down to the employees of the studios, especially its emerging and notable stars. Unfortunately though, great money is often accompanied by great excess. While those living in Hollywood did not invent sin, promiscuity, alcohol, and drug abuse, they most assuredly turned it into an art form. Some of the debauchery even made it onto the screen, drawing moviegoers in but at the same time alienating vast groups of the clergy, temperance unions, and women's groups. So powerful an alliance that in under a year they convinced the nation to swiftly pass the disastrous 18th Amendment banning the sales of liquor, which went into effect on January 17, 1920. Greater restrictions were in store with the disturbing behaviors of many of the stars adding to the growing calls for reform and discipline.

In search of a more exciting life, 18-year-old Olive Thomas left her husband of two years behind in Pennsylvania and moved to New York City. A year later, in 1914, she entered and won a beauty contest and was crowned the "The Most Beautiful Girl in New York City." Actress Mary Pickford, "America's Sweetheart" who in 1917 signed a contract worth a million dollars, described her future sister-in-law Olive as "[a legendary beauty with the] loveliest violet-blue eyes I have ever seen. They were fringed with long dark lashes that seemed darker because of the delicate translucent pallor of her skin."

Olive's career now launched, she found herself posing for several artists, often in the nude. She became the first "Vargas Girl" and joined the famed Ziegfeld Follies. Florenz "Flo" Ziegfeld, who, when he wasn't having sex with her and some of the other Ziegfeld Girls, cast Olive in the after-hours risqué *Midnight Frolic* show, which catered to wealthy men, who spent lavishly on the beautiful nubile women performing scantily clad before them. Many attended, expecting far more than to merely watch an entertaining show. Ziegfeld, who was married at the time to Billie Burke (later the Good Witch of the North in 1939's *Wizard of Oz*) proclaimed Olive as one of the most beautiful women in his show.

The net of her allure now widely cast, Olive, not surprisingly, moved to film, appearing in six movies in 1917, three in 1918, a whopping eight in 1919, and five in 1920. In sharp contrast to her Vargas and Follies background, in the movies she frequently played the innocent, friendly, and naïve country girl. She deviated from that role somewhat in *The Flapper* that last year. There she introduced the flapper lifestyle, which became a cultural craze throughout America during that Roaring decade. Along the path to stardom, she met and married fellow actor, Jack Pickford, the hardy partier and younger brother of superstar Mary.

Jack, appearing on stage at an early age, typically was cast as the model good-looking boy next door, in sharp contrast to his private persona, marked by alcohol, drugs, and philandering. Notably, he joined the military at the outset of World War I. Once in though, he reverted to his less than stellar ways, involving himself in a scheme allowing the wealthy to avoid military service and reportedly also procuring women for some of the officers. Needless to say, his military service ended poorly.

The short and tragic lives of Jack and Olive could have served as a storyline in a movie. Francis Marion, the highly successful and well-paid screenwriter who wrote *The Flapper* and over 300 other scripts, described their relationship as "[t]wo innocent-looking children [who] were the gayest, wildest brats who ever stirred the stardust on Broadway. Both were talented, but they were much more interested in playing the roulette of life than in concentrating on their careers."

With their marriage teetering, they decided to take a second honeymoon in Paris. After a night of partying in the swankier bistros of Montparnasse in early September 1920, they returned to their luxurious hotel at three in the morning. There, Olive somehow came to drink a poisonous solution prescribed to treat the syphilis-caused-sores from which Jack suffered. Five days later, on September 10, she died.

The following day the front page of the *New York Times* blurted out, "Paris Authorities Investigate Death of Olive Thomas." Under that loud headline, a smaller one announced "Police Seek Evidence on Rumors of Drug and Champagne Orgies."

The rumors flew. Suicide caused by Pickford's wanderings! Suicide due to Olive contracting syphilis from her husband! Death due to drug addiction! Pickford murdering wife to collect insurance! Marital strife caused death! Cocaine dealer questioned! And of course, the one to which *The Times* alluded, drug and champagne orgies lead to death!

Pickford, conversely, insisted that the two were in love when she inadvertently ingested the toxic solution, from a bottle labelled in French, which somehow came to be mixed with alcohol. He remained at her bedside for several days. When he asked her how she felt, she softly muttered, "Pretty weak, but I'll be all right in a little while, don't worry, darling." Those were her last words. Dead at 25, her death ruled accidental. Thirteen years later, a twice more married (once to another former paramour of Ziegfeld) and divorced Pickford, ill and emaciated, died of alcoholism.

The public's virginal views of the two greatly differed from their true lives. Once that hitherto unknown aspect came to light, the public recoiled. How could these two sweet and gentle and likeable people so portrayed in their movies and the press be so disagreeable in real life? Soon, and in quick succession, even more egregious events would turn and further anger the public, leading to calls for censorship and the way in which movies were made. A Supreme Court decision ruling that movies were not entitled to free speech protections didn't help.

Like a spinached-up Popeye punch-punch-punching a now overmatched Bluto, the scandals tumbled forth.

One year after Olive's death, Roscoe Fatty Arbuckle, recently estranged from his wife Minta, decided to leave Los Angeles to spend the Labor Day Weekend partying in San Francisco. Imagine the biggest star in America today and that was Arbuckle in 1921. While heavyset, he was surprisingly light on his feet with a voice of an angel and possessing brilliant comedic timing. He dazzled America with his Keystone-cop-slapstick-pie-in-the-face antics, making millions along the way and living ostentatiously. Despising his nickname, he was subdued, pleasant, and surprisingly shy around women. When he drank, however, his mood turned dark.

By Labor Day Monday, aspiring actress Virginia Rapp, delirious and highly intoxicated (despite it being Prohibition), after partying for days with a host of others in a suite of rooms, found herself unconscious in Arbuckle's room. He didn't even know how she got there. Four days later she died. Quickly, the press and the overly ambitious District Attorney Matthew Brady, with eyes on the Governor's Mansion, accused Arbuckle of her rape and murder. Lurid stories of his fatally crushing her during intercourse spewed forth, as did accusations of his inserting either a champagne or coke bottle into her. Quickly the much-loved personality turned reptilian with all his movies pulled. The press, with William Randolph Hearst leading the charge, made it the (fake news) story of the year. Hearst later crowed that the Arbuckle tales "sold more newspapers than any event since the sinking of the Lusitania."

With tainted evidence, a compromised jury, and lying witnesses, the juries in the first two trials could not reach a unanimous ruling. On the third, a not guilty verdict resulted after ten or so minutes of deliberations. Along with their decision, the jurors issued a missive declaring Arbuckle "entirely innocent and free from all blame." The damage, however, had been done. While Arbuckle rightfully won in a court of law, he, along with Hollywood and its randy ways, lost in the, for many the far more important, court of public opinion.

During the height of the Arbuckle imbroglio, his raging story found itself uncharacteristically bumped from the top of page one to its bottom, for on February 2, 1922, the papers led with the shocking murder of 49-year-old famed movie director William Desmond Taylor, the Steven Spielberg/Martin Scorsese of his day. Taylor died of a single gunshot wound.

Several suspects appeared, including his recently missing manservant Edward Sands, who turned out to be a military deserter, thief, and criminal; angered drug dealers who Taylor railed against and banned from his movie set; two former soldiers who Taylor reprimanded while in the military during World War I; famed actress, and cocaine-addicted, Mabel Normand, who co-starred with Arbuckle in many of his movies, and was the last person to see Taylor alive; and the overbearing and most unpleasant stage mother Charlotte Shelby, who weeks before accosted Taylor on his movie lot, screaming, "If I ever catch you hanging around Mary again, I will blow your goddamned brains out." The Mary in her tirade was her meal ticket daughter, Mary Miles Minter, the 19-year-old adorable teenaged star of the day, whose picture sat on Taylor's piano—as did three strands of her hair on Taylor's jacket when he was found dead. Discovered in his bedroom were Mary's monogramed MMM pink flimsy nightgown and her lace handkerchief, along with love letters hidden in Taylor's riding boot. That Taylor may have been gay and wished to disengage himself from an awestruck teenager adds to a mystery that will never be solved. After the murder was discovered, employees from Paramount studio quickly arrived and swept the area, carrying away who knows what. Additionally, the less than scrupulous District Attorney, Thomas Lee Woolwine, a good friend of both Charlotte Shelby and the studios, strangely relieved the homicide detectives working on the case and ordered the evidence delivered to him, which he somehow lost.

As with Arbuckle, the press stormed in, saturating the public with stories of a lecherous old man having his way with an innocent young actress and sensationalizing other aspects of the case. Stories even turned Taylor's anti-drug campaign into one in which he used drugs to enslave defenseless young women.

Wallace Reid and Charlie Chaplin rounded out the onslaught of cases influencing and infuriating the public. Wallace Reid's allure may be summed up in the caption accompanying one of his still pictures in a magazine. "The only reason why they don't let Wally play in dress-suit roles all the time is that the casualties among the ladies would soon empty the picture houses. In fact, we feel that we're toying with the fan hearts even to print this picture."

Reid typified the All-American boy. Hollywood handsome, he possessed athletic powers accompanied by an interest in music. He played various instruments and seemed to be as happy behind the camera as he was in front of it. Born in 1891 to show business parents, he participated in well over a hundred movies, often as an action hero figure. Today, he would be Captain America. He married a fellow actress Dorothy Davenport in 1913, with whom he had two children. En route to a shoot in 1919, he was injured and received morphine to relieve his severe pain. Soon, and sadly, he quickly became addicted and over the course of the final four years of his life spiraled downward, often using the same drug dealer who serviced Mabel Normand. He died in 1923 in a padded sanitarium cell, shocking an adoring and unsuspecting fanbase.

As for Charlie Chaplin, simply, he liked young girls. His first two wives were 16 when they married. He was 29 and 35.

With a fed-up public roaring for reform, state legislatures around the nation enacted various censorship laws. Faced with the daunting prospect of adhering to many differing, and conflicting, laws in the various states, the studios attempted to counter the legislation by announcing a shocked recognition of the problem and a solution of self-regulation. Like baseball naming Judge Kennesaw Mountain Landis as commissioner to clean up that sullied sport in the aftermath of widespread gambling and the scandalous fixing of the 1919 World Series, the studios designated Will H. Hays in 1922 to clean up the movies. (Although Reid died and Chaplin married his second wife after Hayes was named, the reported antics of the Hollywood stars continued to alienate the public.)

Hays, born in Indiana in 1879, carried impressive political credentials. He chaired the Republican Committee, successfully managed Warren G. Harding's 1920 presidential campaign, and subsequently served as Postmaster General of the United States. In 1922, he was named chairman of the newly organized Motion Picture Producers and Distributers of America (MPPDA) at a generous salary. Given his conservative reputation, the studios hoped to mollify the public. In time, he devised guidelines called, "The Don'ts and Be Carefuls," which listed eleven subjects to avoid and twenty-six areas to be delicately handled.

Dissatisfied with the reach and enforcement of the guidelines, many leading Catholic figures, in 1929–1930, met and refined the Don'ts and Be Careful list. Hays enthusiastically adopted the recommendations, which came to be called, variously, The Production Code, The Code, or The Hays Code. While the studios begrudgingly accepted the new regulations, they conspired to sidestep and get around them. Until 1934. At that point, the religious leaders, still highly upset with what was coming out of Hollywood, turned up the pressure. As a result, Hays was given full authority to enforce the Code, which he did with relish. Foreshadowing Senator Joseph McCarthy's infamous 1950s list of subversives, Hays identified over a hundred actors and actresses whose personal lives made them unfit to appear in the movies. Many of those named were gay.

To avoid governmental intrusion, censorship, and oversight, the industry, having little choice, supported the Code. It regulated not only what could and could not be shown in the movies, but actively promoted family and high-minded values. Criminals were never to be portrayed as sympathetic, sex outside of marriage was taboo (sex inside of marriage was only slightly better off), and bad people who did bad things always met a bad end. Later described as "a Jewish-owned business selling Catholic theology to Protestant America," the Code weakened over time and died in the 1960s.

Divided into two sections, it defined and limited for three decades what could and could not be made and seen. As before, the bosses sought to circumvent its limitations.

The first section, "General Principles," read:

> No picture shall be produced that will lower the moral standards of those who see it. Hence the sympathy of the audience should never be thrown to the side of crime, wrongdoing, evil or sin.
>
> Correct standards of life, subject only to the requirements of drama and entertainment, shall be presented.
>
> Law, natural or human, shall not be ridiculed, nor shall sympathy be created for its violation.

The second section, "Particular Applications," was more specific:

Nudity and suggestive dances were prohibited.

The ridicule of religion was forbidden, and ministers of religion were not to be represented as comic characters or villains.

The depiction of illegal drug use was forbidden, as well as the use of liquor, when not required by the plot or for proper characterization.

Methods of crime (e.g., safe-cracking, arson, smuggling) were not to be explicitly presented.

References to sex perversions such as homosexuality and venereal disease were forbidden, as were depictions of childbirth.

The language section banned various words and phrases that were considered to be offensive.

Murder scenes had to be filmed in a way that would discourage imitations in real life, and brutal killings could not be shown in detail.

Revenge in modern times was not to be justified.

The sanctity of marriage and the home had to be upheld.

Pictures shall not infer that low forms of sex relationship are the accepted or common thing.

Adultery and illicit sex, although recognized as sometimes necessary to the plot, could not be explicit or justified and were not supposed to be presented as an attractive option.

Portrayals of miscegenation were forbidden.

Scenes of Passion were not to be introduced when not essential to the plot.

Excessive and lustful kissing was to be avoided, along with any other treatment that might stimulate the lower and baser element.

The flag of the United States was to be treated respectfully, and the people and history of other nations were to be presented fairly.

Vulgarity, defined as low, disgusting, unpleasant, though not necessarily evil, subjects must be subject to the dictates of good taste.

Capital punishment, third-degree methods, cruelty to children and animals, prostitution and surgical operations were to be handled with similar sensitivity.

To enforce the regulations, the Production Code Administration (PCA) was created. It reviewed all films and, if deemed appropriate, stamped it with the MPPDA seal of approval. Joseph I. Breen, a prominent Catholic layman, oversaw the PCA and ruled with a stern eye. For instance, the flapper-like sexuality of the cartoon character Betty Boop was de-sexed and neutered, with her being reduced to wearing a matronly outfit.

Evidence of the creativity in sidestepping the Code, as well as showing how some of its restrictions sometimes got it right, may be found in the classic movie *Casablanca*. Made in 1942, while it was never verbalized or shown outright, there is no question that Rick and Ilsa slept together; so too the various unsavory illicit carnal liaisons of Captain Renault. And, of course, given the sexual background, indeed impropriety, of Rick and Ilsa's relationship, coupled with her adultery, mandated that they could not fly off happily in love and together. Instead, Rick had to act nobly at the end, allowing Ilsa and her god-like husband Victor Laszlo to get on the plane together to fly off in the fog to Lisbon to save the world. Given that unforgettable and wonderful ending, following the restraints this time did no harm.

Under the umbrella of the Code, the studios continued to make and release movies. Despite the limitations placed upon it, movie-making reached its apex in 1939. And each studio had its formula and preference for the types of pictures made.

When Jack Warner passed in 1978, many of the obituaries written about him highlighted how he and his three brothers left the family butcher shop in rough and violent Youngstown, Ohio, for the movies that they shaped, revolutionized, and glorified. Perhaps those obits also noted Jack's highly strained family relationships—going behind the backs of his brothers Harry and Albert and selling the studio to a syndicate secretly loyal to him; fights and a falling-out with Harry so severe that not only did they stop talking but Jack didn't attend Harry's funeral in 1958 opting instead to go on his annual vacation; divorcing his first wife Irma after two decades of marriage to marry a second woman, Ann Page, who the Warner family didn't accept, and his cheating on her; estrangement from his son whom he fired from the company and didn't mention in his 1964 autobiography.

Film director and writer Gottfried Reinhardt, who fled Germany in 1932, and wrote *Bridal Suite* in 1939, a comedy about how a playboy finds the value of hard work and true love, observed that Jack Warner found pleasure in humiliating his underlings, whom he often treated poorly and fired constantly. "Harry Cohn was a sonofabitch but he did it for business; he was not a sadist. Mayer could be a monster, but he was not mean for the sake of meanness. Jack was."

Perhaps Jack, the youngest of his brothers, turned into the person he was when his beloved older brother, Sam, a visionary, died in 1927 at the age of 40 of infections and illnesses initially caused by severe dental problems. The day after he died, on October 5, 1927, his baby *The Jazz Singer* was released. The movie, the first major talkie, revolutionized the industry. Jack's right-hand man, Darryl F. Zanuck, and Warner Bros. won an honorary Oscar for producing the film at the very first Academy Award ceremony, held in May of 1929, honoring the films of the previous two years. The movie rescued a financially ailing studio in dire need of a hit. The last time the studio found itself in such dire straits, Rin Tin Tin raced in to save the day. The lovable German Shepherd was so popular and so smart that a bedazzled Jack Warner tartly branded him smarter than some of his employees. Soon the pooch was earning a thousand dollars a week in becoming the studio's top star.

With money in hand, Warner Bros. churned out action movies and crime films featuring guns galore. In 1931, it released one of the very first full-fledged gangster films, *Little Caesar*, which made the studio money and Edward G. Robinson a star. Playing hoodlum Caesar Enrico "Rico" Bandello, the street thug works his way to the top of organized crime in Chicago only to disintegrate into failure, poverty, and the gutter. At the end he is gunned down and utters the memorable line, "Mother of mercy, is this the end of Rico?"

Following up on the movie's success, just a few months later, *The Public Enemy* was released which catapulted James Cagney, playing bootlegger Tom Powers during Prohibition, to stardom. The most notable scene in the movie involved Cagney, while sharing a meal and argument with his soon to be ex-girlfriend, smashing a half grapefruit in her face. He quickly finds a new girlfriend in Gwen Allen, played by the blonde bombshell Jean Harlow, who, a year later, would be living her own real-life tragedy with the murder of MGM executive Paul Bern, her husband of just a few months. Needless to say, Cagney too dies in the end. Zanuck produced both films. Shortly thereafter, following a salary dispute with Warner, he left and created 20th Century Fox.

In 1939, Warner Bros. released over fifty movies. They released two on July 22 alone. The entertaining *Daughters Courageous* involved an engaged woman having to decide whether to marry her boyfriend or her long ago declared dead husband Jim Masters, who returned after a twenty-year absence. *Casablanca*'s future Captain Renault, Claude Rains, played Masters. The award-winning Michael Curtiz, who discovered and cast John Garfield (born Jacob Garfinkle in NYC), directed it. A few years later Curtiz would again direct Rains in *Casablanca.*

The second movie released that day, *Each Dawn I Die*, would turn out to be one of the studio's most popular movies that year with Jimmy Cagney playing a crusading reporter fighting political corruption. For his efforts he's framed for manslaughter and given a lengthy sentence. In prison he meets "Hood" Stacey, played by George Raft, whose electric performance earned him a long-term contract. In the end, as per the Code, Hood is killed, the crooked governor is brought to justice, and Cagney is freed.

Mining its rich vein, Warner made *The Roaring Twenties*, starring the had-to-be overworked Cagney, this time paired with an equally busy Humphrey Bogart. It was the second movie that year featuring Cagney and Bogart, who earlier together made *The Oklahoma Kid*.

The Roaring Twenties spanned the years from 1919 to 1933 and is considered a classic gangster film, featuring World War I, friendship, Prohibition, crime, wealth, the Depression, betrayal, poverty, a few tough but loving dames including one Panama Smith, blasting guns and murder. In the end, a once-wealthy but now-downtrodden crook Cagney goes to big boss Bogart, asking him to call off a hit on their once good friend turned prosecutor. A fight ensues in which Cagney beats Bogart to the draw and kills him. While escaping, Cagney is shot in the back by one of Bogart's henchmen. He staggers and falls dead by a church. Panama Smith who had been on the scene, rushes over and cradles Cagney. When a cop asks who he is, she replies, in timeless end-of-a-gangster-film talk: "He used to be a big shot."

Adding to the Warner's All-Star list of actors—Robinson, Cagney, Bogart, Raft—may have been the best of them all, Bette Davis. Born Ruth Elizabeth (Betty) Davis in 1908 in Lowell, Massachusetts, to middle-class parents who divorced when she was around 7, she caught, like many, the acting bug upon seeing a play. She changed the spelling of her name to mirror that of *La Cousine Bette*, from the Balzac novel. After appearing in a series of plays, her notable talents were recognized, and she was signed by Warner Bros. where she remained for eighteen years. Around the same time she married the first of her four husbands, Harmon "Ham" Nelson. The marriage was rocky, he was overshadowed by a wife earning considerably more than him, and her affairs, with Howard Hughes and director William Wyler, and abortions.

In 1939, she made four movies. *Dark Victory*, in which she plays a wealthy, young headstrong woman who finds, in short order, redemption, purpose, love, and death, was her best, garnering another Academy Award nomination. Initially the rights to the project were controlled by MGM's David O. Selznick, who sold them to an unenthusiastic Jack Warner ("Who wants to see a dame go blind?"), who thankfully relied on the advice of others. The hope of pairing Davis's with Spencer Tracy went unfulfilled as securing his services could not be arranged. In his stead, the dependable, steady, and charismatically challenged George Brent came aboard. Joining him were an Irish-accented Humphrey Bogart playing Michael O'Leary, the horse trainer working for Davis' character, Judith Traherne, and secretly in love with her; Geraldine Fitzgerald as best friend, Ann, who visits Judith in her large mansion complete with servants; a young Ronald Reagan, not yet 30, playing Judith's playboy friend who seemingly always carries a drink while looking dashing in his ever-present tuxedo throughout the entire movie; and Henry Travers (better known as the bumbling and lovable Clarence the angel in *It's a Wonderful Life*, made in 1946 with Jimmy Stewart), who plays kindly old Dr. Parsons who delivered Traherne twenty-three years earlier.

Concerned about Traherne uncharacteristically passing out on a few occasions, Dr. Parsons seeks out a friend and brain surgeon, Dr. Frederick Steele (Brent), to examine her. Steele, who is literally closing his office—yet nothing is packed and his nurse appears to be still busily engaged—and leaving for Vermont within an hour to begin a new brain research career, reluctantly agrees. At first, she is cold, evasive, and flippant—"I'm well and strong and nothing can touch me."—but quickly warms to the kind and concerned doctor. Tests lead to surgery which leads to consultations and a "prognosis negative"[1] for her brain tumor. Traherne cannot be cured and will be dead within a year, losing her sight right before she passes. Steele speaks with Parsons and the decision is made not to tell her, wanting her to enjoy the final year of her life.

At a party in Judith's mansion, Dr. Steele cannot hide the truth from Ann, who also agrees not to alert her best friend of her bleak destiny. Soon Judith and the good doctor fall in love and decide to marry. With Steele finally making good on his desire to relocate to Vermont (in the hope of finding a cure for those who suffer from Traherne's ailment), Judith goes to meet him at his office, which this time is clearly being packed up. There she stumbles upon her devastating medical file. Feeling that Steele is marrying her out of pity, she breaks up with him and returns to her wild, hedonistic lifestyle. Soon, however, she comes to her senses and marries the man she loves and the two move to scenic Vermont, where they are blissfully happy.

After several months, Ann comes to visit and finds a content and fulfilled couple. Steele privately tells her that, "We just pretend that nothing's going to happen." But it is and it arrives quickly. Digging with Ann in her garden, Judith observes that it's getting darker but the sun is still warm on her hands. Suddenly, the reality of her observation sinks in. She is going blind. Death is near.

Hiding this from her husband, who is leaving to accept a prestigious medical award in New York, she convinces him to go without her. As for his work, whatever he achieves, tell the world that, "This was for Judith, my wife." After professing her love and happiness, she adds, "Nothing can hurt us now. What we have can't be destroyed. That's our victory. Our victory over the dark."

After bravely seeing Steele off, Judith bids goodbyes to Ann and her loving housekeeper, pets her two loyal dogs before sending them away, and retires to her room, where she prays and then lies on her bed, staring out as the movie slowly blurs and fades to black.

Schmaltzy and corny and milked to the end, yes, but impossible not to be hopelessly and completely drawn in, so good, so convincing, so brilliant a performance by its star.

As it turns out, Davis had much to draw on emotionally while filming the movie. Her marriage had earlier collapsed as did her love affairs with Howard Hughes, and her director on *Jezebel*, William Wyler, whom she described as the love of her life. So despondent was she that she asked producer Hal Wallis to release her from her contract. Up to that point her performance had been so notable that Wallis replied, "I've seen the rushes—stay sick!"

During filming, Davis turned to her co-star, George Brent, who had recently split from the third of his eventual five wives, for love and support. Their affair so satisfied Davis that she later remarked, "Of the men I didn't marry, the dearest was George Brent." They made many movies together including another in 1939, *The Old Maid*.

His family having fled Poland due to antisemitism, Jack Warner was particularly affected and alarmed by the rise of Nazism in Europe. While other studios shied away from addressing the subject for fear of alienating powerful groups, Warner jumped in. Wishing to make a movie that involved concentration camps, the Production Code Administration nixed the idea as it shed an unfavorable light on another country's institutions and leaders. Finally, with the encouragement of FBI Director J. Edgar Hoover, Warner Bros. released *Confessions of a Nazi Spy* starring Edward G. Robinson in 1939. The movie, based on an actual FBI case in which a Nazi spy ring was exposed, featured many German actors, including some who fled Germany.

Filmed in documentary-like form, the movie depicts the FBI investigating its first major international spy case, taking down an extensive Nazi ring and charging them with espionage. The film also tells of the severe beating, which actually occurred in April 1938, of some American veterans who stood up for democracy and freedom at a Bund rally in New York City celebrating Hitler's birthday. After the successful trial, U.S. Attorney Kellogg tells FBI Agent Renard, played by Robinson, that, "when our basic liberties are threatened, we wake up." The film closes with the playing of *America the Beautiful*.

The film outraged Hitler, who instructed the German Ambassador to lodge a formal complaint with Secretary of State Cordell Hull. The Roosevelt Administration, joined by Hays and some isolationist lawmakers, strongly requested that such pictures not be made in the future. Congressman Martin Dies Jr. of Texas condemned the studio for defaming a friendly nation. (The year before, Dies criticized Shirley Temple and other Hollywood figures for reaching out to a French newspaper sympathetic to the communist cause. Temple was 10 at the time.) Several countries around the world banned the movie while Germany banned all Warner Bros. productions. Despite winning the National Board of Review Award for Best Film of 1939, the movie flopped.

Waiting in the wings were an onslaught of other, soon to be classic, movies. As always, the studios were looking for ways to improve their product. The talkies constituted a momentous leap forward. A second invention centered around the sound quality of those talkies. And in a small garage in northern California, on January 1, 1939, two young men came together, flipped a coin to decide whose name would go first in the company name, and with $538 formed a company that changed not only the movies, but the world.

3

The Birth of Silicon Valley

Bill Hewlett and David Packard met in 1930 in college, Stanford University in Palo Alto, to be exact. They shared a love of electronics and the drive and intelligence to see their young dreams grow old with success.

David Packard was born a hundred miles south of Denver in Pueblo, Colorado, on September 7, 1912, to successful and intelligent parents, his father being an attorney. Like many early western towns, Pueblo had its share of problems prior to the law settling in. Once considered the world capital of saddle-makers, it soon evolved into a steel town, bringing in various ethically and culturally diverse workers looking for employment. Pueblo also served, sadly, as the location for the final speech given by President Woodrow Wilson who was barnstorming the country to gather support against a hostile Congress for the creation of the League of Nations that he had championed at the end of World War I. Immediately after delivering his latest plea he stumbled, suffering a near fatal blood clot resembling a stroke. He quicky became incapacitated and was essentially never seen again, closeted in the White House with his wife, Edith Bolling Galt Wilson, overseeing his every move—including who and what he saw. In effect, she became the de facto president. Meanwhile, despite Wilson's efforts, Congress voted against joining the League.

Keen of mind, with an interest in radio, electronics, and engineering, Packard also possessed a western toughness, brought out by his athletic feats, playing football, basketball, and running track in high school. With fate driving the car of life, Packard, who planned to attend college in Colorado, found himself on a family vacation in California where a young lady singing the high praises of Stanford University persuaded him to change his plans. He enrolled in 1930 with his father able to scrounge up the high tuition of

$114 a quarter in depression-torn America. Once in school, he continued his engagement with sports—playing at times, football, track, and basketball. He majored in electrical engineering and met the three people who would become the most important influences for the remainder of his eighty-three-year long life—his classmate Bill Hewlett, his professor Fred Terman, and his future wife Lucile Salter.

Not wishing to have sports dominate his rigorous studies, he nonetheless recognized their value—competition, fair play, and teamwork. On the freshman football field he met his teammate Bill Hewlett, who recognized the additional benefits of sports—organization and practice.

William Hewlett was born in 1913 in Ann Arbor, where his father, Walter, taught at the University of Michigan's Medical School. When Walter secured a similar position at Stanford, the family left the cold of the upper Midwest for the far warmer West Coast. Unfortunately, Walter died when his young son Bill was just 12 years old. Perhaps recognizing the value of the Hewletts, Bill was later accepted to Stanford where he majored in engineering.

In college, the two highly motivated students shared common interests in science, radio, and the great outdoors—canoeing, fishing, skiing, and hiking—and quickly found their paths unsurprisingly crossing. A common denominator turned out to be a beloved professor, Dr. Frederick Terman, who quickly turned into a friend, benefactor, supporter, mentor, and later, business consultant.

Frederick Terman was born in 1900 to overachieving parents. His father Lewis came to find himself on the Stanford faculty, where he taught psychology. Concentrating on gifted children, he popularized the IQ test. His mother, upon graduating college, taught English at a local school in Indiana before moving to California with her husband and 10-year-old son Fred, whose hobby was ham radio.

When the time came, Fred remained at the university in which his father taught and gained undergraduate and graduate degrees in electrical engineering. He moved to MIT in the Boston area, in Cambridge, where he received a Doctor of Science advanced degree, the equivalent of a PhD, in the same field. In 1925, he returned to Stanford, also joining its faculty, where he revolutionized the study of radio, teaching and authoring the leading articles and books on the subject. Of note, he sought out the smartest of the students, past and present, and the young leaders in the field, strongly encouraging them to spread their wings in their chosen field by opening their own companies, which he himself strongly supported, including his own investments. Three such people were Charles Litton and the Varian brothers, Russell and Sigurd.

Although young at the time, not even thirty, Charles Litton built vacuum tubes and the first practical glass blowing lathe. He founded Litton Industries, which ultimately became a major defense contractor. Along the way, Cecil Howard Green worked for him and eventually started Texas Instruments. In 1937, the Varian Brothers invented the klystron—a vacuum tube used in microwave relay communications as well as in television transmitters, satellite communications, radar transmitters, and generators powering particle accelerators. In 1948, they started an early high-tech company, Varian Associates, and moved into Stanford Industrial Park, the world's first university research area. Called "an engine for Silicon Valley" as well at "the epicenter of Silicon Valley," over 150 companies located there.

Every so often, but not often enough, a group of unknown people, typically young, come together on a project or in a field and unexpectedly perform miracles, climbing a mountain so high that no one saw it coming nor could have predicted it. And it happens in all walks of life. In baseball, the 1969 Miracle Mets, tabbed prior to the start of the season to finish again dead last, or close to it, as they had futilely done every year during the decade of their creation, won the World Series. Led by a then bunch of unknowns, quickly Tom Seaver and Nolan Ryan developed into Hall of Famers, while other lesser knowns had career years—Cleon Jones, Tommy Agee, Little Al Jackson, Jerry Koosman, Tug McGraw, and Buddy Harrelson to name just a few.

In 1973, the movie *American Graffiti*, starred a cast of relative unknowns, except for a now almost 20-year-old Ron Howard, who played Opie on the *Andy Griffith* television show. Some of the newbies had lead roles and would become major stars—Howard, Richard Dreyfuss, Cindy Williams (Shirley of *Laverne and Shirley* in three years), Mackenzie Phillipps, and Wolfman Jack. Others had minor parts consisting of a few minutes of screen time—Kathleen Quinlan, future *Three's Company* television star Suzanne Somers playing "The Blonde in the T-Bird," and a then working carpenter who didn't want to cut his hair so they had him wear a cowboy hat in his few scenes, Harrison Ford. The movie received superb reviews and is in AFI's Top 100 movies of all time. George Lucas, its co-writer and director, like the others, was also a stranger to the public. Four years later, in 1977, Lucas gained immortality with *Star Wars*. Perhaps the best-known person at the time *American Graffiti* was released was its producer, *The Godfather*'s Francis Ford Coppola. Fred Terman is the Lucas and Coppola of his profession.

While still a junior at Stanford in 1933, Dave Packard trudged up to a ham radio station in which he was involved. Housed in the same building as Terman's laboratory, the two would pass one another in the halls or see each other either going in or coming out of the building. Chance encounters bred familiarity and soon they were stopping and talking. It quickly became evident that the professor knew far more about the student than the other way around. In time, Packard enrolled in Terman's radio education class, joining Hewlett.

After graduating Stanford and gaining membership in Phi Beta Kappa, Packard left to work at General Electric, in 1935, in Schenectady, New York, where he joined three dozen or so other engineering graduates, who were placed in various departments. Terman kept in touch, even visiting when he happened to be in the area, checking up on him and relaying the latest news from Stanford. Hewlett, from his temporary new home in Boston where he attended MIT, worked on his master's degree and also visited Packard where the two discussed, among other things, their future plans.

While Packard quickly distinguished himself at GE, Hewlett after MIT and a short stint in the army, found himself with few job prospects. Terman, upon hearing this, arranged some freelance work and before long Hewlett was back in California and designing an electroencephalograph, which discerns disorders by measuring brain waves, for a local doctor. Not busy enough, he also worked on another Masters.

With one genius in the fold, Terman worked on getting the other. Given his tenacity, it took little time. A fellowship arose involving an idea of Russ Varian, with research taking place at Charles Litton's lab. Offered the position, a newly married Packard grabbed it and "temporarily" left Schenectady and GE, much to its bosses' chagrin and puzzlement given his great success with the company and a concomitant bright future. He never returned.

Hewlett found a new home—367 Addison Avenue in Palo Alto—for Dave Packard and his new wife Lucile, who lived on the first floor, while the landlady stayed on the second. Bill lived in a small cottage behind the dwelling. Most importantly, with the house came a garage, from which a seed would be planted; in time it grew thousands of times over into a technological Amazon Rainforest. The garage became a lab, furnished with the tools and instruments Dave and Lucile lugged in their 3,000-mile journey from one end of the nation to the other.

On January 1, 1939, Bill Hewlett and David Packard formalized their relationship and started their company. They flipped a coin as to whose name went first. Bill won, and Hewlett-Packard came into existence, destined to forever change the world and make their creators billionaires.

The first planted seed grew into the Model 200A oscillator, their first product. The invention tested sound equipment using a simple light bulb as the temperature-resistant resistor. Feeling that the simplicity, efficiency, and cost of the device would take the marketplace, including Hollywood, by storm, the two next turned their inventor caps into business ones.

They decided not to call their first model 100A or 1A, fearing that it indicated a new company peddling a new product. Instead, they dubbed it the Model 200A. To publicize the smallish item, they took pictures of it, placing it on the mantel above the fireplace in their living room. Lucile typed out the specifications and their sales pitch. Now all that remained was finding customers and deciding how much to charge. Once again Professor Terman came to their aid, furnishing them with a long list of potential buyers. As for cost, being fans of history, they somehow settled in on the presidential campaign of 1844 in which James Polk, wishing to expand our nation by adding the Oregon territory, uttered the battle cry, "54-40 or fight." The numbers delineated the latitude and longitude of the land in question. Thus, the first price, $54.40.

Their first mistake. It wasn't enough. To their surprise and delight, raising the price did not deter sales. They also started advertising, placing a small ad in a magazine. When Chicago's talented and ambitious Al Crossley saw it, he came calling and soon became their Midwest representative. With its revolutionary invention, with many to follow, the company took off, greatly aided by the creator of Mickey, Minnie, Pluto, Donald, Daisy, and Goofy.

The legendary Walt Disney constantly searched for innovation and improvement. From his creation of Mickey Mouse in 1928, followed by other beloved Disney characters, to colorization, improved music, art, and camera angles, and expanding the cartoon shorts into full-length movie features, he next sought to improve the quality of sound in his movies. With continuing planning and hard work, it all came together in the classic film *Fantasia*, which featured eight animated segments set to classical music, performed mainly by the Philadelphia Orchestra. Disney wanted the sound to be of the highest quality, as if the audience were hearing the luxurious music live. To aid in that lofty goal, Disney purchased eight or so newly called and slightly altered, HP200B oscillators at $71.50 each from the newly formed Hewlett-Packard Company.

After a year, Hewlett-Packard moved out of its garage, into the Tinker Bell Shop, across the street from its landlord John Bell who ran Tinker Bell's Fix It Shop. In time they owned a good portion of the street. A quarter of a century later they introduced their first computer.

Few today realize the extent to which electronics played a part in World War II. Indeed, it arguably was the world's first electronic war. In the movies, fighters and bombers are filmed heroically flying over a bomb site in

Germany with the bombardier studying his sight and meticulously dropping his payload, much of which lands on the intended target. In fact, often the bombs fell far short, sometimes even miles away from where they had been aimed. As the pilots were engaged in their mission, they found their planes being shot down at alarming rates, from 4 percent to an astronomical 20 percent. Accordingly, for every hundred-strong flights leaving their base, anywhere from four to twenty would not return. With a crew of ten or so, the number of flyers killed, injured, or missing was staggering. With the average age of those serving being 19–22, the toll was even more sobering.

The German adroitness at inflicting such damage was due in large part to its extensive air defense system. Effectively using radar, ground control targeted incoming bombers and relayed the information to its own fighters. Soon radar systems were extended to German pilots who, while in the air, could seek out the allied aircraft from afar and plot their plan of attack. They met with great success.

To counter this drubbing, the government created a top secret 800-person test center—the Harvard Radio Research Lab—located on the campus of Harvard University in Cambridge, Massachusetts. It was headed by the dean of electronics Fred Terman, who moved east to serve his country. The goal of the group was simple, yet seemingly impossible to accomplish—invent, establish, and create a system to jam and confuse German signal intelligence. And do it in six months.

They first built a radar map. Joining bomber and fighter units, unarmed planes armed with electronic monitoring devices recorded and monitored all German radar signals. With this information in hand, the next problem was countering the German defense system. A simple, yet ingenious, solution was devised. Tin foil throws off radar detection. Thus, 10-inch strips of tin foil were cut up and dropped from the planes as they flew their missions. In the beginning, this consisted of simply opening a window on the plane, sticking one's hand out, and dropping handfuls of tin foil strips. The first time it was used, in July 1943 over Hamburg, Germany, not a single Allied plane was lost. With so much tin foil needed, acquiring it became a necessity, without tipping off why it was so needed. Under the guise that it was necessary for supplying our troops with objects made of tin—which was true—the War Production Board mandated that every town, whose population exceeded 25,000 residents, have a process for collecting tin cans. Little did many know that much of what was collected was being modified and thrown out of planes to offset the enemy's radar. Soon, the tin-foil-out-the-window strategy was improved upon, with radar jammers built into every bomber. In all, 30,000 or so were manufactured.

Terman, who could be dubbed the Father of Electronic Warfare, witnessed the emerging relationship between government and universities. No longer was the need to draft specialists—professors and students—in the scientific field; rather, allow them to work at their schools, in their labs with their colleagues, under a contract with the government paying the schools which paid its employees. To do so, the government created the Office of Scientific Research and Development in May 1941, to manage scientific research for the military. It spent nearly half a billion dollars on research and development with $117,000,000 of it going to MIT, $83,000,000 to Cal Tech, and $30,000,000 each to Harvard and Columbia. Terman's beloved Stanford received $50,000, which undoubtedly stuck in his craw.

At the end of the war, Terman returned to Stanford, bringing with him some members of his working group. In effect, he duplicated and created a new Harvard-like entity, this one still under his leadership, but at Stanford. Government money flowed in for research, especially with a new post-World War II enemy, the Soviet Union and its Iron Curtain. Working with the CIA, NSA, and the military, Terman's program grew to 400 members. So secret were their dealings that 75 percent of all PhD theses were classified. Accomplishing his goal of making Stanford the MIT of the West, Terman, in addition to his other parentage, might also be considered a father of the emerging Military-Industrial Complex.

He wasn't done yet. Terman also changed the relationship between schools and start-ups, encouraging his graduating students to go out into the scientific world, start their own businesses, with the full and continuing support of their school, Stanford. Students were free to use school labs and facilities while professors were encouraged to consult with, and even invest in, the new entities. The manner in conducting business was also altered—failure was acceptable, a price paid for learning and advancement—unlike other business models where failure resulted in criticism and dismissal. Work hard, be creative, think big, and learn from your mistakes. With the students and supportive faculty of Terman pollinating Silicon Valley, it was on its way to what we know it to be today. Two additional events put it over the top, and they both occurred in 1956.

The first came when Lockheed moved to Sunnyvale, which was 12 or so miles away from Palo Alto. Once there, Silicon Valley sharpened its focus. In four short years, the area grew from zero to 20,000 engineers. Lockheed was by far the largest employer in the area, concentrating on satellites and submarines.

The second seminal event that year arrived when the research director of an anti-submarine combat group, who led a radar training unit during the war, moved back to California. William Shockley came from an impressive family. His father was a mining engineer who spoke eight languages. His mother graduated from Stanford and became the first female U.S. deputy mining inspector. Their son William was brilliant but flawed, with a hot temper. Homeschooled, perhaps due to his parents' dislike of public education, he eventually attended Cal Tech as an undergraduate and MIT, where he received his doctorate in 1936. In the next few years, he published numerous notable papers in physics and received his first patent. Recognizing his brilliance, the government utilized his services during World War II. His report in 1945 on the number of Allied casualties if Japan were to be invaded—1.7 to 4 million injuries with 400,000 to 800,000 deaths and 5 to 10 million Japanese dying—was a factor in deciding to drop atomic bombs on Hiroshima and Nagasaki. For all his accomplishments and responsibilities, Shockley received the Medal for Merit in 1946, from the Secretary of War, Robert Patterson. Ten years later, in 1956, he won a Nobel Prize.

Upon returning to California, Shockley opened the Shockley Semiconductor Laboratory, bringing with him the very best young engineers in the nation, who worked on the first silicon semiconductor devices. In contrast to his brilliant mind and spotting of talent, he was an awful manager, despised by many who worked for him for his autocratic, unpredictable, and even paranoid manner. One year later, in 1957, the "Traitorous Eight" left his employ and started Fairchild Semiconductor, destined to become an innovator and leader in transistors and integrated circuits, with locations throughout the nation and world. Over the next two decades, sixty-five new related and similar companies formed, all of which, including Fairchild, could be traced directly back to Shockley, "the man who brought silicon to Silicon Valley."

Shockley died at 79 in 1989, estranged from his first wife and their three children, who he thought all intellectually inferior to himself. An avid rock climber, he forged a novel and popular route across an overhang in the Hudson River Valley. The site, called "Shockley's Ceiling" in many guidebooks, was disgorged of its moniker in 2020 due to his outspoken beliefs in eugenics and voluntary sterilization and the inferiority of the intellect of African-Americans. And in another footnote to history, as a child, he took Dr. Lewis Terman's IQ test measuring child geniuses. He did not make the grade.

While there are many fathers and mothers of success, with numerous people holding the baton of creativity and achievement, a few certainly stand out. Dr. Terman, a pioneer of modern electronic warfare, Silicon Valley, the military-industrial complex, and a father figure to Bill Hewlett and Dave Packard, who on the first day of 1939 started a business that, among other things, changed how movies were and continue to be made. And on their journey, they, and their confederates, created far more.

4

Earhart, Capone, and "an arm torn out by the roots"

Amelia Earhart

"The best way to do it is to do it."

On January 5, 1939, the world's foremost female pilot, and, indeed, one of the world's best pilots in her day, Amelia Earhart was officially declared dead. To this day, her disappearance remains one of the great unsolved mysteries.

Born in 1897 in Kansas, Amelia Mary (often called either Meeley or Millie) Earhart had an independent streak, fostered by her mother's desire to not raise her two young daughters to be "nice little girls." Close to her younger sister Grace Muriel (Pidge), the sisters frolicked in the woods, climbed trees, hunted, and shot rats, and flew downhill on their sleds on the local snowy hills.

In life, some are mesmerized by a childhood experience and develop an obsession with that encounter. Such was not the case with Amelia and flying. When she was 10, her family visited the Iowa State Fair and saw an aircraft. Despite her father's urging to take a flight, Amelia demurred, saying that the biplane "[looked] like a thing of rusty wire and wood and not at all interesting."

Although her childhood was far from smooth—her mother and alcoholic father moved to Iowa, then Minnesota and Chicago for work while she and her sister temporarily lived with their maternal grandparents—she loved to read and developed an interest in women working in male-dominated fields. Her education was also rocky; home-schooled initially and then attending a few different schools. In Chicago, she chose to go to a high school further from where she lived as the closer one had a poor science lab. While there, however, she was not particularly happy and kept to herself, graduating in 1916. Briefly attending junior college, she dropped out and worked as a nurse's aide. In 1919, on the cusp of entering Smith College, she instead decided to go to Columbia to study medicine. After a year, she dropped out and moved to California where her parents had relocated. Along the way she experienced some serious medical issues, dealing with her sinuses, from which she convalesced for a year.

In sharp contrast to Amelia's pedestrian reaction upon seeing an aircraft a decade earlier, she experienced a radical departure while taking a ride in a small aircraft in 1920, where she felt her soul lift along with that of the plane. Minutes into the flight she "knew I had to fly."

Working odd jobs, she earned money for flying lessons. Her first was from a fellow female flyer, Anita "Neta" Snook, who accomplished many firsts in her illustrious career—first female aviator in her home state of Iowa, first female student in a Virginia flying school, first female to run both her own aviation business and a commercial airfield, and first woman to enter a men's air race at the LA Speedway. Despite these lofty accomplishments, she would in time come to be best known for her warm relationship with Earhart, as indicated by the title of Snook's autobiography, *I Taught Amelia to Fly*.

Once Earhart took to the skies, she flew many noteworthy missions and slowly gained recognition for her accomplishments. She set a female world altitude record of 14,000 feet and was just the sixteenth woman in the United States to earn a pilot's license. The event that made her a household name ironically did not involve her piloting a plane but by travelling with two others—Wilmer Stultz and Louis Gordon—and maintaining the flight log on a transatlantic flight in 1928, duplicating what Charles "Lucky Lindy" Lindbergh had done just one year earlier. Despite the danger of the journey, Earhart demonstrated her modesty by observing, "Stultz did all the flying—[he had to as the flight involved instruments of which I had no training]. I was just baggage, like a sack of potatoes.... [M]aybe someday I'll try it alone." In 1932 she did just that.

She and her two partners received a heroes' welcome, including a ticker-tape day parade in New York City and a presidential meeting with Calvin Coolidge. Dubbed "Lady Lindy," due to her accomplishments and resemblance to the famed flyer, she was now a celebrity, the "Queen of the Air." In that same year, she flew solo across North America and back, becoming the first female to do so.

Earhart quickly entered a world of whirlwind activity—writing, lecturing, and touring the nation. Along the way she endorsed and promoted products, including fashions for females. She became an associate editor at *Cosmopolitan* magazine where she promoted air travel, joined Lindbergh in working with what would become TWA, and served as vice president of National Airways. She educated the public about the feasibility and common use of airplanes and air travel, nudging its perception of flight as only involving stunts performed by daredevils. She worked with a group, The Ninety-Nines, which supported female aviation.

Publisher George P. Putnam, who had recommended a slowly emerging Earhart for the transatlantic flight, stayed with her, and promoted her literary and promotional efforts. Putnam's role was a familiar one. As head of a book publishing company bearing his name, he published and promoted Lindbergh's autobiography *We*, which Lindbergh himself wrote in less than two months. It became an international bestseller. Putnam did the same for Earhart and her book, *20 Hrs., 40 Min.*. As it turned out, Putnam and Earhart shared more than a love of flying; they enjoyed the great outdoors and all that it had to offer—camping, hiking, swimming, riding, golf, and tennis. Given their compatibility and shared interests, it came as no surprise when they married in 1931. Keeping with her feminist beliefs, she kept her last name and insisted on equal responsibilities in the union. Given his wife's fame, Putnam often found himself being called Mr. Earhart.

After duplicating Lindbergh's solo flight in 1932, Earhart received even greater acclaim, winning prestigious awards from both the American and French governments. Her exploits continued. In 1935, she became the first aviator to fly solo from Hawaii to California. She later flew nonstop from Los Angeles to Mexico City and then from Mexico City to New York City. While routine today, back then it was like going to the moon—unheard of, undreamed of, yet made. From 1930 to 1935, Earhart set seven aviation records for women in speed and distance. With so many conquests, she set her sights on yet another—a flight around the world. Tragically, it would prove to be her last.

Flying a Lockheed Electra, on March 17, 1937, Earhart and three others departed Oakland, flying to Hawaii. Once there, they encountered problems that required a few days to repair. Taking off again, now with Earhart and navigators Fred Noonan and Harry Manning, a skilled radio operator with a knowledge of Morse Code, aboard, the plane's landing gear and/or tire blew. The plane's propellers hit the ground and skidded on its belly. The project was cancelled at which point Manning, who had other engagements, dropped out.

Not to be deterred, Earhart, on May 20, left Oakland with Noonan accompanying her. Noonan, destined to be William Dawes to Earhart's Paul Revere, was equally accomplished in the air and on the high seas, where he earlier had spent two decades, becoming a respected navigator.

Due to the weather conditions and winds, the flight flew west to east, from Oakland to Burbank, Tucson, New Orleans, and Miami. On June 1, they departed for Puerto Rico. Flying over the Atlantic Ocean, they eventually encountered Africa, then Asia, and Australia. On June 29, having travelled over 20,000 miles, New Guinea hosted them. Only 7,000 miles and a flight over the Pacific Ocean remained. After thirty stops, only three remained—Howland Island, then Hawaii and California and another hero's welcome.

At midnight on July 2, Earhart and Noonan took off. Their destination Howland Island, a sliver of land in an ocean of emptiness, over 2,000 miles away. They never made it.

The whys, whats, and hows remain hotly debated to this day. Was it the weather, the lack of a skilled radio operator with Morse Code abilities, and/or tragic miscalculations? Did the plane run out of gas and crash, killing the two? Did they try to land on another island? Did they survive the crash and die as castaways? Were they captured by Japanese forces and killed?

Reacting to the tragedy, the government immediately launched an expensive and extensive search and rescue operation. Nothing and no one were ever found.

With fame comes recognition and with recognition comes a great sense of loss to the masses when that person dies, especially unexpectedly and at a young age. Think President John F. Kennedy or Princess Diana. Most of us never met these charismatic people yet when they perished many felt great sadness. Something had been taken, never to be replaced, akin to the death of a beloved parent or close friend. In time and with one generation replacing the next, the once great dissipate into the fog of history with the next generation left reading and watching movies and documentaries about people they never knew. Today, while the legend of the shy, charismatic, and brave Amelia Earhart may vaguely be known, she personally no longer is. People today don't breathe the air she breathed, share a common world, and personally revel in her exploits and accomplishments. For those of her generation, when she passed everyone felt the emptiness we all feel when a treasured icon dies.

Amelia Earhart was officially declared dead on January 5, 1939. One day later, someone as well known, but for all the wrong reasons, left the harshest prison in the nation.

Al Capone

> "You can get a lot farther with a smile and a gun than you can get with just a smile."

On January 6, Al Capone was released from Alcatraz and taken to the Terminal Island jail to complete the remaining months of his prison sentence for, of all things given his murderous disposition, income tax evasion. Released in

November, his mind was addled and destroyed by his long-term syphilis which went untreated until the very end when he was one of the first people to receive the new wonder drug, penicillin. By then it was too late, the damage having already been inflicted. He died in Florida, a residence he had taken up years before when he sought to escape all of those trying to kill him in Chicago. One wonders what he thought while aimlessly shuffling around his house and pool in his pajamas and slippers. Did he even recall his glory days, those in which he was as well-known as Babe Ruth, Charles Lindbergh, and the most famous movie stars who also commanded the attention of an entire nation?

Alphonse Gabriel Capone was born in Brooklyn on January 17, 1899. His parents came from Italy. His father, also named Gabriel, worked as a barber; his mother, Teresa, a seamstress, when she wasn't giving birth to seven sons and two daughters. Although a bright youngster, he found trouble in his parochial school, which he left at 14 after striking a female teacher. He worked odd jobs before falling under the spell of the ever-present street gangs, joining them in their often-violent criminal mischief. One of their leaders, the physically unintimidating Johnny Torrio, was an anomaly. Calm and cool, he preferred peaceful solutions to any problems that arose. Believing that there was enough to go around, he did not see the need to fight his way out of every tough jam. He would, if necessary, resort to murder if the situation called for it, but he was hesitant to do so, perhaps fearful of events spinning even further out of his control. Seventeen years older than Capone, he took the youngster under his wing.

Capone worked in brothels and bars as a bouncer and bartender. On one occasion he insulted the sister of a fellow Brooklynite and low-level con, Frank Galluccio, who, not taking kindly to the insult, took out his pocketknife and slashed the left side of Capone's face. The permanent scar gave birth to the nickname Scarface, which Capone hated. He preferred Snorky, which translated to one being a sharp dresser.

At a social club in 1918, he met a salesgirl from a local department store, Mae Coughlin, who at 21 was two years older than Capone. Irish, she came from a hard-working and well-respected family. Despite antagonism towards such mixed unions, the two married. A year later she gave birth to their only child, a boy who they named Albert Francis, known as "Sonny," who suffered from severe hearing problems. Named godfather, Torrio generously gifted Sonny $5,000 each year on his birthday.

One year later Torrio moved to Chicago on a fulltime basis at the behest of his aunt's husband, James "Big Jim" Colosimo. Also tagged "Diamond Jim," he possessed a love of women and money. A husky man, he favored lily-white suits and expensive, extensive, and flashy jewelry. Married to Victoria

Moresco, a successful madam and businesswoman in her own right, she helped with some of his business affairs in running Chicago's burgeoning crime market—prostitution, gambling, loansharking, and any other illegal activity in which money reared its tempting head. With an ever-expanding empire and money pouring in, additional support and muscle were needed. Colosimo summonsed Torrio who in turn called Capone, who gladly left New York, where he was a suspect in some murders.

With the advent of Prohibition, Torrio foresaw the vast business opportunities it presented. Colosimo was neither on board nor particularly interested, having gone gaga over 19-year-old aspiring opera singer Dale Winter, who, needing the money, worked in one of his clubs. When the church in which she sang discovered her new place of employment, she was asked to leave. She was so talented that Flo Ziegfeld and famed opera singer Enrico Caruso, at Colosimo's request, heard her sing and came away suitably impressed. Colosimo, ignoring business, lavished his attention on Winter. Despite an over two-decade age difference, the starry-eyed crime boss left his wife to marry his new love. Proving that blood is not always thicker than water, especially when it runs green, the unassuming Torrio had his uncle murdered, a move undoubtedly seconded by Aunt Victoria.

At Big Jim's lavish funeral, priests and police bigwigs, arm in arm with local mobsters, paid their respects, joining his honorary pallbearers of judges, aldermen, a congressman, and an assistant state's attorney. Torrio, who was normally unemotional, wept, telling the press that "Big Jim and I were like brothers." The *Chicago Daily News* observed that "The murder of James Colosimo, vice lord on the south side since 1912 ... marks the ending of one epoch and the beginning of another in the history of vice in Chicago." Little did people suspect that Big Jim was a mere novice compared to the exploits of his successors.

Johnny Torrio—the Professor Fred Terman of misconduct—approached crime like a business, organizing the different factions. Joining with one with similar ideals, New York's capo di tutti capi, Charles "Lucky" Luciano, they created a board of directors to run a national crime syndicate. The matrix originated then is still in practice today.

An entrepreneur at heart, Torrio led a low-key life. He neither drank, smoked, gambled, or chased women. Happily married and devoted to his wife, he was home at six for dinner with her. He rarely swore or even raised his voice. He'd walk to work if he could, wearing a nondescript suit and his only piece of jewelry, a wedding ring. He did not carry a weapon. Once at work, he'd confer with his underlings, review what had occurred the night before and plan what to do next. Like many who run successful enterprises, he was cold and cutthroat, loyal only to the bottom line. The many prostitutes who worked in his brothels were not humans but commodities, to be ditched when their looks and usefulness waned. If someone had to be beaten, make sure it was for a good reason and then beat him (or her). Murder was to be eschewed, unless necessary. A nondescript devil.

As is frequently the case with those in organized crime, someone has what someone else wants, or takes umbrage at some remark and reacts wholly out of proportion, or demands more, more, and then more still. Despite the crime coffers overflowing in Chicago, two assassins Hymie Weiss and Vincent Drucci, perhaps at the behest of the revenge-seeking successors of the murdered North Side Gang leader Dion O'Banion, pommeled Torrio with a barrage of bullets. Rather than react with blind revenge and violence, Torrio recovered from his wounds and coolly assessed his prospects for a long life. Unlike nearly all crime lords, he up and quit and moved to Italy, leaving his empire to 26-year-old Al Capone. When Mussolini took over Italy Torrio returned to America, where he assumed the role of a respected elder statesman. He could not escape his past, however, and like the fate awaiting the newly anointed Capone, he was charged with and convicted of tax evasion. Sent to prison in 1939—the year Capone was leaving confinement—he served two years.

Once Capone took over from Torrio in 1925, business continued to expand and boom to meet a seemingly endless thirst for booze, gambling, and women. The number of brothels and gaming establishments expanded, as did liquor routes, including outside the United States to avoid Prohibition agents. The violence Torrio eschewed became a mantra for Capone. For bar owners not wishing to buy the liquor Capone peddled, messages were sent in the form of threats, bullets, and/or bombings. Businesses, whether legitimate or not, were shaken down and forced to pay for protection, often from the very people who were victimizing them. Large chunks of all that money flowed to Capone, who had the seemingly good sense to never keep any of it in his own name, lacking even a bank account. Where he stashed it all and what became of it was a well-guarded secret. Not surprisingly though, much of what came in went out to overhead, given the high cost of paying off politicians, policemen, and judges, not to mention the expenses of running a widespread criminal organization.

A self-professed man of the people, he freely granted interviews to the press and was constantly in the public eye, even setting up soup kitchens to promote a Robin Hood persona. As he explained to some eager reporters, "I am just a businessman, giving the people what they want." A snappy dresser, hence his nickname Snorky, he frequented jazz clubs and sporting events, making himself and his entourage comfortable in the best seats while mingling with the masses and associating with people who wished to be seen. He ate in upscale restaurants and smoked expensive cigars. Leading a charmed life, he lived openly and for all to see, including attractive women, who readily joined him.

In sharp contrast to the low-profile ways of Torrio, Capone failed at keeping the calm, leading to bitter rivalries and frequent attempts on his life. For self-protection, Capone set up a getaway mansion on Palm Island, Florida, which he frequently visited. It also gave him an airtight alibi for the criminal activities that he planned and others carried out, the most obvious being the Saint Valentine's Day Massacre.

At 10:30 in the morning on February 14, 1929, two men dressed as policemen, accompanied by two other well-attired men, walked into a garage located in Lincoln Park's 2122 North Clark Street in Chicago. A gathering spot for George "Bugs" Moran's North End gang, seven men inside were lined up in front of a brick wall. Their thoughts of being harassed and arrested abruptly ended as bullets from two Thompson submachine guns rattled out.

News of the brazen and brutal slayings quickly ricocheted around the nation. The front page of the *New York Times* told of "7 Chicago Gangsters Slain by Firing Squad of Rivals, Some in Police Uniforms"; "Victims Lined Up In Row"; "Hands up, Faces to Wall of Garage Rendezvous, They are Mowed Down"; "All Took It For A Raid"; "Four Machine Gun Executioners Wearing Badges, Made Swift Escape in Automobile"; "Moran's Staff Wiped Out".

The target of the raid, George "Bugs" Moran, fortuitously decided to sleep in that morning. When a lookout for the killers spotted Albert Weinshank, a Moran crony who fatally bore a strong resemblance to his boss, he signaled for the attack to begin. Weinshank and five others died immediately. A seventh, Frank Gusenberg, lingered for three hours before dying. Keeping with the code of criminal silence, he refused to name who shot him. While Moran remained in control of a greatly reduced gang, his role diminished. In the end, he left the area but continued his criminal ways. On April 30, 1939, he was convicted of conspiracy to cash stolen checks.

The audacious Massacre shocked a public used to being shocked. When the utter disgust reached the White House, Capone's days were numbered. Newly elected President Herbert Hoover set in motion a multi-agency assault on America's #1 criminal. In the end, Capone was caught, not for the killings, extortions, or any of his strong-arm tactics, but for income tax evasion. Everyone has to pay taxes, even criminals who make their money illegally. Capone lived lavishly yet lacked any legitimate proof of where the cash came from, leading to the unassailable conclusion that he had vast amounts of money, on which no taxes were paid. Capone received an eleven-year sentence. His mind already quivering from the effects of untreated syphilis, his reign was over. Released from prison in 1939, he slowly withered away before dying in his beloved Florida mansion in 1947, at the age of 48.

While some might place the monstrous Al Capone in the class of the Son of Frankenstein, that classic movie came out one week after Capone left Alcatraz.

The Super Stars of Horror

"One doesn't forget, Herr Baron, an arm torn out by the roots."

On January 13, Universal Studios released *Son of Frankenstein*, bringing together the superstars of horror. Basil Rathmore plays one whose very name brings shivers, Baron Wolf von Frankenstein, as does Bela Lugosi's Ygor, a crazed workman whose neck was broken when he came to be unsuccessfully hanged. Rounding out the trio is the dead but soon to be resurrected monster himself, played by Boris Karloff.

Although Karloff often received top billing when appearing with Lugosi, both were equally compelling. Perhaps Lugosi's best picture was the bloodsucking *Dracula*, released in 1931, which contained many memorable lines, including the rather chilling, "I never drink ... wine." His heavily accented voice found a home in horror movies, although as demonstrated in *Ninotchka*, he appeared in non-horror movies as well. Sadly, after suffering some injuries and prescribed painkillers, he became seriously addicted. With his film appearances and career dwindling, he found a second life with Ed Woods, the god-awful, cross-dressing director of ghoulish and truly terrible films. Woods's movies were so bad that he was dubbed, after he died, the Worst Director of All Time, along with one of his films, *Plan 9 from Outer Space*, the worst movie of all time. With that notoriety came a renewed interest and a cult-like following of both Woods and his so-bad-they're-good movies, resulting in a 1994 Tim Burton biopic starring Johnny Depp. Martin Landau, playing Bela Lugosi, won an Academy Award.

In all, Lugosi and Karloff appeared in seven horror movies together throughout their careers. Indicative of both the high number of films the actors appeared in, as well as their fleeting faithfulness to marriage, Lugosi was married five times and made five films in 1939, while Karloff was a six and six man.

Son of Frankenstein travels a familiar horror road. Baron Wolf von Frankenstein returns with his wife and young son to the family castle and due to the havoc previously wreaked by his father's creation, not surprisingly finds the locals rather hostile. One surprising supportive native is Inspector Krogh, who lost an arm to the monster. The Baron meets the deranged Ygor, finds the monster's comatose body and resurrects it. Responding to Ygor, the monster goes on a killing frenzy, murdering jurors from an earlier trial involving Ygor. In turn, Ygor is shot by the Baron. Meanwhile, the monster kidnaps the Baron's son and is hunted down by the Baron and Inspector Krogh whereupon, during a struggle, the monster rips out Krogh's false arm. The Baron kills the monster, saves his son, gives the castle to the villagers, who cheer the family as they depart town. At the time, this and other horror movies had to be mindful of the Hays Code. In retrospect some of the scenes are almost comical and most worthy of Mel Brooks's 1974 brilliant satire, *Young Frankenstein*.

Universal Pictures, founded in 1912 and the oldest surviving film studio, had fallen on tough times. One of its original founders, Carl Laemmle, was president and started actively billing its stars. He also astutely hired the boy wonder Irving Thalberg to essentially run the studio. So successful were his talents that Mayer lured Thalberg to MGM, where he continued to spin his magic. With Thalberg's leaving, Universal floundered. While some ventures proved successful—an Academy Award for Best Picture in 1930 for *All Quiet on the Western Front* and a niche for making horror movies—Laemmle was forced out.

Hiring teenage singing sensation Deanna Durbin and placing her under the wing of producer Joseph Pasternak, helped rescue the studio with the 1936 musical comedy, *Three Smart Girls*. That same year Durbin also made *Every Sunday*, appearing alongside an also very young Judy Garland. Three years later the studio went to the well again with Durbin starring in *Three Smart Girls Grow Up*.

Also in 1939, Universal released Jimmy Stewart's first Western, *Destry Rides Again*, which at times, like some horror movies, seems more like a comedy than a Western, once again bringing to mind Mel Brooks and his *Blazing Saddles*, also released in what had to be a most fruitful year, 1974.

Tom Destry Jr., played by Jimmy Stewart, is asked by the new sheriff, Washington "Wash" Dimsdale, to help him bring law to the town of Bottleneck. Dimsdale, the town drunk, replaced Sheriff Keogh, who has gone missing. Wash was appointed to his new position by the town's crooked mayor, Hiram J. Slade, an ally of the equally despicable saloon owner Kent. Working in the saloon is Frenchy, played by the marvelous Marlene Dietrich, the hard-nosed dame who sings and entertains the patrons. In his new position of authority Wash swears off liquor. Meanwhile, the laid-back Destry refuses to wear a gun, maintaining, like Sheriff Andy Taylor of Mayberry, that disputes can be handled civilly and with reason. Meeting resistance at first, he slowly proves himself to the skeptical townspeople.

Suspecting that the missing Sheriff Keogh has been murdered, Destry tricks Frenchy into spilling the beans. Without a body though, Destry has no case. Enter Boris, the henpecked Russian émigré who literally lost his pants to Frenchy in a card game. With a ruse in hand, Destry falsely hints to the evil Kent that he knows the location of Keogh's body. An alarmed Kent orders one of his cohorts, Gyp Watson, to check the site where the body was dumped. As Gyp heads out, Boris and Sheriff Wash follow him. When the site and body are located, Gyp is arrested and charged with murder, the hope being that he'll implicate Kent.

When the crooked mayor orders a trial over which he'll preside, Destry plans for a circuit judge to appear. His plans are dashed however when Boris mindlessly reveals it in the saloon, resulting in the bad guys going to the jail to break Gyp out. Frenchy, now in love with Destry and knowing what's going to happen, seeks to protect him, sending a message for him to come to her home. While there and bashfully flirting, gunshots ring out. Destry rushes back and discovers his prisoner gone and Wash mortally wounded. Strapping on a gun belt, the now radicalized deputy sheriff sets out to the saloon where the gang is holed up.

He gets there. Shots ring out. Frenchy attempts to intervene but is caught in the middle of the melee. Kent fires at Destry. Frenchy dives over to protect him and fatally takes the bullet. Destry shoots and kills Kent. And peace is brought to Bottleneck.

Like many movies at the time, any sexual attraction was downplayed, the parties very shyly interacting, seemingly embarrassed and put off by their mutual attraction. In fact, during the making of the movie Stewart and Dietrich were sleeping together. Allegedly when she found herself pregnant, she got an abortion.

While perhaps somewhat out of character for Stewart, Dietrich was in her element, famous for her multiple affairs with both men and women. As she explained, "In Europe, it doesn't matter if you're a man or a woman. We make love with anyone we find attractive." And that she did. Included in the long and non-exhaustive list were alleged liaisons with Yul Brynner, Kirk Douglas, John Wayne, Gary Cooper, Douglas Fairbanks Jr, Eddie Fisher, Maurice Chevalier, Adlai Stevenson II, Edith Piaf, Frank Sinatra, Edward R. Murrow, George Patton, Burt Bacharach, Michael Wilding, Harry Cohn, Kay Francis, Barbara Stanwyck, Marlon Brando, John Kennedy and perhaps his father Joe, and perhaps Greta Garbo, who was 19 at the time.

As always, the studios did all that they could to ensure that the adventures of Dietrich and her fellow stars remained private. With Dietrich, they had to work overtime.

Three days after the release of the *Son of Frankenstein*, far more serious events were occurring again in Europe, but this time not involving Germany.

England's Difficulty—Ireland's Opportunity

"[It] fizzled out like a damp and inglorious squib."

On Monday January 16, 1939, eight bombs exploded in England, five in London and three in Manchester. A 27-year-old fish porter, Albert Ross, died as a result. During his demise, Ross fell on Thomas Walsh, a postal worker, who was injured. A third man was also hurt when glass from a blown-out building struck him.

Immediately the British knew the culprits: Irish nationalists. The feud seemingly had gone on forever. The implementation of The Acts of Union in 1800 was supposed to unite England and Ireland. Instead, it alienated many Irish citizens who resented the union and sought to undermine it, which they attempted to do repeatedly.

Perhaps the most violent unrest, the Easter Rebellion, or Rising, started on April 24, 1916, and ended five days later on the 29th. While taking place mainly in Dublin, it spread to other areas, with the aim of driving the British, at the time immersed in World War I, from Ireland. In the end, due mainly to a failure of coordination, unified leadership, and manpower, the revolt failed; 485 people perished with five times that number wounded. The Irish forces unconditionally surrendered, leading to over 3,500 arrests, including 425 for looting. Many of its leaders, or those believed to be, were tried and convicted. Over a dozen received the ultimate penalty and executed over a span of ten days in May. The cases against some were weak as they were neither leaders nor killers.

The reaction of the locals initially varied. As the uprising sprang up so suddenly and without warning, many lacked the time for reflection. Many also had loved ones fighting for the British during the Great War. With lives interrupted due to the violence, destruction, and resulting food shortages, hostility focused on those who seemingly caused it: the Irish rebels. Soon however, public opinion started to turn. Many civilians had been killed at the hands of the British. The brutality of almost daily executions for a week and the incarcerations of some innocent people, coupled with stories of British atrocities, lent credence to a demand for freedom from British rule. In the end, one's natural loyalty toward fellow citizens outweighed support for foreigners occupying their country.

As for those incarcerated, placing them together provided the opportunity to meet and plan future strategies. And that they did, culminating years later in the ambitious S-Plan. Also dubbed the Sabotage Campaign, or England Campaign, it laid the groundwork for targeting mainland England's military, economic, and civil capabilities. As before, the goal was Irish independence.

On January 12, 1939, an ultimatum was issued. Written by leaders of the Irish Republican Army (the IRA) to Lord Halifax, the British Foreign Secretary, it demanded British withdrawal from an independent Ireland. Hearing no response, three days later notices posted throughout Ireland declared war. The bombings started on the 16th, and over the following eight months hit power stations, gas mains, railway stations, department stores, an aqueduct, bridges, cinemas, hotels, post offices and boxes, and banks.

As in 1916, the insurgents reached out to Germany for aid. Back then, a plan was presented to the Germans to land on the west coast of Ireland, rendezvous with a supporting force of Irish fighters, and advance to Dublin. The Germans rejected it, offering instead to provide significant arms and ammunition. The British learned of the subterfuge and stopped the vessel carrying the weaponry. Twenty-three years later, the Germans again found fault with another proposed Irish alliance, determining that the S-Plan's targeted bombings were of little use in either deterring England's capability to wage war or providing meaningful military intelligence.

To combat the assaults on its infrastructure, the British authorities beefed up security considerably and made arrests. Although detonations continued into 1940, the campaign effectively ended on August 25, 1939, with the tragic and ill-advised bombing in Coventry.

Coventry is located in the middle of England, 19 miles from Birmingham, 24 miles from Leicester, 11 miles from Warwick, and 94 miles from London. Given its high concentration of plants producing military armaments, it was a natural target for the IRA or any enemy of England.

At around 1:40 pm a bicycle with a bomb in a basket was left by a shop in a busy area of the city. Within an hour, the bomb exploded, killing five people and injuring seventy. The explosion did not discriminate, in terms of sex and age, of those blown apart. John was 15, Elsie 21, Rex 30, Gwilym 50, and James 82.

As civilians had not been specifically targeted in the past, Coventry marked a milestone. While some believe that the civilians here were not the intended target and were killed due to the ineptness of the one placing the bomb, others opine it was the IRA demonstrating to Germany its strength and value as a potential ally. Regardless, tensions ran high against the locals of Irish descent as a manhunt sought those responsible for the blast. Eventually, murder charges were levied against five defendants. Two were found guilty and hanged. In a demonstration that even in harsh times the justice system can work, the remaining three defendants were acquitted.

In summing up the S-Plan on August 23, the man who authored it observed that it was "hastily conceived, scheduled to a premature start, with ill-equipped and inadequately trained personnel, too few men and too little money [and] unable to sustain the vital spark of what must be confessed to have fizzled out like a damp and inglorious squib." One imagines that the same could be said of the Easter Rebellion of 1916.

A week after the bombing, World War II started. Shortly thereafter, during the German Blitz of 1940, Coventry was heavily targeted and devastated.

Even in harsh times, people seek out entertainment and a break from the bleakness. Hollywood once again came to the rescue, producing an action movie, whose themes resonate to this day.

A Movie and an Earthquake

"You're a better man than I am, Gunga Din."

On January 24, the frolicking adventure film *Gunga Din*, starring Cary Grant, Douglas Fairbanks Jr., and Victor McLaglen, premiered in Los Angeles. On the same day, a devastating earthquake hit Chile.

Loosely based on Rudyard Kipling's 1890 poem, *Gunga Din* centers around the exploits of three British soldiers, Sergeants Cutter (Cary Grant), Thomas "Tommy" Ballantine (Douglas Fairbanks Jr), and "Mac" MacChesney (Victor McLaglen). The role of the lowly water carrier who aspired to advance his lot in life was filled by Sam Jaffe.

Since Gunga Din was Indian, the producers initially sought a real-life rag to riches young Indian actor, Sabu, who had been born into poverty in 1924. After his father died, Sabu, only 9 years old, worked in an elephant stable. Fate intervened when a British film crew discovered and cast him in *Elephant Boy*, in which the shy, timid youngster dazzled. Unfortunately, his studio would not release him to RKO and the key role went to Jaffe.

The movie contains many of the classic hallmarks of adventure films. Carefree and wisecracking buddies working closely together against a bogeyman of an enemy; fights featuring chairs smashed over heads and punches to the face, none of which seem to cause any real physical signs of injury to the good guys other than the occasional trickle of blood down one's smiling lips; bullets fired at the heroes but just missing them, the response to which is return fire, single bullets fatally blasting the bad guys, who fall from buildings or cliffs; limitless shots fired from guns that rarely need to be reloaded; the escape from the impossible-to-escape predicament; the comely love interest who loses out in the end to the loyalty the hero has for his buddies and chosen life; and virtue triumphing over evil.

The enemy in *Gunga Din* were the Thuggee, or Thugs, based on once real-life bands of robbers and killers who patrolled and victimized those living in, or travelling through, the Indian subcontinent. In the movie, the climatic last battle has the overmatched three sergeants and Gunga Din battling the Thuggee. After being mortally wounded, a heroic Gunga Din gathers all his strength to make his way to the top of a temple where he sounds his bugle, alerting nearby British forces who rush in and defeat the foe. At his funeral, Gunga Din is posthumously inducted into the British military as a corporal and Kipling's words are read: "You're a better man than I am, Gunga Din." As the film closes, we see a proud and saluting military-clad Gunga Din.

Today, and even when the movie was released, it gathered stereotypical criticism for its portrayal of the characters. Many Hindus were offended, leading to its ban in different areas. One critic thought the movie "imperialist propaganda of the crudest, the most vulgar sort [depicting Indians] as nothing better than sadistic barbarians."

While subsequent movies, especially those currently made, are sensitive to, and avoid, such depictions, *Gunga Din* directly influenced the making of adventure movies, as demonstrated in *Star Wars* and *Indiana Jones*. In the clearest example, *Indiana Jones and The Temple of Doom*, the second in the series, set in India in 1935, has many of the features of *Gunga Din*, including the enemy being, unlike the Nazis in the first film, the Thuggee.

On that same January 24th day, very shortly before midnight—11:32—to be exact, the earth trembled and shook apart in Chillan, Chile, and its surrounding towns. Suddenly awakened, its terrified and confused residents felt helpless in not knowing what was occurring or how to respond. Before even being able to react, somewhere between 28,000 to 30,000 people perished, the exact numbers unknown. Sadly, as has been said before, a single or small group of people dying is a tragedy, tens of thousands a statistic. Nearly the entire area was obliterated by an earthquake measuring a mind-numbing 8.3; electricity and power ceased to function while fires raged. After the shaking stopped and the dead were buried, the town was rebuilt with changes made, adhering to newly devised safety codes. Notwithstanding the gross loss of life, the disaster by and large melted away.

Thunder and tumult in the world are savage and disturbing. Thunder and tumult in the boxing ring, in contrast, are a marvel. And perhaps the best fighter ever to enter the ring was the one known as "The Brown Bomber."

Joe Louis

"Everyone has a plan until they've been hit."

On January 25, 1939, Enrico Fermi, the architect of the atomic bomb, and his team met in the basement of Pupin Hall on the campus of Columbia University in New York City to conduct the first nuclear fission experiment. A couple of miles away in Madison Square Garden, boxer Joe Louis retained his heavyweight title when he knocked out John Henry Lewis in the first round of their heavyweight bout. It was the first heavyweight championship fight featuring two Black boxers. A highly respected fighter in his own right, Lewis, who would later find himself enshrined in boxing's Hall of Fame, previously held the World Light Heavyweight title from 1935 to 1938. He was no match, however, for the man he fought, both in and out of the ring. Few were.

Destined to be one of the greatest, if not the greatest, boxers of all time, Joe Louis Barrow was born in Alabama on May 13, 1914. When he was 12, his family moved to Detroit in search of a safer life and economic opportunity. Five years later he was in the ring. Dropping his last name, he fought fifty-four bouts as an amateur, winning fifty—forty-three of which came via knockout. He found even greater success as a professional, winning sixty-six of his sixty-nine bouts, with fifty-two KOs. He dominated the sport, being the world heavyweight champion from 1937 until 1949, and defended his title successfully in twenty-five straight matches. In 1939, he fought four times. Today a boxer might fight once every eighteen or so months. Back then, like movie actors, he toiled at his craft. In 1935, he fought nearly every month.

Louis's second fight in 1939 found him in Los Angeles where he battled Jack Roper, who fought six times that year. Louis KO'd him in the first round. Louis's third fight in 1939, this time on June 28th in Yankee Stadium, came against one of boxing's most colorful characters, Tony "Two Ton" Galento.

Two Ton's moniker came, not from his shortish-for-a-boxer height of 5 feet 9 inches or his 233-lb keg-like girth, honed with a steady diet of chicken, pasta, and burgers washed down with copious amounts of beer and wine—but his explanation for almost missing one of his fights: "I had two tons of ice to deliver on my way here." Utilizing his dem and dez vocabulary, he promised his foes to "moida da bum." He also refused to shower prior to matches, figuring that his overwhelming body stench would put opponents at a decided disadvantage. If that didn't work, he'd hit them below the belt, try to gouge their eyes out, head butt, rabbit punch, kidney punch, and/or elbow his opponents into submission, all of which was probably not needed given the ferocity of his left hook, the power of which Fermi might have been trying to duplicate in his Columbia lab.

While disliked by those he fought, his audiences remained highly entertained by the antics of the happy-go-lucky brawler, more so when he crossed over to the bizarre side. Over his career, he boxed a kangaroo, fought a bear, and wrestled an octopus. Another time he faced three human opponents, drank beer between rounds, and then knocked them all out. On a ten-dollar wager, only minutes before a fight he wolfed down fifty hot dogs. He won both the bet and the bout, knocking out his 6-foot-3-inch opponent with one punch in the fourth round. He did admit, however, being a bit sluggish at the outset.

His fight with Louis, who Tony told the reporters, "I never hoid of da bum," would turn out to be as compelling as many of his stunts. While Louis, as usual, remained the soft-spoken gentleman who prepared, Two Ton Tony Galento swore off alcohol for all of two days prior to meeting the world champ.

Both the highly favored Louis and the 30,000 strong crowd in attendance were stunned in the first round when Galento landed one of his trademark cement-shattering left hooks, staggering Louis. In the second round, regaining his composure and legs, Louis landed his own hard-to-believe-even-more-lethal left hook, improbably lifting Two Ton off his feet and, for the first time in his career, onto the canvas. In the third round, a pummeled Galento struck Louis with a wild left hook, knocking Louis down. Perhaps deciding that enough was enough, the fourth round found Louis all over a now thoroughly over-matched opponent, who repeatedly got smashed and mashed, so much so that the referee ended the bout. Requiring nearly two dozen stitches to stop his flowing blood, Galento complained afterwards that the fight should not have been stopped. In a bloodlust that saw more action in four rounds than ten fights today have in twelve, it definitely should have.

Louis's climb to the top did not come easy, not because of any talent deficiency, but due to the racism of the times. America did not want another Black boxing heavyweight champion, or so it thought, after having "suffered" through the vastly talented Jack Johnson, who was the heavyweight champion from 1908 through 1915. Adding to the disdain of the bigots, Johnson had the temerity of dating, sleeping with, and marrying white women, and leading an extravagant lifestyle complete with racing cars, snappy attire, and expensive jewelry.

Pressured by many to rescue the white race, former undefeated world champion, James J. Jeffries, who retired rather than fight Johnson, foolishly came out of retirement in 1910, explaining that he was "going into this fight for the sole purpose of proving that a white man is better than a Negro." In the "Fight of the Century," Johnson controlled the bout, clearly outdueling his opponent. In the fifteenth round, Jeffries's corner threw in the towel and conceded defeat. Afterwards, Jeffries respectfully observed that "I could never have whipped Johnson at my best." The nation was not as magnanimous, with riots breaking out in twenty-five states and fifty cities, with nearly two dozen people killed.

With this in mind, Louis's shrewd handlers arrived at a strategy. Knowing that as resistant as the nation was to a Black boxer, it still loved boxing, which had fallen on tough times due to fixed matches, mediocre fighters, and the negative influence of organized crime. Simply, the people were hungry for a great champion. To cull his image, Louis avoided having pictures taken with white women, did not gloat over a defeated opponent, fought honestly, gave his best, and lived, for the world to see, a wholesome life.

Perhaps Louis had little trouble adhering to guidelines that he would have naturally followed given his character. Regardless, the press and the public reacted favorably to the modest, clean living, pleasant, and talented athlete. Over time he was given various nicknames—the Chocolate Chopper, the Safari Sandman, the Mahogany Mauler, the Coffee-Colored KO King, and the one that stuck: The Brown Bomber.

Louis won the world championship on June 27, 1937, by knocking out the reigning champion, James J. "Cinderella Man" Braddock, in Chicago's Comiskey Park in the eighth round. A staggering right hand broke Braddock, and, for the only time in his career, knocked him out. That single punch rocked the world. Langston Hughes, the prolific writer and leader of the Harlem Renaissance, an intellectual and cultural society championing African-American influence—from music and dance to literature, fashion, the arts and politics—summed up Louis's influence.

> Each time Joe Louis won a fight in those depression years, even before he became champion, thousands of Black Americans on relief or W.P.A., and poor, would throng out into the streets all across the land to march and cheer and yell and cry because of Joe's one-man triumphs. No one else in the United States has ever had such an effect on Negro emotions—or on mine. I marched and cheered and yelled and cried, too.

One year later, many whites experienced similar emotions.

One of the greatest bouts ever fought, as much for outside the ring as inside, occurred on June 22, 1938, in Yankee Stadium, when Joe Louis fought Germany's Max Schmeling. The fight was the second between the two. Two years earlier, Schmeling temporarily derailed Louis's methodical march to the heavyweight title, by improbably knocking him out in the twelfth round, handing Louis a rare professional loss.

Schmeling's victory made him a national hero in Hitler's Germany, allowing Goebbels and the Nazis to herald the victory as further proof of racial superiority over an inferior race. The rematch transcended sports. Louis travelled to Washington to meet the president, who told him and the nation, that "Joe, we need muscles like yours to beat Germany." Meanwhile, Nazi officials accompanied Schmeling to New York, boasting that no Black man could ever defeat a great German fighter, whose money earned in victory would go to building tanks for his nation.

Over 70,000 spectators filled Yankee Stadium while millions throughout the world anxiously listened to the fight on radio. Louis was on a mission and his training showed as much. This time he would not underestimate an opponent. This time he would not spend as much time on his new love, golfing. "I knew I had to get Schmeling good. I had my own personal reasons and the whole damned country was depending on me."

Louis won, the fight lasting all of two minutes and four seconds.

As the war in the ring ended quickly, prospects for worldwide peace, notwithstanding Hitler's ramblings to the contrary, dimmed on an almost daily basis.

Hitler's State of the Union

"Germany Wishes to Live in Peace."

On January 30, 1939, the sixth anniversary of his rise to power, Hitler spoke for over two hours to the members of the Reichstag, assembled in the ornately decorated Kroll Opera House. He pledged support for his allies, Italy and Japan, and demanded, as rightfully belonging to Germany, the return of its colonies. He bellowed about the continuing need to expand its borders, Lebensraum, in order to feed and serve its people. He chided the United States and others for interfering with Germany's internal affairs. His main vitriol, as was often the case, centered around the Jews, who he continued to belittle and blame for all woes, real and imagined. He added churches to his rage, who sought to undermine the German government and people, and vowed to "exterminate all priests who are enemies of the State."

He observed that "Germany wishes to live in peace and on friendly terms with all countries, including America," and any beliefs to the contrary were due to "a campaign of defamation carried on to serve obvious political and financial purposes" promulgated "by the gigantic Jewish capitalistic propaganda through press, radio and films ..., [of which] there is not one word of truth in all these assertions." Ominously and prophetically, he concluded that, if war were to come it would result in "the annihilation of the Jewish race in Europe."

As before, the world heard his words, but either did not listen or did not care. Outside of a few nations, the world leaders ignored the pleas of those in dire need of help. As the *New York Times* reported, Hitler "twitted the democracies on having profuse pity for the Jews but refusing to take them [in]...."

The observation was right. In 1938, several countries gathered at the Evian Conference in Evian-les-Bains, France, to discuss what to do with the hundreds of thousands of Jews fleeing Germany and Austria who were stripped of their rights and their citizenship. No longer welcome in their homeland they needed somewhere to go. While sympathetic, no nation, other than the Dominican Republic, offered any substantial aid. The Australian delegate revealed the feelings of many. "[A]s we have no real racial problem, we are not desirous of importing one." It did not help that those representing various Jewish groups had no coordinated plan and at times worked at cross purposes, even if they agreed with the sentiment that "the world seemed to be divided into two parts—those places where the Jews could not live and those where they could not enter."

Hitler was evil not blind and spoke out.

> I can only hope and expect that the [outside] world, which has such deep sympathy for these criminals [the Jews], will at least be generous enough to convert their sympathy into practical aid. We, on our part, are ready to put all these criminals at the disposal of these countries, for all I care, even on luxury ships.

In the spring of 1939, which is discussed below, 937 Jewish passengers on a Nazi ship, sailed from Germany in search of a new home. The Voyage of the Damned didn't find one. With nowhere to go, the liner returned to Europe. As one survivor later sadly observed, "We were not wanted [and] abandoned by the world." Hitler clearly realized that the vast number of nations joined him in not wanting what he didn't want. With few countries willing to take the Jews wishing to leave Germany, Hitler was left with few options. He, not surprisingly, chose The Final Solution.

5

Sinatra, the Pope, and a Nazi Rally

Frank Sinatra

"You want the singer, take the name. "

On February 4, 1939, a skinny Frank Sinatra married Nanicia "Nancy" Rose Barbato in New Jersey's Our Lady of Sorrows Church. Together they would share three children. After their divorce in 1951, he wed three more times, the first just months later to movie temptress Ava Gardner. Nancy, meanwhile, never again walked down the aisle.

Some are gifted, in both good and bad ways, sharing a common destiny of immortality, forever engrained in the fabric of America. George Washington (despite never cutting down that cherry tree), Honest Abe Lincoln, Paul Revere (but not William Dawes), Al Capone, (Where Have You Gone) Joe DiMaggio, Marilyn Monroe (but not the seemingly equally glamorous and blond Jayne Mansfield), swivel-hips Elvis Presley, and, of course, The Voice, Ol' Blue Eyes Frank Sinatra, who bedded as many women as Marlene Dietrich.

Sinatra was born in 1915 and grew up in Hoboken to a father, Antonio Marino "Marty" Sinatra, who once boxed under the name of Marty O'Brien, and a domineering mother, Natalina "Dolly" Garaventa, whose hard-driving demeanor more than made up for her 4-foot-11-inch stature. She also ran a tavern with her husband and performed abortions on the side. While their only child Francis Albert Sinatra was born quite heavy, weighing over 13 lb, he didn't stay that way, being small and noticeably thin as a child. He also suffered from scarring to his neck, cheek, and ear, which was also perforated, due to a difficult delivery at birth, requiring forceps. Unlike his overmatched father, Frank developed a steel will of his own matching that of his mother. It too would serve him well. He was also, at Dolly's insistence, exceedingly well-dressed despite the bleak economic times.

Working various jobs but taking none very seriously, above all else Frank wanted to sing, just like his idol Bing Crosby. And that he did, at any joint that would have him, and there were many in Jersey at the time. The summer he turned 19, he ventured down to the Jersey Shore to enjoy the beach, sand, and sunshine. There he met Nancy, two years his junior. From a large and hard-working family, she liked the attractive and seemingly talented young man. The attraction was mutual. Her father, on the other hand, was not impressed with Frank's career goals, and pointedly informed him that an interest in Nancy carried an equal interest in working. The next morning Frank appeared for work at his future father-in-law's plastering business. He lasted but a few weeks. With that, his relationship with Nancy went underground.

With his drive and the support of his mother, Frank soldiered on, seeking and securing various singing opportunities. Soon he wrangled himself a spot with the 3 Flashes, whose singing successes required the use of a car to travel to some of their non-local appearances. Frank happened to own a spiffy green Chrysler convertible. Soon they were the Hoboken Four.

Modern and popular television shows featuring unknowns performing—from *The Gong Show* to *American Idol and America's Got Talent*—can trace their lineage to the *Major Bowes Original Amateur Hour*, an exceedingly well-received radio show heard throughout the nation. Every week, the avuncular Major Bowes either brought out an act or spun the Wheel of Fortune, uttering what would become his trademark "Round and Round she goes, and where she stops nobody knows." When it stopped on a name, that person or group was called upon to perform. An on-stage applause meter allowed the crowd to participate and determine the best performer. Bowes grouped the various winners, and obviously there were many, into touring shows that crisscrossed America, raking in crowds and money.

A talent agent had seen the 3 Flashes and before long the now-named Hoboken Four improbably found themselves on the stage of the second largest theater in the world, NYC's Capitol Theater, which held 5300 seats. Far more importantly, millions listened in, glued closely to their radios. Sunday night, September 8, 1935. With Sinatra singing lead, the Hobokens sent the applause meter off the charts and the group became part of the Bowes family, signed to tour the nation.

As they did, Sinatra grew more and more comfortable sharing a voice that stirred the crowd, especially those of the opposite sex who dreamingly imagined Frank singing only to them. That he stood only a tad over 5 feet 7 inches and looked in dire need of a meal, did not deter women, both young and old, married and unmarried, from wanting to sleep with him—and oftentimes succeeding; Sinatra did his best to satisfy their desires. So skinny, with no ass at all, Sinatra did not cut a sharp image, despite his stylish dress and manner. When he wound up in the sack however, his lover for the night undoubtedly experienced another Sinatra asset. As Ava Gardner later allegedly opined, "There's only ten pounds of Frank, but there's a hundred and ten pounds of cock."

Tired of travelling and living on the road and performing with others he felt beneath his talent, Sinatra quit and moved back in with his parents, with whom he surprisingly stayed for three years, while continuing to ply his trade. A break came when he was hired, once again due to his assertive mother making a few phone calls, as a singing waiter and emcee at the Rustic Cabin in Englewood Cliffs, New Jersey. The establishment had a wire to a radio station, WNEW, which broadcast some of the club's music on its show, *Dance Parade*.

With Dolly's approval Frank continued to see Nancy, who came from a decent family and perhaps more importantly posed no threat to her future mother-in-law. Frank, however, still young, had other ideas. One came in the form of an attractive, sexy, and outspoken Antoinette "Toni" Della Penta, three years Frank's senior. Needless to say, she did not meet with Dolly's approval, which meant her days with Frank were coming to an end. No one messed with Toni though, who took the news of the breakup badly. In November 1938, in short order she swore out a complaint for Sinatra, who was arrested and charged for "being then and there a single man over the age of eighteen years, under the promise of marriage, did then and there have sexual intercourse with the said complainant who was then and there a single female of good repute for chastity [ahem] whereby she became pregnant."

One small problem appeared though when the news dropped that Toni was at the time still legally married, albeit separated. The charge was dropped, but Toni, perhaps with "no" not in her vocabulary, persisted. Soon a new charge was levied—adultery, and Sinatra was again arrested. A local newspaper, smelling blood in the water and money in the bank, headlined, "Songbird Held on Morals Charge." A rather upset Frank called the paper and raged. "I'm coming down there and I'm gonna beat your brains out, you hear me? I'm gonna kill you and anyone else who had anything to do with that article! And by the way, I ain't no songbird, you idiot! A dame—that's a songbird!" The charges were eventually dropped.

Despite the fracas and with Nancy's disapproving family, with Dolly's blessing a madly in love Nancy and an in-love Frank tied the knot. The marriage barely slowed Frank down; 1939 would soon to be an even more eventful year for him.

In March, Sinatra cut his first record in a recording studio. In June, his rendition of *Night and Day* at the Rustic Cabin, broadcast on WNEW's radio show, happened to catch the ear of a true songbird, Louise Tobin. She woke her newly married husband, bandleader Harry James, and told him, "Honey, you might want to hear this kid on the radio."

Bandleaders and those that sang with them ruled the land in those days. In the various clubs of New York City, one might hear Tommy Dorsey, Artie Shaw, Louis Prima, Count Basie, Fats Waller, Art Tatum, Billie Holiday, Ethel Waters, and a host of other supremely talented musicians and artists. Harry James fit the bill, a gifted trumpeter and orchestra leader.

James, born a year after Sinatra and, like Frank, still in his early twenties, spent his entire life performing. Both his parents were circus performers; his father the bandleader and his mother a performer, whether it be on horseback or an acrobat holding on by her teeth as she dangled far above. At 3, Harry was also performing. At 19, he married 17-year-old Tobin. As seemed to be the modus operandi of the day, marriage barely put a dent in his social carousing. His big break came when he joined the king of swing, Benny Goodman. When he decided to start his own band two years later, in 1939, Goodman helped finance Harry James and His Orchestra. He was flying high. As perhaps another sign of the times, where people all seemed to age prematurely, James looked far older than his twenty-three years.

James traveled to the Rustic Cabin where he learned that the singer his wife wanted him to hear, also waited tables and emceed a bit. After hearing Sinatra sing, Frank's waiter days were behind him, signing a one-year contract at $75 a week. There was just one catch, he'd have to change his name. "Sinatra" just sounded too ethnically Italian. James suggested a new one, Frankie Satin. Frank basically told James what he could do with his suggestion. "You want the singer, take the name." James took both.

On June 30, Frank debuted with the James Orchestra. When the women in the audience started swooning and screaming, all knew that Sinatra was no ordinary singer. He was hot, unlike the cool singers of the time like Bing Crosby. Still though, it was not all smooth sailing. His first recording flopped. Some reviewers, not used to his style, were slow to embrace it. Being on the road with James, who suffered frequent financial setbacks, was often difficult. Knowing that it might be time to move on, Sinatra jumped when the legendary bandleader Tommy Dorsey came calling. By the end of 1939, the career of one of the greatest crooners ever had launched. It was also the year that wife Nancy became pregnant.

Pope XI dies at 81

"We still have so many things to do."

On February 10, 1939, Pope Pius XI died. At the time of his death, he had been planning on issuing an encyclical denouncing antisemitism, colonialism, Nazism, and racism wherever it might be found. His successor, Pope Pius XII, perhaps for diplomatic reasons, chose not to publish it.

Ambrogio Damiano Achille Ratti came into the world in Desio, Milan, on the final day of May 1857, four years before the start of the American Civil War. His father, Francesco, owned a silk factory while his mother, Teresa, tended to their six children. Ordained in 1879, he followed a scholarly path, studying theology, philosophy, canon law, and ancient church manuscripts. Not surprisingly, he taught and worked in church libraries. In his spare time, perhaps symbolically in a quest to get closer to his God, he skillfully scaled mountains. In 1911, he moved to the Vatican to work in its Library. Within a few years, he headed it.

In 1918, Pope Benedict XV asked him to take on a new challenge, that of a diplomat in post-World War I's reconstituted state of Poland. Along with the move came a promotion to archbishop. As the Weimar Republic was finding in Germany—that being in the middle often results in attacks from both the right and left—a neutral Ratti faced similar blowback from competing forces in Poland. In the end, he was asked to leave. Far from diminishing the respect his church seniors held for him, Ratti was promoted to cardinal. Six months later, in January 1922, Pope Benedict fell ill and unexpectedly died.

Demonstrating that politics exists everywhere, even among those promoting the kindly words of God, the cardinals had to determine which of two men, each representing different factions, should be elevated to Pope. Deadlocked and enduring what would be the longest conclave in the twentieth century, Ratti emerged as the compromise candidate. On February 6, 1922, Ambrogio Damiano Achille Ratti became Pope Pius XI.

Keenly aware of the office he now held, the intelligent, blunt, and demanding Pontiff chartered his course in increasingly choppy waters. Recognizing the future forces of science and technology, he oversaw the creation of Vatican Radio in 1931, allowing him to address a worldwide audience. While conciliatory to other religions and factions within Christianity, he, understandably, thought the Catholic Church to be the supreme one.

Most challenging, however, was his relationship with a world headed toward war. Initially his efforts bore fruit. With France, he reached a reconciliation with its anti-clerical government. With Italy, he entered into the Lateran Treaties, which recognized the sovereignty of Vatican City (plus $100 million) in exchange for the Church abandoning its demand that Papal territories seized more than a half a century before be returned. Further, Catholicism became the official religion of Italy (recognizing the obvious), paid salaries to certain church personnel, accepted Church marriages, and brought religious instruction into the public school, regardless of the religious make-up of the student population. In return, the bishops, over which the Italian authorities had veto power, swore allegiance to the Italian government, which like the Church, was fiercely anti-Communist. It quickly became apparent, however, that fidelity to Mussolini's fascism and growing closeness to Hitler was unworkable.

Wishing at the outset of Hitler's rise to power to work hospitably, resulted in the Reichskonkordat in 1933, signed by Cardinal Eugenio Pacelli (who would succeed Pope Pius XI), which granted the Church freedom and independence. It was quickly tossed away by Hitler, who ordered the arrest of clergy members who did not toe the Nazi line, dissolved the Catholic Youth League, and instituted a sterilization law that ran counter to church theology.

Relations with Austria, where a Catholic majority prevailed, initially proved workable, but then deteriorated when its chancellor, Engelbert Dollfus, was assassinated by a group of local Nazis in 1934. While his successor, Kurt von Schuschnigg, was also supportive of the Church, Hitler's march into Austria ended von Schuschnigg's career, with him being arrested and imprisoned. Once in power, the Nazis brutalized the Catholic clergy, closing its institutions and organizations, and sending many of its priests to concentration camps. Even local Cardinal Innitzer's residence was ransacked, notwithstanding his earlier support of the annexation of Austria by Germany, in which he, along with other Austrian Catholic bishops, not only signed the supportive statement, but added "Heil Hitler" for good measure. Needless to say, the Pope and Cardinal Pacelli were angered and ordered Innitzer and the others to issue a new statement, reading in part: "The solemn declaration of the Austrian bishops ... was clearly not intended to be an approval of something that was not and is not compatible with God's law."

Prior to the Nazi violence, Cardinal Innitzer, in celebration of Hitler's birthday, ordered that church bells be rung, that Nazi flags be flown, and prayers for Hitler offered. Six months later, perhaps either after having been taken to the woodshed by his superiors, or recognizing the evil of Nazism, he declared at a sermon attended by nearly 9,000 people, that there is only one true Führer—Jesus Christ. During the war, he condemned the treatment of Jews and Gypsies and the harsh treatment of the clergy.

While Pope Pius spoke out against Nazi policies, its antisemitism, and its sending priests to concentration camps, the West engaged in what the Pope labelled a "conspiracy of silence." Equally infuriating was the silence of the Western powers in the face of savage Catholic repression in the Soviet Union, Spain, and Mexico, which Pius labelled a "terrible triangle." In a godless Soviet Union, despite more than half of its population identifying as openly religious, religious leaders were killed, church property seized, and places of worship shuttered. In Mexico, thousands of priests were murdered. While the situation in Spain was not as dire, many Jesuits were expelled along with Catholic education being discouraged and minimized.

When Mussolini moved closer to Hitler and his vile views on race, the Pope moved further away, publicly condemning the growing racism. He was swimming upstream, however, as the torrents of hate and racism in Germany and Italy appeared overwhelming. Even some members of his church sided with the forces of evil. Despite open hostility to his views, he planned to publish an encyclical condemning the wrongs of the day. Having so much to do, he never got the chance to complete his agenda. Pope Pius XI died at the age of 81, succumbing to heart disease and the often-inevitable ailments of age. Some, however, speculated that the Pope was murdered due to his beliefs

Unlike the long Conclave that named his predecessor, Cardinal Pacelli was quickly elected on March 2, 1939, to replace him, and chose to be called Pope Pius XII. Many thought the Cardinal's past relationship with Germany and other foreign powers would help smooth relations. Given the times, though, whatever he did led to distrust and criticism from the divided nations. To this day, many argue he did not do enough. One author even called him Hitler's Pope. Others believe that he did all that he could and found success in saving countless Jews and those aligned against Hitler. In all likelihood, it is a debate that will never be resolved.

Stagecoach

"[S]truck down by a foul disease called social prejudice."

On February 10, 1939, the movie *Stagecoach* premiered in Miami before opening the following month at Radio City Music Hall in New York City. The movie revitalized the Western, re-enforced John Ford's reputation as a brilliant director, gave birth to a superstar, John Wayne, and influenced moviemakers for decades to come. Orson Welles, in making his classic *Citizen Kane* a few years later, told of how he watched *Stagecoach* dozens of times to hone his vision and skills for *Kane*.

The story itself was not much different than the Westerns made during the Silent Era and afterwards. Ford took what was common and elevated it to greatness, as the super talented are wont to do. He took limp bodies and stuffed them with character, range, humanity, and magic. The social outcasts—The Ringo Kid, a prison escapee, played by Wayne; "That creature" Dallas, a prostitute forced to leave town by the sanctimonious Ladies of the Law-and-Order League; the frequently intoxicated Doc Boone, who "couldn't doctor a horse," kicked to the curb by his shrill of a landlord for not paying the rent; and a well-dressed and groomed Hatfield, a southern "hardly a gentleman [who is] a notorious gambler."

Seemingly respectable citizens, who bleed hypocrisy when pricked, joined them—the huffy, older white-haired banker Henry Gatewood—whose wife was one of the instigators driving Dallas away—leaving town with a bagful of money he stole from the bank; the pregnant and lofty Lucy Mallory, travelling to meet her military husband; and Samuel Peacock, a milquetoast of a whiskey salesman, whose goods are frequently usurped by the devilish Doc Boone. Rounding out the group were the stagecoach driver and U.S. Marshall, owners of two prototypical Western names—Buck and Curley.

The characters slowly come into focus as Dallas and Doc Brown are essentially being driven away by the stern-looking ladies of Tonto. When a clearly distressed Dallas asks an inebriated Doc, whom she plainly respects, why she can't stay, why they're making her leave, he replies, "We have been struck down by a foul disease called social prejudice, my child. These dear ladies of the Law and Order League are scouring out the dregs of the town. Come, be a proud, glorified dreg like me."

As the camera pulls back, the expansive and bustling western town comes into view, with horses and buggies hustling over the clean and well-maintained streets, totally clear of any litter or horse manure whatsoever; apparently these horses, like those in every television and movie Western, have been potty-trained as there is never a hint of any excrement.

As Dallas and Doc eventually amble over to the Lordsburg-headed stagecoach, Marshall Curley Wilcox decides to ride shotgun after getting word that the Ringo Kid has broken out of jail and headed to that very same town "to get even with them Plummer boys [whose] testimony sent him to the penitentiary" and, for good measure, murdered Ringo's father and brother. The kind-hearted but somewhat slow Buck, played by the always gravelly voiced Andy Devine, is happy Ringo, "a fine boy," escaped. As it turns out, Sheriff Curley also has warm feelings for the Kid and wants to capture and save him from any sure to be fatal confrontation with the murderous Plummers.

As Mrs. Mallory boards the coach, Hatfield, in the midst of a poker hand, spots her, "an angel in a jungle," whose Confederate father he served under during the Civil War. With the stagecoach about to depart, ten cavalrymen gallop into town, announcing that Geronimo and the Apaches are in the area. As the passengers debate whether to proceed—with Buck and Peacock the whiskey salesman against the trip—Lieutenant Blanchard tells the concerned riders that his squad will escort them to their first stop, where another army detachment will meet and accompany them to their next destination. The decision to leave made, Hatfield, having left his poker game, joins the scene, shouting "Make room for one more!" and gallantly announces, as he doffs his hat to Mrs. Mallory, that "I'm offering my protection to this lady."

Just as they're leaving town, banker Gatewood—"What's good business for the banks is good for the country"—appears, flagging them down and asking to be let on board. While Curley is suspicious, they depart only to shortly find Ringo, whose horse has come up lame. Curley makes the arrest and places him in an already far too cramped stagecoach, now housing seven people as they travel through the majestic and imperial Monument Valley.

As Doc puffs away on his ever-present cigar that clearly irritates Mrs. Mallory, Hatfield chides him. "A gentleman doesn't smoke in the presence of a lady," and offers Mallory some water, which she gratefully accepts. As Hatfield is putting the water away, Ringo asks him whether he's also going "to ask the other lady" if she wants a drink.

Ringo's humanity again presents itself when the coach stops at its first destination, Dry Fork, where the horses are fed and no one uses any semblance of a bathroom. When they see that there is no one waiting to escort them, they are informed that the soldiers, including Mrs. Mallory's husband, had been ordered out the evening before. Again they vote as to what to do, learning that Lieutenant Blanchard insists on following his orders that he return to his base immediately upon dropping the passengers off at Dry Fork. Curley asks Mrs. Mallory her preference and, again, she bravely insists on reuniting with her husband, regardless of the danger that he and she might be in. When Curley then turns to Peacock for his preference, Ringo cuts him off, "Ain't you going to ask the other lady first?"

When they sit to eat, Dallas is unsure whether she can sit with the respectable folks and wanders about. Seeing her discomfort, Ringo invites her to sit next to him and across from Lucy Mallory, who clearly is uncomfortable with the breach of social etiquette and accepts Hatfield's offer to sit elsewhere.

At their next stop, Apache Wells, Lucy learns her husband has been wounded. As Dallas offers condolences that are barely acknowledged, Lucy faints and goes into labor. The always drunk Doc Brown employs the ever-popular consumption of copious amounts of coffee while repeatedly dunking his head into a barrel of water to sober up. A baby girl is delivered with Dallas not only serving as a nursemaid but spending the entire night watching both the baby and mother.

Taken with Dallas, Ringo asks her to marry him and move to a small ranch he owns just over the border in Mexico. Initially fearful that he really doesn't know her past, she demurs. The next morning, however, she accepts his offer, but tells him that she has to remain behind to care for Mallory and her child. She also tells him to escape and go to his ranch, where she'll meet him. Although reluctant, he reacts to her prodding, but barely gets out when he sees Apache smoke war signals.

The group jumps back into the coach and heads off to Lee Ferry which they find, to their horror, has been destroyed by an earlier Apache attack. They continue on their way, cleverly crossing a river despite its bridge having gone down. Relieved and seemingly safe on their way to their final destination of Lordsburg, the Apaches suddenly attack, resulting in a lengthy and breathless death-defying pursuit as worthy as the immortal car chases in *Bullitt* and *The French Connection*. While bumping up and down and side to side in the stagecoach, Ringo, Curley, Hatfield, and the others somehow manage to aim straight and true, improbably hitting many of their pursuers. Peacock takes an arrow to the chest. Buck is shot in the arm, dropping the reins. Ringo climbs out of the coach and quickly jumps from one set to another and then another out-of-control stampeding horses, trying to rein them in while dodging arrows and gunfire and keeping the horses going fast enough to outpace the charging Apaches. Yells suddenly go out that they're out of ammunition and about to be caught. Hatfield saves one last bullet for Mrs. Mallory whom he will shoot and save from being captured by a godless group intent on doing who-knows-what awful thing to her. As he points the gun to her head, the sound of a bugle rings out. The cavalry has arrived. The Apaches are driven off, but not before firing off one last round with Hatfield's name on it.

Arriving in Lordsburg, the Kid is recognized and word quickly spreads to the Plummers. The local sheriff, who has learned about Gatewood's bank theft, arrests him. Mallory, meanwhile, learns her husband is not seriously hurt. She starts to show her gratitude to Dallas but then catches herself. Dallas responds with a sad, "I know." Ringo convinces Curley to briefly let him go. Curley gives him an unloaded rifle. Ringo takes off his hat and retrieves three bullets that he had been saving for the Plummers. As he walks Dallas to where she is staying, she tries to convince him to leave town. Instead, Ringo leaves Dallas, tells her to wait for him, and sets off to do what he came to town to do. A few minutes later she hears shots ring out.

Expecting the worst, she is shocked when Ringo returns. As promised, Ringo surrenders to Curley, who is standing by a small carriage. Ringo asks him to help Dallas get safely to his farm in Mexico, where she'll wait for him. Curley agrees and tells Ringo to get in the carriage and asks Dallas if she wants to ride along with him a bit to which she gratefully agrees. As the two of them are seated, Curley and Buck smack and shout to the horses to giddy-up, allowing Ringo, with Dallas, to escape.

While initially the studio heads wanted better known actors—Gary Cooper and Marlene Dietrich—for the roles of Ringo and Dallas, John Ford recognized the star quality of the unheralded John Wayne and insisted that he be cast. Claire Trevor, who specialized in playing bad girl/hard-bitten characters, played Dallas. Ford was a brutal taskmaster and relentlessly challenged Wayne. When Wayne found it difficult playing a romantic scene with Trevor, Ford told him to wrinkle his forehead and raise his eyebrows, advice Wayne took to heart and used for the next forty years. At one point or another, Ford called Wayne a big oaf, a B-grade actor, a dumb bastard, and even criticized his manner of walking—"Walk like a man, for Christ's sake, instead of skipping like a fairy."

The movie had it all. The vast expanse of Monument Valley, which stood in stark contrast to the cramped quarters of the stagecoach; a classic song track, featuring "Shall We Gather at the River," "Jeannie with the Light Brown Hair," and "Bury Me Not on the Lone Prairie"; a breathtaking chase scene; and a compelling story with compelling characters, many of which are outcasts who find redemption, acceptance, and love. The movie brought glory to Ford and Wayne and revitalized the Western genre. Ford's ability to transform lost characters into winning ones helped satisfy the Hays Production Code, which initially had many objections. To make the movie more acceptable, the words prostitute, harlot, or whore, while alluded to, were never used.

Stagecoach proved to be a hit upon release and was nominated for several Academy Awards—Best Picture, Director, Cinematography, Editing, and Art Direction. It won two for Best Score and Supporting Actor, the honor going to the wonderful Doc Boone's Thomas Mitchell, who would go on to greater recognition, playing Scarlet's father in *Gone With the Wind*.

The Golden Gate International Expo

"Pageant of the Pacific."

On February 18, 1939, the Golden Gate International Exposition: Pageant of the Pacific, or more colloquially, the GGIE or San Francisco World's Fair, opened, celebrating the earlier construction of two nearby great bridges—The San Francisco-Oakland Bay Bridge (1936) and the more famous Golden Gate one (1937), which at the time was the world's longest suspension structure. Located on what was billed as the world's largest manmade island—Treasure Island—it turned an empty area into 403 acres of glowing fantasy. Named after the famous novel, written in 1883 by Scotland's Robert Louis Stevenson, who lived in San Francisco for a short time, the book was made into a movie in 1934. The film was directed by Victor Fleming who would, in 1939, direct *Gone With the Wind* and *the Wizard of Oz*.

With the federal government footing the hefty bill, thousands of unemployed workers, jobless due to the Depression, found steady and valuable work, both building, and later working in, the Fair. Hoping to draw 20 million people, additional monies would hopefully pour into the area. To further justify the expenditure, plans were made to transform the Fair, at its conclusion in two years, into a much-needed world-class airport. As it would turn out, the war scuttled those plans, with the site turned over to the navy.

The Fair, featuring its dominant structure at 400 feet tall—The Tower of the Sun holding forty-four musical bells—highlighted the Pacific nations, Central and South America, with San Francisco serving as its gateway. The Goddess of the Pacific Ocean, Pacifica, found celebration with an 80-foot-tall statue. In all, thirty-six nations participated.

While the Island had 12,000 parking spaces, ferries, at a cost of a dime, were a major source of transportation. Those wealthy enough to own or have access to yachts or private boats had docks to accommodate them. Less than a month after opening, the Fair welcomed its one millionth customer.

Six central courts composed the Fair with pavilions divided into themed classes. There was something for everyone—waterways, fountains, and reflecting pools, flower displays and gardens, glowing colors and costumes, testaments to nations and states, entertainment, art, and food, and a cheerily colored tram pulled by a mechanical elephant. For lovers of college basketball, the NCAA held its very first post-season West Regional Tournament there. In 1939, unlike now, there were only eight teams vying for a national championship: four from the west—Oklahoma, Oregon, Texas, and Utah State—and four from the east—Brown, Ohio State, Villanova, and Wake Forest, playing their regional games in Philadelphia.

In the West Regional, played in the California Coliseum on the grounds of the Fair, Oregon (which had beaten Texas 56-41) played Oklahoma (which had defeated Utah State, 50-39). Oregon won the pivotal game against Oklahoma, 55-37, and advanced to the finals, held on the campus of Northwestern University, where Oregon defeated Ohio State, 46-33, for the National Championship. The Coliseum, which had a capacity of 9,476, was demolished at the end of the Fair as was the Pacifica statue.

A fan favorite, the Gayway featured attractions found in many amusement areas—rides, a Ferris Wheel, a penny arcade, Jo-Jo the Clown, shows, and performances. It also included some popular oddities including racetrack driving monkeys, little people acting in a Western setting, and what had to be a hit, Sally Rand's Nude Ranch, manned with "Nudies" serving as ranch hands.

With 147,674 people attending on its last day, the Fair closed on October 29. In May 1940 it reopened, closing forever in September. In the end, like most World Fairs, it did not meet financial expectations. It did well enough though, with 17 million visitors forking out a little under $8 million. Given increased employment, a diversion from economic and world events, and the sheer excitement of the spectacle, it was a success nonetheless. It paled, however, when compared to a far larger and grander World's Fair on the opposite side of the country, in New York, which opened the same year, six weeks later, on April Fool's Day.

Nazis Rally at Madison Square Garden

> "If George Washington were alive today, he would be friends with Adolf Hitler."

On February 20, 1939, Nazi sympathizers and supporters gathered at a sold-out Madison Square Garden in New York City to hold a "Pro-American Rally," which in reality trumpeted support for Germany and its Führer. With over 20,000 fascists inside the building, thousands demonstrated against them outside. Separating the two stood an army of New York's finest, with over 1,700 police officers outside and 600 inside, in uniform and plainclothes. "We have enough police here to stop a revolution," intoned a police official. Firefighters, armed with a heavy-duty fire hose to disperse an unruly mob if need be, along with bomb squads, added to the security.

With membership declining, leaders of the German Bund hoped a well-publicized event would inspire the masses. In the end, it didn't, although the spectacle was one even Hitler and his cohorts in Germany would admire. As music blared in the background, uniformed Bund members marched in carrying both American and German flags. Audience members, who paid between 40 cents to $1.10, jumped to their feet, greeting them with raucous cheers and Nazi salutes as the ensemble made its way to the stage where a 30-foot picture of George Washington with Nazi insignia flanking him, awaited. Despite assurances in renting the Garden that there would be no antisemitism displayed or verbalized, banners flowed, proclaiming "Wake Up America—Smash Jewish Communism" and "Stop Jewish Domination of Christian America."

As the clock struck eight, Margarete Rittershaush regaled the crowd with her rendition of the Star-Bangled Banner. The Bund's national secretary James Wheeler-Hill then took the podium and proclaimed that "if George Washington were alive today, he would be friends with Adolf Hitler." America, he roared, must be freed and restored to "True Americans." He, and those who followed, taking their cues from Hitler, blamed the world's woes on the Jews and blasted those weak leaders who failed to recognize the threats posed. Jews, who controlled the movies and the press, they charged, moved in lockstep with the godless and evil Communists, "the menace of Anti-National, Gold-Hating Jewish-Bolshevism." Blame went to the nation's leaders, President Franklin Delano "Rosenfeld," New York City Mayor Fiorello "Jew Lumpen," and NYC District Attorney, and future Governor, Thomas A. "Jewey."

The final speaker, the head of the Bund Fritz Kuhn, further egged on the audience. In a decidedly foreign accent, he intoned:

> We, with American ideals, demand that our government shall be returned to the American people who founded it. If you ask what we are actively fighting for under our charter: First, a socially just, white, Gentile ruled United States. Second, Gentile controlled labor unions, free from Jewish Moscow directed domination.

Suddenly, and without warning, a spectator, Isadore Greenbaum, incensed at what was being said, jumped on stage and charged Kuhn. Before he could reach him, Kuhn's stormtroopers intervened and started to beat and stomp on Greenbaum, much to the delight of the crowd. The quick intervention of the police ensured that the sole protester was not severely injured. Kuhn concluded his speech by imploring those gathered that "The Bund is open to you, provided you are sincere, of good character, of white Gentile stock, and an American citizen imbued with patriotic zeal. Therefore, Join!" With the assembled thousands chanting "Free America! Free America! Free America!", the largest Nazi rally held on American soil came to an end.

Thirteen arrests were made that evening, all demonstrators opposed to Nazism and its hateful rhetoric. Isadore Greenbaum, the charging 26-year-old plumbing assistant from Brooklyn, was also arrested for disorderly conduct. When the judge asked him whether he realized that someone could've been hurt by what he did on stage, Greenbaum replied, "Don't you realize that someone is going to be hurt by what was being said on that stage." Greenbaum was fined $25 ($450 today), similar to the penalties given to the other protestors. At the time, Hitler's sixth concentration camp was being completed in Europe.

Years later, Greenbaum explained that he:

> went down to the Garden without any intention of interrupting but being that they talked so much against my religion and there was so much persecution I lost my head and I felt it was my duty to [do something] ... [W]hat would you have done if you were in my place listening to that s.o.b. hollering against the government and publicly kissing Hitler's behind, while thousands cheered? Well, I did it.

Much to the dismay of Kuhn and his followers, the Bund continued to lose support and interest. A few months after the rally, Warner Brother's *Confessions of a Nazi Spy* was released, further tarnishing Germany's image. Like the characters in the movie, Kuhn soon found himself under scrutiny. When it was discovered that $14,000 ($250,000 in today's money) was missing from the funds raised at the event, Kuhn was charged and convicted of embezzlement. It appears he spent the money on his mistress and other personal expenses. Sent off to prison, two people succeeded him. One later fled to Germany in 1941 while the second, also under investigation, committed suicide.

6

Czechoslovakia, Nanchang, and Wives Killing Their Husbands in Philadelphia

Bad Fad

"Preserving (Gold)fish from Cruel and Wanton Consumption."

On March 3, 1939, as the tale goes, Harvard freshman, Lothrop "Lofie" Withington Jr., while running for class president, proclaimed that he'd do anything. Soon, on a ten-dollar bet, he took the dare to swallow a live goldfish. Recorded by a titillated press, news of the event quickly spread, giving rise to a national fad. Soon students everywhere were gobbling the squirming and most unfortunate fish. *Life* and *Time* magazines, in addition to many local newspapers, covered the new and most odd phenomenon.

Upping the ante, rather than swallowing a single living creature, the challenge moved to who could consume the most. Albert Hayes Jr., in upholding the honor of MIT, swallowed forty-two. Michigan's Julius Aisner, twenty-eight; Boston College's Donald Mulcahy, twenty-nine; Albright College football captain Mike Bonner, thirty-three; and Northeastern's Jack Smookler, thirty-six. Not to be outdone, and proving that one need not go to an Ivy League or other well-known institution to achieve greatness, Clark University's Joseph Deliberato whisked down eighty-nine. MIT's Hayes explained the art of the swallow, "You lay the goldfish well back on the tongue, let it wiggle forward till it hits the top of the throat, then give one big gulp. Same effect as swallowing a raw oyster." Aids included milk, salt and pepper, oranges, or whatever got the job done.

In April, demonstrating that a feat accomplished by a male is one equally conquered by a female, journalism major Marie Hensen of the University of Missouri became the first member of her gender to join the goldfish gobbling club.

Local lawmakers in Massachusetts, upset—and rightfully so—at the actions of some of its more raucous college students, enacted legislation "to preserve the fish from cruel and wanton consumption," an action that gained the support of Robert Sellar, president of the Boston Animal League, who threatened to arrest the gulpers. "This is not a subject for levity," he intoned, adding, "I hesitate to bring such a matter to court, but we won't sidestep the issue. There have been too many complaints." At the same time, the U.S. Public Health Service issued warnings about the danger of the act in that it could subject the swallower to tapeworms or disease.

Some went beyond goldfish, expanding the practice to include other rather unfathomable objects.

Lothrop, who is given credit for starting the craze, dropped out of Harvard to join the military. Along the way, he attended MIT's Aeronautical school to learn to fly. In the army air corps he served as a pilot and flight instructor and worked with Igor Sikorsky, the father of the modern helicopter. Sikorsky, whose family fled Russia when the Bolsheviks took over, designed and flew, in 1939 when Lofie was swallowing goldfish, the first US single lifting rotor helicopter, the VS-300, setting standards still in effect today. Lofie later piloted some of the early models and became a pioneer in the field. He also put his fish swallowing escapades behind him.

Czechoslovakia Dies

"We will Germanize the Czech vermin."

At 1:30 am on March 15, 1939, the recently named head of Czechoslovakia Emil Hacha, having arrived earlier that evening to meet Hitler, was kept waiting for hours as the Führer watched a film. Hacha, born in 1872, was a respected lawyer and judge, and the father of a daughter. His wife had died the previous year. A man of culture, he translated English literature, collected art, and wrote poetry, culminating in a book, *Errors and Decisions*, released under a pseudonym in 1939. After the recent travesty of the Munich Agreement, he succeeded Edward Benes, who resigned, realizing the ultimate fate of his country.

Predictably, the meeting with Hitler went poorly. Told that Germany was about to invade, Hacha was given an ultimatum: surrender or see his nation destroyed. Having no choice, he opted for the former. He also had a heart attack and was treated by Hitler's doctors, whose care enabled him to recover significantly enough that by 4 am he had turned over his beloved, once democratic, proud nation of Czechoslovakia to Germany. What was once Czechoslovakia was now Slovakia, the Sudentenland, and the Protectorate of Bohemia and Moravia.

Within days, as the German military entered its latest conquered state and flew its flag, Hitler visited and inspected his spoils. Again, without firing a shot and through bluster and bluff, Hitler got what he wanted. In addition to controlling yet another once formidable nation, Germany also got its gold, assets, and an impressive military arsenal—hundreds of tanks, cannons, and artillery pieces and over a million rifles and pistols accompanied by innumerable rounds of ammunition. The armaments came into great use against France and Britain when World War II started. Chamberlain and his cohorts in France finally realized, now too late, that Hitler could not be trusted. They stamped their feet and prepared for an inevitable war.

Allowed to remain in power, Hacha signed an oath of loyalty to Hitler, legislation fatal to the local Jewish population, and the dissolution of Parliament. Many of his friends and colleagues were either shot or arrested and sent to concentration camps. Surrounded by those loyal to Germany, his puppet administration jumped to the whims of Hitler and his cronies. Any resistance was brutally suppressed. When students protested, their schools were shut and their leaders either executed or sent to concentration camps. The culmination of brutality came after Czech partisans assassinated Reinhard Heydrich.

Next to Hitler, Reinhard Tristan Heydrich might well have been the second most vile person in all of Germany. Born to a well-do-do family, his father, Richard Bruno Heydrich, was a composer and opera singer, while his mother taught piano in a conservatory his father had founded. They named their son Reinhard after a hero in an opera written by Richard, and his middle name, Tristan, after Wagner's *Tristan und Isolde*. Despite his seemingly well-bred background, Heydrich grew into a murderous high-ranking member of the SS and main architect of the Holocaust, a role he savored. Millions died under his direction. Stationed in Prague to rule over the area, Heydrich, variously dubbed The Hangman, The Butcher of Prague, Himmler's Evil Genius, The Blond Beast, the Young Evil God of Death, and, in Hitler's own words, The Man with the Iron Heart, sought to stamp out any resistance by the local populace, which he did with ruthless precision, proclaiming the need to "Germanize the Czech vermin." Plans were made to eliminate nearly two-thirds of the entire population after the war. On May 27, 1942, at the behest of the Czech government in exile, Heydrich was shot in Prague. He clung to life, suffering and dying slowly, which he did a week later, on June 4.

In retaliation, Hitler ordered a genocidal retaliation for any village even remotely connected to the killing; all men were to be executed; all women sent to concentration camps; all children suitable for Germanisation placed with SS families (with the others killed), and the villages burned and levelled completely.

Two Czech towns, Lidice and Lezaky, both falsely linked to the assassination, tragically suffered the consequences. In Lidice, 173 men were lined up and shot, first five at a time and then ten, all morning and afternoon long. Eleven men not in the village at the time were later located and assassinated, as were eight men and seven women already in custody for having relatives supporting the Czech army in exile; 203 women and 105 children were hauled off, the women taken to concentration camp.Four who were pregnant were first forced to have abortions at the hospital in which Heydrich had died, and then shipped out. The children who were not suitable, all but seven, were gassed at the Chelmo extermination camp.

Not satisfied that the dead were somehow escaping retribution, the Nazis went to the local cemetery, dug up the deceased, and stole their gold teeth and jewelry and anything else of value. Even the animals were slaughtered. And with total destruction of all life, the town was incinerated. Two weeks later the very small village of Lezaky met a similar fate.

In the end, over 1,300 people were murdered, some at the outset when over 12,000 men were questioned and 36,000 houses searched. Unlike other brutal killings, the Nazis proudly announced its dirty deeds leading to outrage among the Allies and all civilized people.

As for an impotent Hacha, when the Red Army liberated Prague, he was severely beaten and taken into custody where he died, quite possibly assassinated by his Russian liberators.

Nanchang

"Eight corners of the world under one roof."

On March 17, 1939, the ferocious Battle of Nanchang started, setting off yet another clash in the long conflict between Japan and China. The Second Sino-Japanese War, referred to by Japan as the first step of the eight corners of the world under one roof, began in 1937. Arguably, it was the true start of World War II.

China and Japan had been warring for a long time. In the First Sino-Japanese War, 1894–1895, underdog Japan successfully fought a-thought-to-be-more powerful China over control of Korea and Taiwan. In 1931, in need of resources and space, Japan invaded and took Manchuria, on which it laid claim as a result of an earlier war with Russia.

Nanchang, a railway hub, provided a major supply line for the Chinese, as well as having important airfields. Japan, after its most recent major victory in Wuhan, continued its assault, hoping to take yet another city. Despite suffering grievous losses leading up to the battle, China's military was revitalized with its alliance with the Soviet Union, which supplied pilots, planes, and resources.

With initial success, bolstered by the use of poison gas, Japan pushed the Chinese out of Nanchang. The Chinese forces regrouped and counterattacked. After weeks of intense fighting, and heavy casualties, Japan maintained its grip as the Chinese retreated, ending the battle on May 9. In the end, over 50,000 Chinese were either killed or wounded, with Japan suffering half that number.

Weakened by the fight, Japan could not pursue its retreating enemy. Adding to its dilemma, border clashes with another area rival, the Soviet Union, took a further toll on the Japanese, which had shockingly defeated the Russians in the 1904–1905 Russo-Japanese War, fought over imperialistic control of Manchuria and Korea.

During this time, diplomatic machinations raged behind the scenes. China and Germany were major trade partners. Seemingly at odds with that arrangement stood the 1936 Anti-Comintern Pact, an agreement between Germany and Japan aimed at isolating the Soviet Union. While Japan and Germany had common adversaries—England, the United States, and the Soviet Union—Japan's main opponent at the time was the nation it was fighting: China, Germany's valuable trading partner. In August 1939 the Soviet Union, Japan's enemy, shockingly entered into a non-aggression pact with Germany. So much for Germany seeking to contain and isolate the Soviet Union through mutually beneficial pacts. Also at odds were German and Japanese views on race, with each nation proclaiming its attitude superior to all others. Indeed, Hitler in *Mein Kampf* specially named the Japanese race as an inferior one.

Despite shifting moves, some elements remained the same, with Germany making territorial demands of its neighbors and terrorizing the Jews. On March 22, Lithuania capitulated to German demands and handed over Memel (Klaipeda), which post-World War I's Treaty of Versailles had taken from Germany. Thousands of Jews fled the country. Germany next turned its attention to taking the Free City of Danzig, also created by the Versailles Treaty. It would take the start of World War II for Germany to accomplish that murderous goal.

The Arsenic Ring Murders

"Just send the guy to California."

On March 23, 1939, a Philadelphia jury returned a guilty verdict against Herman Petrillo in what had been dubbed the "Great Arsenic Murder trial," which captivated the nation. Charged with the murder of Ferdinand Alfonsi, he was the first to be tried and sentenced to death. (Despite the conviction being overturned due to the admission of a mountain of highly prejudicial and irrelevant evidence, Herman was retried, convicted, and again sentenced to death.) His co-defendant, Stella Alfonsi, would be tried separately later for her role in her husband's painful death. With numerous other trials remaining, the public would not be disappointed.

The main players in the "You're tired of your spouse, allow us to aid you" ring included cousins Paul and Herman Petrillo, and Morris "Louie the Rabbi" Bolber, who, when not teaching Hebrew School and training young Jewish students studying for their Bar and Bat Mitzvahs, was arranging various murders.

Paul Petrillo made up for his somewhat overweight and short stature with a charming and well-coiffured appearance. Emigrating from Italy in 1910 at the age of 17, he continued his journey of achieving the American dream, while taking a bride and growing a family. Owning a tailor shop in Philadelphia, he spoke with, and learned from, the many clients who frequented his shop. From those selling insurance to the poor immigrants in the immediate area, he quickly discovered that money could be nearly effortlessly made. Soon, he was selling life insurance policies and collecting their weekly installments of 50 or so cents. Deeply superstitious, as were many of his compatriots, he also held himself out, as his business card read, "Professor P. Patril—Divine Healing, Private Readings."

With far less subtlety, his younger cousin Herman joined Paul in his lust to make a quick buck. Not bothering to engage in any semblance of legitimate work, the conniving conman Herman sought whatever illegality suited his needs, with arson and counterfeiting topping his crimes of choice. Not surprisingly, he attracted the attention of the authorities. When an insured house, under his wife's name, mysteriously burned down, Herman was charged with arson. Despite connecting him to a cache of dynamite, Herman was acquitted. Leaving the courtroom, Herman both mocked the fire marshal—"What d'ya think now, flatfoot?"—and then travelled to the insurance company to collect the $3,000 in insurance proceeds.

With the success of his efforts, Herman proposed expanding his horizons to his cousin, suggesting killing those on whom Paul held policies, or in Herman's quaint vernacular, "Just send the guy to California." Wrangling their way into the scheme was a problem easily solved, whether it be by charm, threats, greed, desperation, or preying upon the naivety of the local population. Paul demurred, more due to his distrust of his cousin's reckless ways than the wisdom of his suggestion.

Not one to be slowed, Herman befriended a disabled 50-year-old vagrant, Raeffele Caruso. Finding him a place to stay, Herman arranged to get life insurance policies for the illiterate Caruso, which Herman paid for, along with the rent, and made himself the beneficiary. Accumulating a sizable nest egg of $3,000 in insurance, Herman decided the time was ripe to send Raeffele to California via a local river. With a cohort, Salvatore Sortino, Herman drowned Caruso, who was found the next day. When Herman tried to cash in, however, suspicions arose. The insurance companies balked, agreeing only to pay funeral expenses. Herman begrudgingly agreed, but in double-billing the companies on amply padded funeral expenses, he walked away with a not-too-shabby $700, or about $13,000 in today's money.

Some months later, he replicated his scheme in killing John Woloshyn, on whose life John's wife Marie had purchased several policies. That Herman was sleeping with Marie made his suggestion to purchase the policies fairly persuasive. The police concluded that John was the victim of a hit and run—which it most assuredly was, but not in the traditional sense. As Herman, accompanied by his 6-foot-3-inch, 250-lb goon "Jumbo" Valenti, and the soon-to-be-dead victim, travelled in Herman's car to an after-hours joint, Jumbo hit Woloshyn over the head with a lead pipe, dragged him in front of the car, at which point Herman proceeded to run him over a few times.

The Russian born Morris "Louie the Rabbi" Bolber rounded out the group. Rotund, sloppy in dress, the 40-or-so-year-old Bolber held himself out as a scholar, mystic, and wise man, who spoke several languages. Married with four children, he even advised Salvatore Sortino, who aided in killing Raeffele Caruso. Sortino, suffering from a run of bad luck (but not as bad as the man he helped kill), sought to change his fortunes. Bolber told him to put an egg under his arm for nine days. It must have worked as Sortino came back for additional advice.

Given mutual connections and a fondness for the occult, Bolber and Paul Petrillo became close friends and partners in crime, with each catering to, and exploiting, the superstitions of the local populace.

Over time word spread that Petrillo and Bolber had magic in their veins and successfully provided help. Women sought out the two, seeking advice as to how to address certain marital woes. Paul and Louie lent a sympathetic ear while providing life insurance and magic powders, which was, in fact, arsenic. The wife, as dutifully instructed, stirred the poison in with her husband's food or drink. At times the wives were merely dupes, doing as they were told, relying on the healing power of those providing the advice. At other times, the wives were neck deep and fully aware of what they were doing—ridding themselves of a problem and making some decent cash in depression-hardened times. The one constant were the ringleaders, who always got their cut of the insurance money. Indeed, at times they took the entire amount, leaving the widow both husbandless and even poorer.

The murder of Ferdinando Alfonsi broke open a case that quickly mushroomed. Ferdinando, a cement contractor who saw his business disappear during the depression, became a day laborer to (barely) help ends meet for his attractive, and angry, wife Stella and their two young sons, Ralph and Leo. Befriending Herman, he leaped into easier, yet more lucrative work, moving counterfeit money and stolen goods.

Stella had good reason to be mad, bitter that her father sold her, at 17, to Ferdinando, who was ten years older, for $2,000. She was young and pretty and liked to have a good time. If that meant leaving her young sons home alone while she was out, so be it. Since her husband was also always out without her, she did not want to miss out. And she certainly did not need the company of her loveless husband, with whom she fought and occasionally left—for four years on one occasion.

Herman Petrillo, who liked the ladies almost as much as his criminal ways, saw an opening and quickly ingratiated himself with her. With two life insurance policies in hand, Herman knew what had to be done, as did Stella. Unfortunately, offing a good friend presented somewhat of a moral dilemma, which was quickly solved when Herman decided to have someone else do the killing. He recruited an ex-con, George Myer, whose real name was Newmyer, on the good word of another ex-con. When Myer asked Herman why he didn't do what appeared to be an easy job, Herman explained, "Well, I know this man and I can't do it but I just knocked a guy off five days ago, but I didn't know him so good."

Unfortunately for Herman, Myer was also an informant. Hoping to get in with the feds, who wanted Herman for his counterfeiting misdeeds, Myer dropped a dime. Soon, Myer and undercover agent Stanley Phillips were dealing with Herman, plotting murder and counterfeiting schemes. Clearly the Phillips-Myer team had no interest in knocking off Ferdinando and continually put off the hit, meeting frequently with Herman to endlessly discuss how to best do it. Eschewing the tried-and-true arsenic route,

Herman discussed what also worked well—a trip to a river or a hit and run accident combined with an equally lethal lead pipe to the head. With much dithering and little happening, Herman grew tired of the wait.

When Myer and Phillips later met Herman in a bus station in New Jersey to pick up some bogus money, Ferdinando's name again came up. This time though, Herman told them not to worry about it.

As Ferdinando writhed in pain, with bloodshot eyes bulging and his innards exploding teems of vomit and diarrhea, his seemingly loving wife dabbed his forehead to comfort a man burning up with fever. Mercifully, he soon died. As Herman later related, "The fools in the hospital think he got influenza or pneumonia ... I gave him enough arsenic to kill six men."

The police were not so gullible and shortly Herman and Stella were arrested. While Stella clammed up, her cohort surprisingly did the opposite. Rather than tell the police to pound sand, Herman opened up and sold everyone down the river, excluding himself. He told of all the people who had been "Petrillo-ized," including one of Paul's girlfriends: Rose "the Kiss of Death" Carina, who had killed three significant others and was in the process of killing #4; and Maria "The Wicked Witch of North Philadelphia" Favato, who had killed her husband, and finding that to her liking, knocked off her teenaged stepson and a third victim, the husband of a neighbor. With the body count at twenty, the prosecutor, Vincent McDevitt, could not keep up with the litany of victims and defendants, who in the end totaled thirty. Soon Favato talked, as did Peter and Louie, who, like Herman, greatly downplayed their involvement.

Throughout 1939 there were trials and pleas, and pleas during trial, with a mass of women involved, nearly all of whom were reported as being uneducated, unattractive, and unassuming. All, that is, except Stella, who was the opposite—attractive, smart, and cunning. When she didn't like her court appointed attorney, she demanded, and got, a new one: Raymond Pace Alexander, who was highly respected and very competent. He was also Black and would be one of the first of his race to try high profile and capital cases.

Her trial, which was substantial yet circumstantial, started in October. The insurance agent testified about meeting with Stella, who would not allow him to meet with her husband; the treating doctor, who told of Stella refusing to send her obviously ailing husband to the hospital; Myer, who outlined the plot to kill the victim; the toxicology results indicating a deadly amount of arsenic; and Maria Favato, now a cooperating witness, who got the poison from Herman and gave it to Stella, who knew what to do with it.

Despite the onslaught of evidence knocking them to the ground, Alexander and his client rose to the occasion. Alexander stressed the unworthiness of some of the state's obvious unsavory witnesses; that Stella, unlike many of the other defendants who made incriminating statements to the police, had never admitted to anything; and persuasively, and fortuitously, that the insurance policies had lapsed due to non-payment prior to Ferdinand's death (probably due to oversight or cheapness on the part of Herman, who paid for the policies), thus eliminating a motive for the killing.

More than anyone or anything else, however, the comely defendant held sway. "A picture of poise, ebony-haired Stella Alfonsi took the witness stand yesterday," one newspaper reported. She calmly told the jury that those who testified against her had lied. Even a lengthy and withering cross-examination did not derail her.

Not guilty.

When all was said and done, the cast of characters could have come from a dark, dirty, and engrossing film noir, highlighting sordid backgrounds, human frailties, and tales hardly worthy of belief. Justice, for the most part, prevailed with Paul and Herman Petrillo dying in the electric chair, and Bolber, given a life sentence instead of death for his cooperation, dying in prison in 1954. Some of the women got off, like Rose "The Kiss of Death" Carina, who was also brilliantly represented by Alexander—who she later stiffed on his fee.

7

The Spanish Civil War and a Concert in Washington

Spanish Civil War Ends

"The dress rehearsal for World War II."

On April 1, 1939, shortly after the fall of Madrid, came the end of the Spanish Civil War, which had started in 1936. Sadly, like many civil wars, massive numbers of civilians and innocents died, often in retaliatory horrific manners. While an encyclopedia could be written about the war, suffice it to say that the left-leaning Republicans (supported by the Soviet Union and Mexico) fought and lost to the right-leaning Nationalists (supported by Germany, Italy, Portugal, and conservative Catholics). Francisco Franco, who led the Nationalists, would remain in power until 1975. Surprisingly, yet Machiavellian, despite the assistance of Hitler and Mussolini during the Civil War, Franco attempted to remain somewhat neutral during World War II, as Spain had done in the first war. While leaning toward those who helped him, as the tides of victory shifted so did Franco. In dealing with Franco, Hitler complained that he preferred having some of his teeth pulled.

Spain experienced great turmoil for over a century, with those bent on reform clashing with conservatives favoring the status quo. Uprisings and coups were common. Alliances often shifted, reflecting the mantra that the enemy of my enemy is my friend (until my friend reverts to again being my enemy). In the 1930s, the schisms split wide open once again with bloody clashes on the streets. Many abandoned the idea of changes made via a democratic peaceful process in favor of violent upheaval and anarchy, thereby creating in opposition yet another group with no strong political bent other than restoring security. With the kettle of discontent boiling over, civil war erupted in the summer of 1936.

Depending upon which side one favored, the clash came down to the Republicans viewing the fight as between fascist tyranny and freedom. Conversely, those favoring the Nationalists saw the battle as against Communist lawlessness intent on destroying Christian society. Foreign nations intervened, with Germany, Portugal, and Italy actively favoring the latter, while Mexico and the Soviet Union threw their support behind the former. So-called International Brigades, with the often-tacit permission of the nations from which they came, also fought with the Republicans, while the Catholic Church, reacting to the burning of Spanish churches and the killing of priests by the left, supported Franco.

While actively backing the Nationalists, Hitler walked a tightrope; he sent German air and ground troops, which gained invaluable combat experience, testing its war weaponry and technology, but was careful not to provoke a wider war that he was not yet ready to fight. Further, Hitler had ulterior motives, as German documents later revealed, "A hundred per cent victory for Franco was not desirable from a German point of view; rather were we interested in a continuance of the war and in the keeping up of the tension in the Mediterranean."

France was also in a delicate position, not wishing to alienate large swathes of its populace backing one side or the other. Fearful of Germany further encroaching and surrounding it, covet assistance was, at times, offered to the Republicans. The United States, meanwhile, while sympathetic to the Republican cause, was officially neutral. Some Americans, however, volunteered to join the fight, forming the Lincoln Battalion, which suffered high casualties. As one volunteer described his experience, "They give me a gun and they give me 100 bullets and they send me to fight."

The Republicans, who hoped to forge an anti-fascist alliance, saw that hope dashed when England, France, and Germany entered into the Munich Agreement. With that, and Franco's successful military advances, the conflict ended. While the number of military and civilians injured and killed varies widely, from the low hundreds of thousands to the high hundreds of thousands, it cannot be denied that many greatly suffered. The civil war was indeed, as U.S. Ambassador to Spain Claude Bowers later observed, the precursor of what was shortly to follow.

Less than a week later, on April 7, in homage to Hitler's Germany moving against Czechoslovakia in March, Mussolini's Italy invaded neighboring Albania, which had at one point in history been a part of the Roman Empire. When the Albanian people caught wind of the coming invasion, they took to the streets and demanded that the government resist. It did little good, as the nation was no match for the invading army. With Albania's leaders fleeing, Italy easily conquered the nation. The war lasted less than a week.

Albania thankfully was spared the horrors of Italy's 1935 invasion of Ethiopia, which saw the illegal use of mustard gas and the brutal slaughter of thousands of Ethiopians, who frequently fought a twentieth-century war with nineteenth-century weaponry. The war ended in 1937 with the Addis Ababa Massacre, wherein an Italian official proclaimed, to avenge a failed assassination attempt on a high-ranking officer, "Comrades, today is the day when we should show our devotion to our Viceroy by reacting and destroying the Ethiopians for three days. For three days I give you 'carte blanche' to destroy and kill and do what you want to the Ethiopians." The Italians troops followed the missive. Although disputed, approximately 20,000 people, or 20 percent of the local population, were randomly murdered, making it the worst massacre in Ethiopia's history.

With murder the norm in many parts of the world, in America at least, for one shining moment, beauty rang out as Marian Anderson, after overcoming many hardships, thrilled the masses.

Marian Anderson

"A voice heard once in a hundred years."

On Easter Sunder, April 9, Marian Anderson sang before approximately 75,000 people at the Lincoln Memorial Monument in the U.S. capital in Washington. Her journey to that day and location was anything but smooth.

Born to hard-working, middle-class and devout Christian parents in Philadelphia in 1897, she started singing at an early age. Despite demonstrating a unique talent, after graduating high school she was denied entrance to the local music academy, where she was succinctly told, "We don't take colored." Undeterred, she took private lessons, which paid off. In 1925, she won a competition which landed her a role performing with the New York Philharmonic orchestra. Her path, occasionally upended due to racial prejudice, was set, appearing in Carnegie Hall in 1928, the Orchestra Hall in Chicago a year later, and then throughout a more racially tolerant Europe where she blossomed. In Salzburg in 1935, the famed conductor Arturo Toscanini exclaimed that "[she had a voice] heard once in a hundred years."

While she sang many arias, she declined to perform in operas as she felt she lacked the appropriate training. Returning to America, she travelled throughout the nation, still suffering the pangs of racial intolerance. While eagerly sought after to sing in Princeton, New Jersey, she could not stay in a local hotel there. Albert Einstein, a champion of both physics and civil rights, came to her rescue and hosted her, a practice and friendship that endured the remainder of his life.

When her manager Sol Hurok tried to book Marian at the DAR Constitution Hall in Washington in 1939, he encountered resistance. As the head of the Daughters of the American Revolution explained, "The rules governing the use of Constitution Hall are in accordance with the policies of theaters, auditoriums, hotels and public schools of the District of Columbia." As such, Marian was denied entrance to perform.

When word got out, an uproar ensued. Membership in the DAR plummeted, led by the socially aware first lady, Eleanor Roosevelt. In her letter of resignation, Mrs. Roosevelt wrote:

> I am in complete disagreement with the attitude taken in refusing Constitution Hall to a great artist. You have set an example which seems to me unfortunate, and I feel obligated to send in to you my resignation. You had an opportunity to lead in an enlightened way and it seems to me that your organization has failed.

Newspapers around the nation joined in the condemnation. The *Richmond Times-Dispatch* editorialized, "In these days of racial intolerance so crudely expressed in the Third Reich, an action such as the D.A.R.'s ban ... seems all the more deplorable." Meanwhile, the *Philadelphia Tribune* intoned, "A group of tottering old ladies, who don't know the difference between patriots and putridism, have compelled the gracious First Lady to apologize for their national rudeness."

Mrs. Roosevelt implored the Secretary of the Interior, Harold Ickes, and her husband, a sympathetic president, to act. They did, arranging for Marian to perform on the steps of the majestic Lincoln Memorial. That no one had ever performed there previously served as no barrier.

Despite somewhat uncooperative weather—it had snowed the day before and was cold, yet clear—Marian captivated an unexpected crowd of tens of thousands, a number dwarfed by those listening via radio. Marian was overcome by the moment:

> There seemed to be people as far as the eye could see. I had a feeling that a great wave of good will poured out from those people, almost engulfing me. And when I stood up to sing ... I felt for a moment as though I were choking. For a desperate second, I thought that the words, well as I know them, would not come.

They came.

Marian Anderson died in 1993 at the age of 96, leaving behind a bevy of appearances throughout the world, a mountain of prestigious awards, and her image adorning both a postage stamp and savings bonds. She also got to perform in Constitution Hall.

The Forgotten Castles

"The best-dressed woman in America."

On April 28, RKO released the movie, *The Story of Vernon and Irene Castle*, starring Fred Astaire and Ginger Rogers. As is often the case, movies made about worthy people often fall short, if for no other reason than no movie can adequately capture the enormity and essence of the subject's life and accomplishments. The movie admirably tried though, opening: "In a fabulous and beloved era, near enough to be warmly remembered, two bright and shining stars, VERNON and IRENE CASTLE, whirled across the horizon, with the hearts of all who loved to dance. This is their story."

Vernon was born William Vernon Blyth in 1887 in England. His future wife, Irene Foote, came into the world six years later in 1893. Vernon, the son of a pub owner, was on his way to becoming a civil engineer when he detoured, emigrating to New York and taking to the stage, thanks to his sister and her husband who were both actors. Meanwhile, Irene, born in New Rochelle, New York, to a physician father, studied dancing and acting. Given their common interests it comes as no surprise that they met. A year later they married, on May 28, 1911.

Both gifted dancers and charismatic actors, Vernon often played the comedic role of an elegant drunk, stumbling around on stage as he mightily attempted to hide his inebriation. Looking to expand their horizons, they travelled to Paris and quickly ingratiated themselves with the elite, introducing the latest American dance moves. Their glowing reviews sailed back with them to the United States where they returned to glory and recognition, performing in those new-fangled silent motion pictures as well as on stage and in vaudeville.

On Broadway, they starred in a musical written for them, *Watch Your Step*, featuring Irving Berlin's very first score. Berlin, with his career already soaring with the earlier success of his major hit, *Alexander's Ragtime Band*, continued its ascent with the new ragtime musical with the Castles polishing and updating the Foxtrot with songs. As one noted, they "[radiated] musical and lyrical sophistication." One such song, "Play a Simple Melody" featured the first of Berlin's famous simultaneous tunes in which two different lyrics and melodies were sung at the same time. In its review, *Variety* called the show, "[a] terrific hit [featuring the] first syncopated musical [where the] sets and the girls were gorgeous," catapulting Berlin, at 26, "[to] one of the greatest lyric writers America has ever produced."

As the nation's, if not the world's, foremost dance team, Vernon and Irene expanded their horizons, opening a dance studio, "Castle House," in which they taught the latest dance crazes; a nightclub, "Castles by the Sea," on the Boardwalk of Long Island's Long Beach; and a restaurant. Setting the tastes of the times, they popularized different high energy dance styles and brought African-American music to the white masses. They travelled with a Black orchestra and employed an openly gay manager, Elisabeth Marbury, a force in her own right, who also guided George Bernard Shaw and Oscar Wilde. Adding to their versatility, the Castles authored a book, *Modern Dancing*. A trendsetter in dance, Irene also became one in fashion, marked by elegance, grace, and style.

When World War I broke out, Vernon did what is unthinkable today among our theatrical, and for that matter sports and other, elite. Determined to join the fight, he left the touring company of *Watch Your Step*, to take flying lessons. Once he became proficient he appeared, before shipping out, with Irene and the highly acclaimed John Philip Souza and his band, in two farewell shows in the Hippodrome Theater in NYC.

Enlisting as a pilot in England's Royal Flying Corps, he flew 300 combat missions. In 1917, he was awarded the highly prestigious Croix de Guerre for bravery. As Vernon fought, Irene appeared in a handful of shows, greatly saddened that she was performing alone. She also promoted war charities.

On February 15, 1918, during a training exercise, Vernon was killed. He was just 30 years old.

Given no choice, Irene carried on. In addition to appearing in a dozen silent films, in 1919 she married the son of a well-known local family, who lost Irene's money through poor investments. After divorcing him in 1923, she remarried again, this time to Frederic McLaughlin, sixteen years her senior, and relocated. Major McLaughlin, a coffee tycoon, had also fought in World War I, commanding the Blackhawk Division, named after Black Hawk, a prominent Native American in Illinois history. When McLaughlin purchased a local hockey club in 1926, he named them the Chicago Blackhawks, destined to become a mainstay in the National Hockey League. Irene designed the team's jersey logo.

Two years after the Blackhawks came into existence, Irene, while looking with a friend for a country estate in Illinois, came across one with an outdated dog kennel. An animal lover, Irene decided to refurbish the kennel and turn it into a sanctuary for stray dogs. She named it Orphans of the Storm, after a 1921 silent movie starring Lillian and Dorothy Gish, based on a French 1874 play about one of France's revolutions. The kennel, now also catering to cats, is still in existence.

In 1944 McLaughlin died, leaving behind Irene and their two children, Barbara (born 1925) and William (1929). Although scaling back her career when her children were born, Irene, still dubbed "the best-dressed woman in America," remained active, appearing in a radio show, "The Life of Irene Castle" about her family's European travels.

In 1939, the movie was released about her life with Vernon, on which she consulted. Being somewhat of a perfectionist she had several problems with the film, including casting white Walter Brennan as their faithful friend and servant, who, in reality, was Black. The film also altered the race of the Black orchestra to white. Due to censorship considerations, the free-flowing costumes, dress, and style of the Castles and their contemporaries were neutered, with Rogers and Astaire donning a far staider and more conservative 1939 look. While brown-haired Irene wore and popularized the short bob haircut style of her time, Rogers wore her long hair blond and bland.

The movie is unique though in that it was far more serious than the other Astaire-Rogers ones, leaving behind the screwball comedy mantra. Indeed, it is the only Astaire movie in which he tragically, albeit heroically, dies.

Two years after McLaughlin passed, Irene married for the fourth and final time, to an advertising executive, also living in Chicago, whom she also outlived.

Thirty years after the movie's release, Irene died. A talented innovator, and indeed a giant in her time, she first married a man equal in stature. The world knew and idolized them, much as they had another icon, Amelia Earhart. Sadly, unlike Earhart, today the Castles are essentially unknown and forgotten.

Other seminal events occurred in April—golfer Ralph Guldahl won the sixth Masters, Native-American Ellison "Tarzan" Brown won the Boston Marathon (in 2:28:51), the Boston Bruins won hockey's coveted Stanley Cup, the public for the first time both heard Glenn Miller's hit tune *Moonlight Serenade* and read John Steinbach's *The Grapes of Wrath*, Stalin signed the British-France-Russian anti-Nazi pact, and Hitler revoked both the Versailles Treaty limiting the size of his naval forces and the German-Polish Non-Aggression Treaty of 1934. Despite these noteworthy occurrences, they were overshadowed by one magnificent event, setting in motion changes still in effect today. For, on April 30, the World's Fair to end all World's Fairs opened in, where else, New York.

8

A World's Fair to End All World's Fairs

That it was larger than life came as no surprise as it was located in a city larger than life, albeit one still struggling, along with all others, due to the effects of the deadly depression. Opening on April 30, its planning began, not surprisingly, years earlier in 1935, when a group of businessmen and politicians came together to formulate a plan to lift both the local economy and spirits. The newly formed New York World's Fair Corporation met in the upper reaches of the Empire State Building. Local luminaries, including former businessman/former police chief/city official/man about town, Mr. New York Grover Whalen; the forward-thinking and energetic Mayor Fiorello La Guardia; and a host of other luminaries, worked with the visionary and autocratic City Parks Commissioner, Robert Moses, to create one of the largest and most expensive international fairs ever.

Fiorello La Guardia is to this day considered one of the best mayors ever to occupy the office, despite his unimpressive 5-foot-2-inch stature and high, squeaky voice. Born in Greenwich Village in 1882 to a Catholic father and a Jewish mother, he was raised Episcopalian. Joining the State Department, he was stationed in Europe where he took advantage of the many languages in which he was fluent—Italian, Yiddish, German, and Croatian. Upon returning to the United States, he attended NYU's Law School, where he graduated in 1910. Entering politics, he was elected to Congress in 1916. He decided to leave, however, when the position of President of the Board of Aldermen opened up in 1919. He defeated a Tammany Hall Democrat and served for a few years before returning to Congress, still as a Republican, and served a decade, leaving in 1933, to successfully run for mayor.

La Guardia's mayoral campaign was energetic, promising to reform the city, root out corruption, and replace patronage with a merit-based civil service program. Wishing to restore economic vitality to the city he loved, he worked closely with the Roosevelt Administration and despite the difference in political parties, forged a close and successful relationship in reworking and rebuilding the city's infrastructure. With an influx of federal funds and the vision of Robert Moses, the many bridges, tunnels, and highways of today's New York City came to life under him. In a dazzling display of construction, the East River Drive, the West Side Highway, Triborough Bridge, and Brooklyn's Battery Tunnel, were all constructed; so too, two airports—New York Municipal Airport, later in 1953 aptly renamed LaGuardia, and Idlewild, later renamed John F. Kennedy, or more colloquially, JFK.

When a Jewish opponent, Henry Frank, ran against him in a mayoral race, Frank accused La Guardia of antisemitism. Not wishing to exploit his mother's religion, La Guardia instead offered to debate Frank entirely in Yiddish. Frank, not speaking the language, declined and, not surprisingly lost an election that he probably had no chance of winning in the first place.

In 1939, in addition to seeing the fruits of his labor realized with the opening of both the World's Fair and the New York Municipal Airport, he oversaw the public takeover and creation of the subway system when the city purchased the two independent subway lines. La Guardia, affectionally known as Little Flower, during a newspaper strike famously took to the radio to read comics to the children listening. He also welcomed the von Trapp family (of *Sound of Music* fame) when they arrived at Ellis Island, having fled Europe.

When the planners of the Fair met in the mid'30s, a first order of business was where to place it. After discussion, a suitable location came into view, focusing on a nearly deserted and desolate foul-smelling marshy ash dump in Queens, where for years the daily refuse of the area came to be delivered. It was a no-lose decision. The residents of the city's borough had long complained that while Manhattan and Brooklyn had large and notable green areas—Central and Prospect Parks respectively, Queens countered with a smelly landfill. Clean up the area, build the Fair, and after it closes, turn the area into a lush, sprawling park. And, as an added benefit, the construction created jobs, paid workers needed money that was taxed and spent, and generated revenues benefiting local businesses.

The optimism of creating the project spilled over to its central theme—"Building a better tomorrow with the tools of today"—and showcased everything America had to offer and dream about. As the official guide explained:

> The eyes of the Fair are on the future—not in the sense of peering toward the unknown nor attempting to foretell the events of tomorrow and the

> shape of things to come, but in the sense of presenting a new and clearer view of today in preparation for tomorrow; a view of the forces and ideas that prevail as well as the machines. To its visitors the Fair will say: Here are the materials, ideas, and forces at work in our world. These are the tools with which the World of Tomorrow must be made. They are all interesting and much effort has been expended to lay them before you in an interesting way. Familiarity with today is the best preparation for the future.

That a new mini-city, comprising 1,216 gutted acres, could be constructed from scratch in just four or so years is astonishing by today's standards, in which it would take that long to address the permitting processes. But it was a different world, one in which great goals could be accomplished in relatively short times, as later evidenced by industry's vital impact on the war effort. The mammoth undertaking included the additional construction of new and existing subway and railroad lines along with the Whitestone Bridge, connecting the boroughs of the Bronx and Queens, and opened two months early to coincide with the start of the Fair.

With lofty goals, the Fair launched on the last day of April, a date purposely coinciding with George Washington's Presidential Inauguration 150 years before, then held in New York City. To commemorate the event, the *New York Times* published two hefty additional sections to its already bulky Sunday paper. It also included a full-page ad in yet another section: "Beginning April 30 in the New York Area RCA and NBC offer you TELEVISION."

The Fair was indeed off to an auspicious start. It also introduced, featured, and popularized, often crude versions of, color photographs, air conditioning, FM radio, international phone calls, robotics, fluorescent lights, fax machines, and nylon pantyhose.

The first day, like all the coming ones, carried a cornucopia of events. The highlights included welcoming speeches by Governor Lehman, Mayor La Guardia, and President Roosevelt. When the president spoke, the crowd saw a seemingly hardy man at the podium, often gesturing with his head. They did not see his hands, which remained hidden and holding two sturdy pegs for support, given his debilitating polio and inability to stand on his own. His speech was the first ever televised, watched by approximately a thousand people on two hundred or so TV sets.

At 4:30 pm, a re-enactment of President Washington's inauguration took place in front of a 65-foot-high statue of him in Constitution Mall. Costumed descendants of those who actually attended the original ceremony also participated. Thirty minutes later, Mayor La Guardia dedicated the nearby large statues of the Four Freedoms—speech, religion, press, and assembly. At 9 pm, a light and sound demonstration lit up the area, showing off the very latest innovations in those areas, as well as an address by Albert Einstein, discussing cosmic rays.

Throughout the day, aerial acts, parades, and music, most notably by the New York Philharmonic-Symphony Orchestra performing in the Hall of Music, entertained the over 200,000 people attending the grand opening. At 11:15 fireworks blasted off, accompanied by billowing water displays from fifteen nearby barges. Midnight found a stage show in the amusement area and a giant street carnival. Finally, after the long day, the Fair closed at 2 am with a light and fountain display on Fountain Lake.

The large Fair came to be divided into seven unique and bold zones and areas, which its designers encouraged to be brash, innovative, and forward-looking in creating big, beautiful, and colorful buildings, containing equally noteworthy exhibits. This encouragement extended even to the Fair's water fountains, benches, and streetlamps.

The Communications and Business Zone housed several exhibits, including a large structure with two oversized 160-foot pylons. Upon entering the AT&T Pavilion, the robot Voder welcomed and greeted visitors with his husky synthesized voice. The Business and Insurance Building held Aetna, MetLife, and IBM exhibits, including new-fangled electric typewriters and a calculator. The Masterpieces of Art, really a museum, featured priceless paintings, including those by Caravaggio, Rembrandt, DaVinci, and Michelangelo, and sculptures assembled from throughout the world.

The Community Interest Zone contained numerous buildings dedicated to the home, including the latest in plumbing, cosmetics, garden, and jewelry. It also featured fifteen homes, an electrified farm, and a working farm, all showing what a Town of Tomorrow might look like.

The Government Zone consisted of twenty-one pavilions, including those from Britain (complete with a copy of the Magna Carta); France (with a world-class restaurant—Le Pavillon—remaining in NYC after the Fair closed); Italy (with 100,000 square feet featuring a 200-foot waterfall and murals celebrating Italy's rich history); Greece (also featuring large murals depicting its unique past); and Japan (housing a shrine and garden, a replica of the Liberty Bell festooned with pearls and diamonds worth over a million dollars, and soon-to-be-ironic signage "Dedicated to Eternal Peace and Friendship between America and Japan"). The buildings of the Netherlands, Pan America, Poland, Jewish Palestine, the USSR, and the US also lavishly vied for the attention of those attending. The Soviet Pavilion—with a life-size replica of the interior of a Moscow Metro Station, a 260-foot statue on a pylon, and a large partially enclosed courtyard—competed with the

US Building with its two 150-foot pylons and several structures devoted to many of its states.

The original Elsie the Cow joined 250 of her pedigreed cousins on the Rotolactor, which mechanically milked, bathed, and dried them in the Food Zone, which featured other food-related subjects. The nation's manufacturing and distribution processes were on display in the Production and Distribution Zone. In one imposing horseshoe-shaped structure with a large tower, the Westinghouse Electric Manufacturing Company Exhibit featured Elektro, which the Official Guide described as "a seven-foot metal man that talks, sees, smells, sings, and counts with his fingers." He also smoked. Possessing a 700-word vocabulary spoken via a 78-rpm record player implanted in his 250-lb body, "moto-man" often hurled mild insults at those around him, such as "My brain is bigger than yours."

Westinghouse also featured The Time Capsule, buried in 1939, not to be opened for 5,000 years in 6939. At 7 feet long, it contained hundreds of pounds of life from the time—different types of fabrics, metals and seeds, a pack of Camel cigarettes, a Mickey Mouse watch, millions of pages on microfilm, money, writings by Albert Einstein and acclaimed Nobel Prize writer Thomas Mann, a Gillette safety razor, a kewpie doll, and issues of *Life* magazine.

Nearby, workers in the Dupont exhibit spun its latest product, nylon stockings. Hoping to replace the current leggings, which were made of either too hot wool, or silk that ran far too easily, nylons were both cooler and stronger. Audiences witnessed how nylons were made followed by models either wearing them or yanking on them to demonstrate their durability.

The 36,000-square-foot Futurama exhibit highlighted the General Motors Building in the Transportation Zone. Futurama visitors were transported over a large diorama of a fictional area of the United States, starting with smallish figures that grew larger as one progressed to the end where they found themselves in a life-sized city intersection, complete with actual auto and appliance stores with GM's latest products. Or as the Guide described it:

> In 600 moving chairs, each equipped with a sound device which serves as a private guide on the Aladdin-like trip, visitors travel over a vast miniature cross-section of America as it may conceivably appear twenty years or more from now.... As they travel on several layers of the building in their magic chairs, they view a continuous animated panorama of towns and cities, rivers and lakes, country and farm areas, industrial plants in operation, country clubs, forests, valleys, and snow-capped mountains. The "futurama" contains approximately 500,000 individually designed houses; more than a million trees of eighteen species; and 50,000

scale-model automobiles, of which 10,000 are in actual operation over super-highways, speed lanes and multi-decked bridges.

Twenty-seven thousand visitors a day took the 15-minute journey, the end of which they received a "I Have Seen the Future" pin.

Meanwhile, on the roof of the Ford building, racing cars sped endlessly around its figure eight track. Nearby, the birth and growth of railroads was reimagined in a live demonstration. Also featured were several historical locomotives, one of which ran in place on a dynamometer, continuously at a speed of 60 miles per hour.

The most fun of all, perhaps, was in the aptly named Amusement Zone, where if one's intellectual spirits were not lifted, certainly their bodies were. Whether whirling on the rollercoaster, weaving on the topsy-turvy bobsled, or shooting up into the sky only to be hurled back to earth on The Parachute Jump (later moved to Coney Island), one's body, not to mention stomach, were constantly in a state of action. For those less inclined to churning adventures, Gimbels Flyer Train (now in Pittsburgh's Kennywood amusement park), carnival acts, and Frank Buck's Jungleland (with elephants, reptiles, birds, animals, camel rides, Jiggs the trained Orangutan, and Monkey Mountain inhabited with 600 monkeys) awaited.

Showman Billy Rose led a life worthy of the many Broadway shows he produced. He also composed a number of songs, including "Me and My Shadow" and the immortal "Does the Spearmint Lose Its Flavor on the Bedpost Overnight." Perhaps more famous today for having been married, from 1929 through 1938, to famed comedian Fanny Brice, who was immortalized by Barbra Streisand in two acclaimed movies, *Funny Girl* and *Funny Lady*, he was a master of entertainment, extending his talents to an ornate water and musical show titled "Billy Rose's Aquacade." Performed in an arena accommodating 10,000 Fairgoers, his shows featured oceans of water, churned out in waterfalls at 8,000 gallons a minute, engulfed in pulsating lights. With an orchestra providing the music, two of the most famous swimmers of the era, Olympian Gold medalists Johnny Weissmuller and Eleanor Holm, dazzled their audiences with their aquatic prowess. When Weissmuller wasn't in the pool, he was out publicizing his latest movie, *Tarzan Finds a Son!*, which MGM released in June. When Holm wasn't in the pool, she was having an affair with Rose, whom she married in November.

Seven years earlier, Eleanor Holm had won a gold medal at Los Angeles's 1932 Summer Olympics. The following year she married Art Jarrett, a fellow graduate from Brooklyn's Erasmus High School. While sailing on the SS *Manhattan* to swim in the 1936 Olympics in Berlin, Holm either drank far too much at a raucous drinking party and passed out, or was the victim of a spiteful Avery Brundage, the powerful and autocratic U.S. Olympic Committee President, whose sexual advances she spurned. Regardless of what truly transpired, she found herself expelled from the team. Heartbroken at the turn of events as she was favored to win another gold medal, she regrouped, returned to America, and appeared in the movies. In 1938 she played Jane in *Tarzan's Revenge*. That same year, Jarrett divorced her due to the embarrassment caused by her expulsion from the Olympics, as well as her sleeping with another man.

As Holm and Rose were marrying in 1939, Weissmuller was also in the throes of marital adventures, culminating in the shedding of one wife, "The Mexican Spitfire" Lupe Vélez, to marry a third, socialite Beryl Scott, with whom he would have three children before again divorcing a decade later. Unlike many movie stars whose public and private personas clashed to the dismay and cover-up of the studios, Olive Thomas and Jack Pickford being prime examples, Lupe's private life was as open and notorious as her public one. So well-known was her reputation that many of her movies centered around and took advantage of it.

Lupe Vélez was born Maria Guadalupe Villalobos Vélez in Mexico in 1908. One of five children, her family was well-educated and financially well off. Deciding to take to the stage, which upset her father, she incorporated her sensual looks and manner into a suggestive singing and dancing routine. When one boss refused to give her a raise she quit; her new boss fired her for being too feisty. She quickly found new employment. Not shy around potential rivals, she openly ridiculed and fought with them, gaining her the publicity she coveted. Attracting a large local following, Hollywood soon beckoned. Upon arriving she met Fanny Brice, who was taken with her outgoing personality. In addition to her strong sex appeal, she also possessed an equally strong comedic streak, shown in her early roles with Laurel and Hardy.

In 1938 Vélez appeared on Broadway in Cole Porter's *You Never Know*, which had a short run due partly to her public feud with her jealous co-star Libby Holman, who recoiled at the publicity Lupe received, especially when imitating, not necessarily in a sympathetic manner, the female stars of the day—Katherine Hepburn, Greta Garbo, Fanny Brice, Simone Simon, Gloria Swanson, Shirley Temple, and Marlene Dietrich, whom Lupe particularly disliked due to both of them (Dietrich and Vélez) having affairs with Gary Cooper. The spat with Holman came to a head with fisticuffs and a black eye during a curtain call. When Vélez returned to Mexico for a film role, 10,000 fans greeted her.

One year later, in 1939, Vélez starred in a B comedy for RKO, *The Girl from Mexico*, where Vélez basically played herself, a 5-foot-tall, sassy, temperamental, highly strung, and sexy singer from a small town in Mexico who is discovered by an ad man from New York, played by Donald Woods, searching for a singer for a radio show. Featuring romance, mayhem, songs, malapropisms, and arguments, Vélez was not only one of the first non-white actresses to play the lead role, but also one featuring a Caucasian-Mexican romance. A surprise hit, Vélez would go on to make seven more "spitfire" movies, the last one being in 1943.

In 1933, Weissmuller divorced his wife to marry Vélez. Less than four months later, the *New York Times* reported their "trial separation." As Vélez explained, "I love Johnnie, and he loves me, but we have two terrible tempers. We fight all the time." They reconciled, but their relationship remained stormy. One perhaps apocryphal tale involved Weissmuller returning home only to find his beloved dog dead. Believing that Vélez killed the pet due to her jealousy over the attention he paid it, Weissmuller retaliated by killing her parrot.

The unpredictable and volatile actress who might either kiss, bite, or spit upon one during an interaction, had dinner with two female friends on December 13, 1944. Upon leaving, she downed over seventy Seconal pills, washing them down with brandy. Her maid found her dead that morning; nearby, a suicide note. On the front Lupe wrote, "To Harald, May God forgive you and forgive me too, but I prefer to take my life away and our baby's before I bring him with shame or killing him. Lupe." On the back, "How could you, Harald, fake such a great love for me and our baby when all the time, you didn't want us? I see no other way out for me, so goodbye, and good luck to you. Love Lupe."

Earlier, Vélez had announced her engagement to fellow actor Arturo de Cordova, who was married with four children at the time. She ended the romance after de Cordova's wife refused to grant him a divorce. She quickly rebounded with an affair with Harald Ramond, an Austrian actor, with whom she unexpectedly became pregnant. Ramond refused to marry her and Vélez, a devout Catholic, recoiled at the thought of an abortion. Weissmuller served as one of the pallbearers for his former wife, whose colorful life ended at 36.

When the crowds filed in by the thousands to see Weissmuller and Holm perform, they were well aware not only of the vast talents of the performers, but their colorful backgrounds as well. The popular and well-known Weissmuller received thousands of letters from fans weekly. Their fame, however, provided little rest from performing. Daily shows started at 3:30, followed by ones at 5:30, 8:30, and 10:45. Joining Weissmuller and Holm were the Aquabelles and Aquadudes, either diving off high diving boards, performing synchronized swimming routines, or other marine spectaculars.

Of all the diversions in the Amusement Zone, one of the quieter, yet probably more popular, ones involved the topless shows, wherein comely women brazenly featured their assets. Although frowned upon, economic considerations allowed for performances at various locales in the area, including Billy Rose's Aquacade. Authorities thought the line was crossed, however, when The Cuban Village held a "Miss Nude of 1939" contest at which the vice squad swooped in and closed the spectacle down. It shortly reopened in a far tamer and more wholesome circumstance.

Of all the Zones and the events going on within them, two structures predominated, with all attention and focus lavished upon the symbols of the Fair—Trylon and Perisphere, the sphere and the triangle—but to the locals: the spike and the ball. The Perisphere, eighteen stories high and a world record 200 feet in diameter, contained an auditorium double the size of Radio City Music Hall featuring Democracity, a towering model of the City of Tomorrow, home to miniatures a million strong, with 250,000 hypothetical workers, all living in its outskirts in five satellite towns, all with many parks and large buildings. Broad highways surrounded by lush greenery allowed for travel in and out of the main hub.

Visitors entered the Perisphere at its base and stepped onto the world's longest moving stairway. Quietly propelled upward and deposited onto one of two revolving balconies moving in opposite directions, the ride lasted for six minutes, showing a city from daylight to evening as the sun set. The darkened sky came alive, alit by a thousand stars accompanied by the chorus of an equal number of voices singing out to the heavens. From ten different points, people dressed in the garments of various workers marched out as the symphony grew louder. When the music ended, the workers all magically disappeared, replaced by an explosion of light. Grand indeed.

After Democracity and the Perisphere, the symbol of the Fair's lofty purpose Trylon beckoned. Standing at 700 feet tall, the three-sided spike of a structure reached far into the sky. Upon passing through, attendees gently descended to the ground via the helicline, a walkway providing wide, clear, and unobstructed views of the vast surrounding areas.

The experience of those viewing the structures, as with most of the exhibits, seemed other-worldly to nearly all. At the time, people did not jet off to Europe, the Caribbean, or some other foreign land for vacation. Most had never left the surroundings into which they had been born and inhabited, never even visiting other parts of the nation they lived. Few had ever been on an airplane. Their knowledge of the world came not from experience but from books, newspapers, newsreels, and the stories and tales told by grandparents and teachers. Visiting world cultures up close and in person in the various exhibits provided an opportunity of viewing an exotic world never before experienced or imagined. Entering tall and wide and imposing brilliantly colored, often enormous buildings, surrounded by gushing fountains, pulsating lights, and lush gardens provided an illuminating and exhilarating new world. Few had ever personally interacted with anything resembling Electro or Voder or Monkey Mountain, or had the option of viewing either a painting by Rembrandt or a topless woman parading around in public. Even the Official Guide to the Fair, at 200 pages, was a handful.

On June 10, when King George VI and Queen Elizabeth came, 2 million fans followed to see them. On July 2, the World Science Fiction Convention held its first gathering. Every day featured something new and different to meet the varying interests of those it wished to attract.

The 1939 "World of Tomorrow Fair" closed in October and reopened in April 1940, to an even more conflicted world, as evidenced by its new slogan, "For Peace and Freedom." The countries most affected by hostilities—Poland and Czechoslovakia and Russia—did not bother to reopen. Germany, citing budgetary considerations, didn't participate at all. On July 4, a bomb exploded in the British pavilion, killing two detectives. Some of the foreign workers found themselves stranded and could not return to their native lands.

When it finally closed on October 27, 1940, it took far less time to break down the Fair than it did to build it: months rather than years. The 40 tons of steel it took to construct the Perisphere and Trylon went to the war effort. Some buildings remained, however. The Belgian Pavilion was dismantled and sold to Virginia Union University in Richmond where it hosts its basketball and volleyball games. The Bendix Lama Temple still sits in storage after proposals for its use at various colleges failed to materialize. The NYC Pavilion served as the early site for the United Nations General Assembly; in 1964 it returned to its roots for that generation's World's Fair, housing a model of all of New York. Today the Queens Museum is located there. On the site where the Perisphere stood a similar-looking structure, the Unisphere, was built for the 1964–1965 World's Fair. It still stands today. Duplicating the time capsule laid in 1939, another Westinghouse one was planted next to it, also to be opened in 5,000 years. Today, fans attending a New York Mets baseball game or the US Tennis Open, use the same station built for those attending the Fair in 1939.

In the end, the Fair proved to be a financial failure. Although around 45 million people came, it was far below the millions more initially predicted. The 70-cent entrance fee (25 cents for children), a quarter to enter Democracity, a nickel for the multi-page daily events newspaper, and various other expenses associated with what one wanted to enter, see, ride, or eat, did not come close to covering the vast costs of building and running paradise. As for the excitement and awe the Fair created and provided though, it was a smashing and unforgettable success.

9

A Voyage to Nowhere

The SS *St. Louis*

"A Voyage to Nowhere."

On May 13, the doomed SS *St. Louis*, flying the Nazi flag, departed Hamburg with 937 passengers, most of whom were Jews seeking to leave Germany to escape oppression and start a new life. Sadly, like the nation they were leaving, no one wanted them.

The ship, named after the American city, was constructed in Bremen, Germany, and launched in 1928. Alternatively referred to as either the MS (Motor Ship) or SS (Steamship or Sailing Ship or Single-Screw, which is a method of propulsion), it was built as a luxury liner and primarily traveled across the Atlantic to New York and Canada. In 1939, under the kind and watchful eye of German Captain Gustav Schroeder, the ship's human cargo purchased visas to Cuba, where they would disembark and then try to gain entrance to the United States. Among the crew were several members of the Abwehr, Germany's military intelligence branch. One such person in particular, Otto Schiendick, was tasked with retrieving secret documents amassed by German agents gathering American defense secrets and taking them back to Germany.

With relief blowing in the wind and believing freedom awaited, the passengers enjoyed a leisurely voyage with ample and previously hard-to-secure food, which the parents often ate while their also well-fed children played with babysitters. Entertainment abounded with concerts, dances, and even a cinema. A swimming pool added to the "vacation cruise to freedom." On Friday evening, religious services were held. Busts and pictures of Hitler were covered.

In blissful ignorance, the passengers had not learned that Cuban president, Federico Laredo Brú, under pressure from various fronts, revoked the visas that had been purchased. Nor did they know that on May 8, tens of thousands of Cubans, in the largest antisemitic rally in Cuba's history, railed against the admission of the Jews, dubbed Communists and revolutionaries who would vie for scant employment opportunities. Spurred on covertly by Nazi spies living there, right-wing politicians and their parties, as well as newspapers which had supported Franco in Spain, demanded that no Jews be admitted. A former president went even further, demanding that the Cubans "fight the Jews until the last one is driven out."

In the early morning hours of May 27, the ship docked in Havana Harbor. Waiting interminably for five days to disembark, the passengers grew increasingly concerned as only twenty-nine travelers were allowed entry. Those allowed off the ship consisted of twenty-two Jews with U.S. visas, four Spaniards and two Cubans, and one medical evacuee who had tried to commit suicide when he learned he could not leave the ship.

Despite pleas from U.S. Secretary of State Cordell Hull, Secretary of the Treasury Henry Morgenthau, and the American Jewish Joint Distribution Committee (the JDC), Brú stood firm. Negotiations with the Cuban government failed. Monies offered were rejected. Fees earlier paid for the visas wound up in the pockets of corrupt Cuban officials.

Not welcome in Cuba, Captain Schroeder set sail for Miami in the hope that the American government would be more receptive. Despite the pleas of Hull and other notable American officials for Cuba to admit the refugees, when it came to America's handling of the humanitarian crisis, it followed Cuba's lead in denying entry.

At night, although the passengers could see the twinkling lights of Miami, they got no closer. As the days passed, cables were sent to President Roosevelt beseeching him to take action. Like Brú, Roosevelt also faced substantial political pressures. Still in the throes of the Depression, pressure came to continue the severe immigration quotas established by the Immigration and Nationality Act of 1924, if for no other reason than to preserve jobs. Nationally, Americans overwhelmingly opposed the relaxation of the law, spurred on by isolationist Republican gains in 1938's Congressional elections. Months before the *St. Louis* left Germany, Congress refused to act on legislation that would have allowed 20,000 German Jewish children to enter America. Even the press, which generally reacted favorably to the plight of the passengers, did not go as far as to call for their admission. With FDR contemplating running for an unprecedented third term, a stand against strong popular opinion was politically disadvantageous. Against this backdrop, along with his desire to work with Congress in moving against restrictive neutrality laws and taking a stand against Hitler, Roosevelt did not respond to calls for action. Instead, the State Department wired a formalistic reply informing those seeking asylum that they "must await their turns on the waiting list and qualify for and obtain immigration visas before they may be admissible into the United States." In defense of this stand, many thought it unfair for the passengers to jump ahead of those back in Germany who had earlier applied for admission and were waiting their turn.

As the *St. Louis* departed the inhospitable waters of Florida, Captain Schroeder thought of grounding the ship. The Coast Guard, acting on orders from Secretary Hull, followed and guarded against this action. Another plan, of landing in Canada, was met with equal obstinance with Frederick Blair, who oversaw immigration, opining, "No country could open its doors wide enough to take in the hundreds of thousands of Jewish people who want to leave Europe. The line must be drawn somewhere."

Despite the adversity, Captain Schroeder continued to try to save those on-board, even entertaining the thought of later sinking the ship on the shores of England, thus forcing that nation to take in the refugees. In the end, he refused to return the *St. Louis* to Germany, docking instead in Belgium. With the help of the JDC and others sympathetic to the cause, including American higher-ups, Neville Chamberlain of England agreed to take in 288 passengers, while France admitted 224, Belgium 214, and the Netherlands 181.

With the ship now emptied of passengers, it returned to Germany. For Hitler, the saga in all probability confirmed his beliefs that no one wanted, nor really cared about, the Jews. Any further hostile and violent moves he made against them might be met, if at all, with the world clucking, but little else. Another seed of The Final Solution had started to sprout.

The passengers who landed in England basically survived the war. Those who settled in the three other European nations later overrun by Germany were far less fortunate, with approximately 254 dying in the Holocaust. Many of those who survived ultimately wound up in the United States.

As for Captain Schroder, a man who studied languages as a hobby, and soon mastered seven, he served Germany during the war working at a desk. At the end of hostilities he was recognized for his empathy and bravery, winning awards, including being named one of the "Righteous Among the Nations" by Israel's Yad Vashem. In the mid-1970s, a book and movie, *Voyage of the Damned*, told the heroic tale. In 2012 and 2017, the American and Canadian governments, respectively, formally apologized for their roles. The ship at the center of the controversy suffered severe damage at the hands of Allied bombers in 1944 and was ultimately scrapped eight years later.

The 5-year-old Mother

"More interested in playing with her doll than her child."

On Mother's Day, May 14, Lina Medina, aged 5 years, 7 months, and 21 days, gave birth via a C-section to a healthy 6-lb son, whom she named Gerardo after the doctor, Gerardo Lozada, who treated her. Needless to say, this came as a great shock not only to her parents but to the medical establishment and world at large.

Lina, one of nine children, was born on September 23, 1933, in a poor Peruvian village. Her father, Tiburelo, a silversmith, and mother, Victoria, became alarmed at the sight of young Lina's steadily expanding stomach. Thinking it was a dangerous tumor, they travelled to a hospital to have her examined. Initially the doctors joined her parents in their early belief and started running tests to ascertain a diagnosis and treatment plan. They soon, to their astonishment, came to a startling conclusion. Lina was seven months pregnant. In disbelief, Dr. Lozado reached out to specialists to confirm that he had not gone over the edge. He hadn't.

Lina, as it turned out, was the victim not only of rape but also of precocious puberty. While not all that uncommon for girls to start puberty at 6 or 7 years of age, it was unheard of that a 5-year-old could fully develop breasts, reach full puberty with regular periods at 3 (some reports had her menstruating at 8 months), get pregnant at 4, and give birth.

As the story ricocheted around the world, cries of hoax abounded. Soon they were shot down as medical experts confirmed the birth, recognizing that it had never happened before. The question remained as to who had impregnated her. Understandably, when questioned young Lina was confused and imprecise in her answers. A likely suspect, her father vehemently denied the allegation and was released after being briefly detained. The family returned to their small village and rebuffed all attempts by the press for interviews.

Treating Gerardo more like a brother than a child, she often preferred to play with her toys and dolls. The two remained with their family, essentially secreted from the world and at ease with their situation. Gerardo learned of the true nature of his relationship with Lina at 10. He died thirty years later, in 1979, of bone cancer. Lina, meanwhile, married, worked as a secretary, and had a second child, thirty-three years after her first one. Despite living an economically poorer life, Lina never sought to capitalize on her story, despite many lucrative offers to do so.

The Pact of Steel

"Two nations, one will."

On May 22, foreign ministers Joachim von Ribbentrop and Count Galeazzo Ciano, representing Germany and Italy respectively, formally signed a pact in Berlin that, as the *New York Times* reported, "produced the most candid and most sweeping alliance in modern times," forging "two nations [into] one will." Originally dubbed The Pact of Blood, it came to be called The Pact of Steel after Mussolini determined the original title too indelicate for the Italian populace.

The Pact culminated after years of meetings and negotiations between Hitler and Benito Mussolini (Ciano's father-in-law), who worked hard to fuse their common Fascist-Nazi ideologies. Three years earlier the two nations secretly agreed to a common foreign policy. That same year, Japan, which had earlier invaded Manchuria, faced the consternation of the Soviet Union, which bordered on the conquered land. To address that threat, Japan and Germany also entered into a pact in 1936. Demonstrating the machinations of the parties involved and their shifting strategies, Japan hesitated to join the Pact of Steel, a position to which Germany agreed. Japan did not sign as its main concern centered around the Soviet Union and, ironically, not the West, against whom it felt the Pact was directed. Hitler, also ironically as events would play out, feared a perceived anti-Soviet Union Pact that might involve Germany in a two-front war, preferring at the time to conquer Europe first before moving east.

With high level dignitaries and military personnel in attendance, it was declared that the Pact created "an invincible bloc of 300,000,000 people [including their anti-communist allies] to obtain a 'just peace'." If war were to come, Germany would control the land while Italy the sea. Speakers for both sides stressed that they wished for peace but would not compromise their right to protect themselves against the "so-called [warmongering] democracies" and its "encirclement policy," as evidenced by England, France, and Russia meeting that very day in Geneva to counter their rivals' positions. Speeches also detailed their right to Lebensraum/living space expansion. and the need to correct past wrongs as evidenced by the horrific Versailles Treaty.

At the end of the signing a smiling Hitler, who had been seated by the two signatories, presented Ciano with the grand cross of the German Eagle in gold, Germany's highest decoration. In return, von Ribbentrop was presented with the Italian equivalent, the Collar of Annunciata.

By its terms the Pact was to last ten years. Instead, it died in 1943 with Mussolini's removal from office and the Italian defeat in World War II.

The USS *Squalus* Sinks

"Hello *Squalus*. It's *Sculpin*. What is your problem?"

On May 23, the USS *Squalus*, a newly minted submarine, sunk off the coast of New Hampshire, potentially dooming the fifty-nine men aboard. At that time, all similar accidents resulted in a near total loss of life as adequate rescue efforts did not exist.

Recently commissioned in March, the *Squalus*, the only navy ship named after a member of the shark family, successfully completed its eighteen test dives. Lieutenant O. F. Naquin expected no problems on the nineteenth when he ordered the sub to dive again at 8:40 that fateful morning. Stabilizing at 60 feet, all seemed well until catastrophe suddenly struck. For unknown reasons, a main air intake valve failed to close resulting in an unstoppable onslaught of water gushing in as the men frantically struggled to gain control. To avert a certain fire or explosion, batteries that provided light and heat were quickly extinguished, plunging the sub into darkness as it fell to the ocean floor, 240 feet below. The operating compartment was also shut, allowing some to survive the initial horror as those less fortunate quickly drowned. Naquin, believing the soon-to-be shivering crew could survive for no longer than forty-eight hours, had a cable-attached buoy with a phone attached sent to the surface to mark their location; a red flare was also fired. He sought to calm the sailors telling them that help was on the way and to try to relax as best they could, mindful that oxygen was in short supply.

At 12:55 pm, a sister submarine, concerned that the *Squalus* had not surfaced, discovered the remnants of the flare, searched the area, and found the buoy. After dropping anchor, communication with the sunken vessel was made. "Hello, *Squalus*. It's *Sculpin*. What is your problem?" As the dire situation was being relayed, the cable snapped.

Quickly made aware of the unfolding tragedy, the navy summoned the legendary Lieutenant Commander Charles "Swede" Momsen. A visionary in submarine rescue, Momsen, who graduated from the U.S. Naval Academy in 1919, developed both the Momsen Lung to help stricken sailors breathe, and a diving bell to rescue them. Taking years to develop the bell, its efficiency was not as yet established. After suffering over 800 deaths because of submarine mishaps, the navy saw the need to seek a remedy, with

Momsen—who would retire a Rear Admiral—leading the way. That remedy was about to be tested.

As the rescue vessel, the USS *Falcon*, set sail from New London, Momsen boarded a seaplane and flew to New Hampshire. Rescue divers who followed were not as fortunate; a vicious storm hit the area, forcing them to land in Newport, where a police escort anxiously awaited. Radio broadcasts were issued telling motorists to keep the roadways clear. Arriving at 4:15 am, they waited for the ship carrying the recently developed diving bell, which finally came six hours later under a now calm and sunny sky.

A never-before-tried rescue mission began. Thirteen hours later, it ended.

In darkened and treacherous highly pressured waters, a diver descended the 240 feet to the hatch of the stricken vessel where the diving bell would attach. Over the following hours a cable was lowered which other divers secured. The diving bell slowly followed, ending with a seal made between it and the hatch. Finally, the hatch was opened and seven of the most weakened crew members were loaded into the bell and slowly brought to the surface. The next two journeys each carried nine men. On the last one, as the remaining eight men, including Commander Naquin, were being raised, the cable broke, sending them back to the bottom of the sea. A new cable was sent down. Finally, after a 4½ hour ordeal that final group surfaced.

Great accolades deservedly came to the rescuers. Four of the divers were awarded the Medal of Honor, while many others, Momsen heading the list, also received formal and prestigious recognition. On July 30, in North Hampton, New Hampshire, a national radio broadcast covered Arthur Fiedler's Boston Symphony Orchestra Memorial Service for the twenty-six men lost.

A second arduous task, again assigned to Momsen, remained in raising the *Squalus* to determine what went wrong with such a carefully designed ship. It took fifty days to bring it up, only to see it slip away from its cables and return to the ocean floor. Twenty days later, after 628 dives, the mission was accomplished. The ship was towed back to Portsmouth, examined, decommissioned, and reborn in February 1940. Renamed the USS *Sailfish*, the first ship in the navy named after a sailfish, it served in the war, sunk seven enemy ships, and was awarded nine battle stars and a Presidential Unit Citation for its outstanding performance.

On June 1, a week or so after the miraculous rescue of the *Squalus*, a British submarine, the HMS *Thetis*, sank during a training exercise. Ninety-nine of the 103 men aboard died.

10

“Pulling a Crater” and the Opening of Baseball’s Hall of Fame

A Judge Goes Missing (forever)

“Pulling a Crater.”

On June 6, 1939, Judge Crater was legally declared dead. Seventy-five years after his disappearance in 1930, the NYPD officially closed the case again, having failed to solve the longest and most extensive manhunt in history. The matter had earlier been shut down in 1979 but was briefly reopened in 2005 upon the report of some seemingly bombshell evidence. As before, nothing came of it.

The age-old saga started on a steamy night in New York City on a Wednesday, August 6, 1930. Despite the heat, Judge Joseph Force Crater was, as always, nattily attired in the hip style of the recently ended Roaring Twenties. With a double-breasted suit, high-choker collar, bow tie, spats, and Panama Hat, he fit right in with the crowd with whom he wished to associate—the high-living (despite the Depression) businessmen, politicians, show people, chorus girls, and gangsters. With all he held his own. Tall and distinguished, though considered unattractive, he was a well-known, respected, and highly successful lawyer, who had just realized his fondest dream. Despite his young age of 41, Crater had recently been named by Governor Franklin D. Roosevelt to fill a temporary opening on the city’s prestigious trial court. Confident on being permanently named in the fall for a full term of fourteen years, he spent much of the summer vacationing in his cabin in Belgrade Lakes, Maine, with his wife, Stella. On Saturday, August 2, he unexpectedly told her that he had to return to the city the next day “[to] clear up a few things” and “straighten out a few people.”

Stella thought little of his departure, as he had often left in similar circumstances to tend to matters he typically did not share with her, and promised to return shortly to celebrate her birthday on August 9. Stella had married Crater in 1917, within days of her getting a divorce, which Crater helped secure. To all, their marriage seemed to be a loving and supportive one. Perhaps like many wives in those years, she knew little of her husband's business and personal dealings. Indeed, she wasn't even invited to his judicial swearing-in, and certainly was not privy to his widespread philandering, particularly with chorus girls and a longtime mistress. What she probably did know is that he was born in 1889 in Easton, Pennsylvania, the oldest of four children of a highly regarded family; staying local, he attended Lafayette College on a scholarship from which he graduated in 1910. He was popular and outgoing and liked women and the nightlife. Not all were enamored of him, though. As the editor of the local newspaper later recalled, "[H]e was a rotter, a debaucher, selfish, egotistical cad who had a venereal disease and transmitted it to the ruination of many girls of the City. To deflower seemed a fixation."

Succumbing to ambition and the sweet fragrances of money, success, and stature, Crater relocated to New York City where he attended Columbia Law School, graduating in 1913. He shared with Stella his belief that to achieve his goal of becoming a judge he'd have to enter politics and make connections, which meant at the time joining Tammany Hall, the highly corrupt arm of the Democratic Party.

Tammany Hall, organized in 1789, personified dirty politics. When Crater joined, the organization was moving away from its specialty of prostitution, gambling, shakedowns, bribery, and other illegal endeavors often associated with organized crime to a seemingly more genteel one—"honest graft." In so doing, it shifted to using, and abusing, the government as the instrument to illicitly make money. Corrupt politicians fueled the con. Scams included sweetheart contracts and deals, inflated fees for licenses, shaking down jobseekers, and the frequently highly lucrative act of tipping off insiders to future government plans. As an example, if the city decided to condemn a certain area in the name of urban renewal or street construction, those in the know purchased the local property before the plan was made public. Once the plan was announced, the government seized the property and paid inflated prices to the new owners, who earned a windfall. Everyone was in the loop. The private investors were tipped off and bought the property; those inside the government ensured that the price paid for the seized property was highly inflated; and if a court were involved, the judge, often also associated with Tammany, would ultimately rule that everyone, except the public and those cheated out of their property, got what they wanted. Kickbacks and bribes oiled the smooth running of the various schemes, with seemingly legitimate businessmen and lawyers ensuring that everything looked legal. Tammany quickly learned that Joe Crater possessed a brilliant legal mind and welcomed the young attorney, who rose quickly up the ranks, eventually becoming president of one of its district clubs. Change, however, was in the wind, spearheaded by the press, some honest politicians, and a fed-up public, now in the throes of the Depression and tired of graft and government mismanagement.

Whoever and whatever it was that necessitated Crater unexpectedly leaving Maine and taking an overnight train back to Manhattan, where his posh 5th, Avenue apartment complete with a cook and maid awaited, can only be surmised.

On the last day he would ever be seen, Crater was busy yet acting mysteriously. Despite the court being on summer break he went to his judicial chambers that morning, which surprised his judicial assistants Joe Mara and Fred Johnson, who were readying for the upcoming fall session. Uncommonly serious, he entered his chambers, closed the door, and was heard shuffling and going through papers, many of which ended up in the trash. At one point he emerged and asked Mara to cash two checks totaling $5,100 (worth approximately $90,000 today) in large denominations. Mara did as ordered and returned with the money, which Crater shoved into one of his pockets. He then took two packed legal briefcases and a few folders and left with Mara. Crater told Mara to go to the street to hail a cab, which he did. When the cab arrived, Crater descended the courthouse steps, glancing around nervously. On the ride to his apartment, Crater was atypically quiet. When they arrived, Mara carried in the briefcases and folders. As Mara was leaving, Crater bid him farewell, mentioning that he "was going up Westchester way" and would return to his chambers the following day. Mara thought little of the Westchester comment, thinking Crater was going to its quiet beaches to escape the oppressive heat.

At six that evening Crater travelled to 1539 Broadway, where his friend Joseph Gransky ran a ticket agency, and asked Gransky to reserve one ticket for that evening's *Dancing Partners*. Gransky thought it strange as just a few weeks before, on July 25, the two of them had travelled to Atlantic City where they met two women and another couple and engaged in a day's long party, seeing a preview of the show along the way.

After arranging for the ticket, Crater eventually wound up at another familiar haunt, Billy Haas's Chophouse at 332 West 45th Street, only a six-minute walk away. The restaurant, also located in his beloved playground, the hedonistic Times Square, seemed immune to the Prohibition laws and other norms of rectitude. There, "Good time Joe" could play.

Upon entering the restaurant, Crater bumped into, and reluctantly joined, a lawyer friend, William Klein, a giant in theatrical law. Klein was dining with his girlfriend, 22-year-old showgirl Sally Lou Ritz, who danced in the nearby *Artists and Models* revue. Earlier that summer Crater had taken his long-time mistress Connie Marcus to the show, known for its nudity and salacious content. Marcus was surprised at Crater's familiarity with some of the performers. As it was, in addition to Marcus, he was spending time socializing with showgirls Alice Wood and Elaine Dawn. Two days before his disappearance, a relaxed Crater stayed out till three in the morning with Dawn, who was also the recipient of gifts and attention from the good judge.

While eating on the 6th though, his mood had changed. Klein thought Crater "very nervous and disturbed," while Ritz described him as "somewhat depressed." The three finished and left the restaurant. Crater bid his companions farewell, got into a cab, and drove off to oblivion.

When Crater did not return to Stella, she was initially unconcerned, believing he was detained on business. Her beliefs quickly changed though when she learned that her husband had missed the opening of the Court's fall session on August 25. Driven back to New York by her chauffeur, she discreetly, not wishing to jeopardize her husband's judicial renomination, reached out to friends seeking to learn of his whereabouts. With nothing learned, the police were finally notified on September 3, nearly a month after Crater's disappearance. Knowing that the news would cause a media frenzy Stella was advised to return to Maine.

On September 4, the *New York Times* ran the story on the top of page one: "WIDE HUNT IS BEGUN FOR JUSTICE CRATER, MISSING FOUR WEEKS." Under this banner ran a smaller one: "Drew $5100 From Banks When Last Seen, Two Days After [Federal attorney] Tuttle Made Ewald Charges."

The charges alluded to an allegation that former magistrate George Ewald was named to the bench only after paying $10,000 to Martin Healy, a Tammany district leader. At the dinner celebrating the 1927 event, then attorney Crater gave the keynote congratulatory speech. Some of the attendees were also involved in the scandal. Indictments resulted against both Ewald and Healy.

Despite the offer of a large reward and a manhunt that stretched the nation, if not the world, nothing solid surfaced. Showing the thoroughness of the investigation, the police went to Washington, Philadelphia, and Atlantic City in search of a woman with whom Crater and Gransky had recently socialized. Finding Marie Miller, she offered little other than that she ate, drank (despite Prohibition), danced, and went to the beach with the group. She thought Crater liked her but seemed more interested in a seductively dressed woman with a southern accent and flapper bob hairdo.

Five thousand missing person posters flooded the nation. The picture used was of his younger self before his excessive lifestyle took its inevitable toll. His description included:

> Age, 41 years; height, 6 feet; weight, 185 pounds; mixed gray hair, originally dark brown, thin at top, parted in middle 'slicked' down; complexion, medium dark, considerably tanned; brown eyes; false teeth, upper and lower jaw, good physical and mental condition at time of disappearance.... Panama or soft brown hat worn at rakish angle, size 6 5/8, unusual size for his height and weight.

In October, a grand jury convened—which Stella refused to attend. After ninety-five witnesses and 975 pages of testimony, the jury reached its non-conclusion: "[T]he evidence is insufficient to warrant any expression of opinion as to whether Crater is alive or dead, or as to whether he had absented himself voluntarily, or is the sufferer from disease in the nature of amnesia, or is the victim of crime."

As the police chased often fruitless clues, the public salivated over the lurid tales of a bigwig leading a notorious secret life. Needless to say, humor also quickly entered the American consciousness. In the stage version of the Marx Brothers' *Animal Crackers*, Groucho exited to "Step out and look for Judge Crater." Comedians used the punch line "Judge Crater, call your office," while "[To] pull a Crater," or "Pulling a Crater," came into vogue for those disappearing.

Even innocent questions went unanswered, such as the lack of full cooperation from Stella, who was understandably highly distraught. In Maine, while she turned over the checkbook Crater used in New York, how did she come to possess it and how did it travel from New York to Maine? When she returned to her New York apartment, she somehow found personal papers and money ($6,690) belonging to her husband in a drawer that the police had thoroughly searched earlier. Some found the discovery a tad too convenient insofar as how greatly it benefited Stella, providing needed money and a will, insurance policies, stock certificates, real estate documents, and bankbooks all necessary to settle an estate. There was also a $500 check, payable to him and then endorsed, made out on August 4, as well as an envelope addressed to his wife and marked "Confidential." Inside was a list with the missive: "The following money is due me from the persons named. Get in touch with them for they will surely pay their debts." They didn't. Two people on the list were involved in a recent very shady and lucrative real estate deal with the city. At the bottom of the note, Crater wrote, "Am very [either 'weary,' 'whary,' or 'wary']. Love Joe."

Over the course of the investigation other information came to the attention of the police. On August 1, Crater was in New York. Just before his chauffeur drove him back to Maine, Crater asked a fellow judge to loan him $3,000 in cash. While that judge agreed, he fell ill and could not complete the loan. That previous spring Crater had sold $16,000 worth of stocks and withdrawn $7,000 from his bank account (cumulatively worth over $400,000 today). It was never shown where the money went, although some surmised it bought his judgeship. Some also alluded to a potential scandal swallowing Governor Franklin Roosevelt, who appointed Crater. Roosevelt was not only running for re-election as governor but had a keen eye on the White House two years later. That Crater was also closely associated with Senator Robert Wagner added to the political intrigue.

On August 5, as per an anonymous letter from Chicago later printed in a New York newspaper, one Lorraine Fay, a young, well-dressed, bleached-blonde, met with NYC attorney Samuel Buchler and told him of an affair with Crater, against whom she now wanted to sue for breach of promise to marry. Buchler confirmed the allegation, but indicated that when he asked her to return the following day with proof, she never did. Fay was never located and Buchler was later disbarred for defrauding clients.

As showgirls often supplied the air that Crater breathed, they were sought out and questioned. Sally Ritz spoke with the police and quickly left town, going to Youngstown, Ohio, to help, as she explained, care for her ailing father. By 1937 she had moved further west to Beverly Hills. Showgirl June Bryce, who had been with Crater on August 5, also dropped out of sight. Nearly a decade later, in a July 1939 lawsuit brought by Stella against a few insurance companies to collect Joe's life insurance policies, Stella's attorney alleged that Crater was murdered by Bryce's mobster boyfriend who was blackmailing the judge over his relationship with her. Bryce was finally located, seriously ill in a hospital on Long Island and too sick to speak, much less testify. The authorities also turned to Vivian Gordon, hoping that she might be able to supply some helpful information. When her apartment was searched, a jacket belonging to Crater was discovered. Gordon, a high-level con artist and sex worker, mixed with many influential people, including the infamous gangster Legs Diamond, who some thought also associated with Crater. After agreeing to testify about graft and payoffs, Gordon was murdered on February 20, 1931. Her killing electrified the city.

In the end, Tammany Hall was essentially neutered, Mayor Walker resigned, and the police department dirtied.

As the years went by the thousands of tips from throughout the U.S. and then the world naturally started to dwindle. While sightings of Crater were numerous, no one came forward with any concrete specifics. Until deathbed confessions started to roll in.

Harry Stein, before going to the electric chair for murder, stated that he and others had killed Crater, whom they had bribed to give a reduced sentence to a confederate. When Crater reneged on the deal, they killed him. The murder that resulted in Stein's death sentence was that of the aforementioned Vivian Gordon.

In 1954, Harry Krauss, a retired butcher dying in his mid-80s, "[wanted to] get something off his chest." He told of owning a house in Westchester County that he used on weekends. He let the politically connected George Ewald, Martin Healy, and Joe Crater use it at other times as a party house, in which women and sex workers frolicked. Once, the three men brought $90,000 in cash from a crooked city deal and buried it in the backyard. When Krauss returned to the house the week Crater disappeared, he found it in shambles, with broken liquor bottles and glass and blood scattered throughout the kitchen. His caretaker brother-in-law was not present and would never be seen again. The area in which the money had been buried was dug up and empty. A week later, Krauss received a phone call to meet with Ewald and Healy. At the meeting he was told that there might be some trouble, which might involve the police. If so, he should clam up and deny he ever knew Crater—something he testified to before the grand jury. In his latest tale, he added that Crater was dead, and buried in Bronxville. That Krauss had a poor reputation and often walked on the wrong side of the tracks with the wrong people detracted from his story. Still, the police sought to verify it, without success.

Nearly a half century later, in 1979, the NYPD closed the case. Until 2005.

When 91-year-old Stella (same name as Stella Crater but a different person) Ferrucci-Good died, her family read some withered notes she had left behind. In them she related that her late husband told her that police officer Charles Burns and his taxi driver brother Frank admitted picking up Crater outside the Chophouse, driving him to Coney Island, where they killed and buried him under the future home of the aquarium.

That Officer Burns was one of the police officers guarding Murder, Incorporated killer turncoat Abe Reles added to the intrigue. Reles, who agreed to testify against various mobsters, including crime bigwig Albert Anastasia, was under exceedingly tight watch at Coney Island's Half Moon Hotel. Despite the heavy police presence, somehow at 4:30 am on November

12, 1941, Reles plunged to his death from his sixth-floor encampment. How exactly the "canary who could sing but not fly" died has never been resolved.

As before, the police investigated the new information, could not substantiate it, and again closed the matter.

We have come no farther today than the grand jury investigating Joseph Crater's fate in 1930. What forced him to return to New York to straighten some fellows out? Was he killed because he knew too much (especially about the innards of the pending Healy-Ewald matter that promised to expose Tammany and, in the process, drag him and others down, destroying his reappointment to the bench)? Did he commit suicide for some of the same reasons? Did he run off with one of his many lady friends to start a new life? Why did he seemingly place his affairs in order for Stella? Why was she so uncooperative? Why was he so nervous and out of sorts? Why did he make the comment about Westchester? Was he being blackmailed? Or quite simply, did he just rile the wrong person who took murderous umbrage to something, or someone, he did? And who was he? The cad the editor of the Easton paper depicted him, or how the judge who swore him in:

> I'm shocked and mystified. He was a highly qualified lawyer and jurist and I regarded him as a scholar and almost ascetic. What I have been told about his being a frequenter of night clubs and the subject of a proposed breach of promise suit is entirely at variance with my estimate of his character.

What we do know is that in all likelihood, we will never know.

The same day Judge Crater was declared dead, June 6, saw the birth of an American institution: Little League Baseball. On that day its very first game was played with Lundy Lumber beating Lycoming Diary, 23–8. Later in the season Lycoming Diary gained revenge, winning the best of three championship series, defeating Lundy. There were only three teams, Jumbo Pretzel being the third, making up the League started by Carl Stotz, a lifelong resident of Williamsport, Pennsylvania.

Inspiration came to Stotz when he banged his leg against a lilac bush while playing catch in the backyard with his two young nephews, Jimmy and Harold "Major" Gehron. While nursing his wounds, he suddenly yelled to the boys, "How would you like to play on a regular team with uniforms, your own cap, a new ball for every game and bats your size?" And from that, three teams, a handful of youngsters and a few sponsors in the small town of Williamsport grew to the world's largest youth program, with approximately 200,000 teams playing in every American state and more than eighty countries around the world.

One week later, another seminal event involving baseball sprang to life.

The Baseball Hall of Fame and Museum Opens

"The grand game founded by Abner Doubleday (not)."

On June 12, 1939, the Baseball Hall of Fame and Museum opened in Cooperstown, New York, thanks to the vision of the multi-talented Stephen Carlton Clark who sought to revitalize his beloved area which, like elsewhere, suffered from the Depression.

Clark came from money, a lot of it, and unlike many who hoard and crave its collection and accumulation, he spent it generously and wisely in various areas. As an heir to the Singer Sewing Machine fortune, he and his three brothers and mother inherited $30,000,000 (worth over a billion dollars today) when his father died in 1896.

Clark's education reflected that of the elite—Andover Academy, Yale (1903), and, beating Judge Crater by six years, Columbia Law School (1907). Upon graduation, he succeeded in a number of endeavors—executive with Singer Sewing; building, with a brother, what would become of the historic, and rumored to be haunted, Otesaga Hotel in Cooperstown; elected to the New York State Assembly; serving, and winning acclaim, during World War I; owning three newspapers; opening art museums; and serving as a trustee of the Metropolitan Museum of Art and the Museum of Modern Art. (Two of his brothers, Sterling and Ambrose, were also avid art collectors with impressive collections. Sterling's collection is today housed in the Clark Museum, also known as the Sterling and Francine Clark Art Institute, located in Williamstown, in western Massachusetts.)

Married with five children (one of whom died in infancy), Stephen lived in different areas, including New York City, where he built a mansion at 46 East 70th Street. After his death in 1960, the home was eventually sold to the renowned Explorers Club, where it currently resides.

As early as the late nineteenth century, baseballer Sam Crane floated the idea of honoring his beloved sport. While bandied about for decades, it solidified in the 1930s with the guidance of a handful of individuals, including the president of the National League, Ford Frick. Stephen Clark, seeking a way to bring money and tourists to his economically downtrodden and beloved town, agreed to fund the project. In 1936, the very first class was named—Babe Ruth, Ty Cobb, Honus Wagner, Christy Mathewson, and Walter Johnson—even before the building was opened. When the Hall launched three years later, the classes of 1937–1939 added twenty-one additional ballplayers, including Connie Mack, John McGraw, Tris Speaker, Cy Young, Charles Comiskey, and Lou Gehrig.

One reason the founders focused on 1939 was the belief that the game was founded one hundred years earlier, in 1839 by Abner Doubleday. As it turns out, neither is true. Baseball historian David Block writes of baseball being played as early as 1344. Four hundred years later, in 1744, the game was described in a children's book by English author John Newbery. The years 1749 and 1755 carried tales of the game in England. In 1791, the elders of Pittsfield, Massachusetts, banned its playing near the town's new meeting house. Five years later a German book on pastimes described "englische Base-Ball" as a competition between two teams in which "the batter has three attempts to hit the ball while at the home plate." If the ball is hit, the batter runs to the "next post" and eventually scores at "home." There were only three bases played on a triangular field, with each team only having one out per inning. By 1848, another base had been added.

As for Abner Doubleday, he accomplished many things, which was not surprising as he came from an impressive military family. Following in their footsteps, he graduated from West Point in 1842. His great-grandfather was a Minuteman, while both of his grandfathers served in the Revolutionary War. His father fought in the War of 1812. Abner saw action in the Mexican-American and Seminole Wars and was second in command at Fort Sumter when the Civil War broke out. In response to the attack, he fired the first shot in defense. He fought or stood in reserve in the major battles of Bull Run, Antietam, Fredericksburg, Chancellorsville, and Gettysburg, where a monument today stands in his honor. When President Lincoln delivered his famous Gettysburg Address, Doubleday travelled with him. After the war, he was stationed in California where, as his *New York Times* obituary reads, he "suggested and obtained the first charter of a street cable railway in the United States [that] was built in San Francisco." He ended his career commanding an African-American regiment in Texas. Retiring in 1873, he located to the East Coast where he served as an attorney and authored two books about the Civil War. He died in 1893, leaving his wife (they had no children) and is buried in Arlington National Cemetery. Nowhere was it mentioned that he had anything to do with baseball.

In the early 1900s, a group of baseball executives and aficionados gathered to determine who invented the grand pastime. Due to incompetence and laziness (let's not believe the ramblings of Abner Graves—later committed to an insane asylum after killing his wife—who remembered Doubleday inventing the game in Elihu Phinney's cow pasture in Cooperstown in 1839, despite Doubleday attending West Point at the time and never in his lifetime making such a claim), and special interests and patriotism (we Americans invented baseball, not the rounders- and cricket-loving English), the well-respected Doubleday was wrongfully dubbed the inventor of baseball. And to this day, as in director John Ford's masterpiece *The Man Who Shot*

Liberty Valance, "When the legend becomes fact, print the legend," nearly everyone believes the legend.

Eugen Weidmann

"Then the Blade Fell."

On June 17, 1939, Eugen Weidmann became the last man publicly guillotined in France. Many thought it a fitting end to a murderous spree. Others, put off by the violence and spectacle of cheering crowds seemingly attending a sporting event, thought it wiser to simply move it away from the bloodthirsty masses to a quieter and more private domain.

Weidmann was born in Germany and lived with his grandparents during World War I. While with them, he, for whatever reason, entered the criminal world. In his twenties he was convicted of robbery and sent to prison where he met his future problematic partners, the aptly named Roger Million and Jean Blanc. Hatching a plan to victimize visiting tourists, they moved to France.

Given his good looks and charming ways, he most assuredly could have found a more benevolent occupation and lifestyle. Jean De Koven, a 22-year-old dancer from Brooklyn visiting her Parisian aunt, met Weidmann. She wrote to a friend of that encounter: "I have just met a charming German of keen intelligence who calls himself Siegfried. Perhaps I am going to another Wagnerian role—who knows? I am going to visit him tomorrow at his villa in a beautiful place near a famous mansion that Napoleon gave Josephine."

During their meeting, they laughed and smoked while she playfully snapped pictures of him with her new camera. When he killed her, he stole her 300 francs and $430 in Traveler's checks, which Million's girlfriend Colette Tricot trudged off to cash. Adding a dose of additional evil, Jean's aunt was contacted and told that Jean had been kidnapped and would be released upon the payment of $500. A few months later, in September 1937, Weidmann hired Joseph Couffy's cab to drive him to the French Riviera. Along the way, Weidmann fatally shot Couffy and stole his cab and cash, 2,500 francs. Two days later, Weidmann and Million, under the guise of a job offer, lured private nurse Janine Keller to her murder, wherein they stole her 1,400 francs and diamond ring. On October 16, the two murderers tricked theatrical producer Roger LeBlond into meeting with them, promising an investment. Instead he got a bullet in the head and his wallet containing 5,000 francs stolen. Blanc aided in their criminal endeavors.

Two more murders quickly followed. In November, Fritz Frommer met his end. Frommer, a Jew earlier imprisoned for his anti-Nazi views, met Weidmann while they were serving time in Germany. His body joined Jean's, both buried in the basement of Weidmann's residence. The last victim, real estate agent Raymond Lesobre, was killed while showing a house to Weidmann.

A business card left by Weidmann at Lesobre's office, plus the pictures taken from Jean's camera, led to the arrest and demise of Weidmann and his cohorts. Weidmann surprisingly eagerly cooperated with his captors, confessing everything. Of all his murders he only had feelings for Jean: "She was gentle and unsuspecting. When I reached for her throat, she went down like a doll."

The Weidmann-Million-Blanc-Tricot trial in March 1939, matched that of France's spellbinding one nearly two decades earlier, that of notorious mass murderer Henri Désiré Landru, the Bluebeard of Gambais, who romantically met or corresponded with nearly 300 women, many of whom disappeared. The nation again stood mesmerized as the three men were found guilty, with the fourth defendant, Colette Tricot, exonerated. Weidmann and Million received death sentences while Blanc was given twenty months. Million's sentence was eventually commuted to life. Weidmann did not fare as well.

Given the ideals of the Enlightenment Era in France, the guillotine came into vogue and use to counter the brutality of capital punishment. In the past, it could often take several whacks to disengage one's head from his, or her, body. Other forms of putting the guilty to death were also typically gruesome, the goal often being to further punish and agonize the convicted. The guillotine, or so it was thought, made death instantaneous and relatively painless. It was also considered egalitarian, with both the rich and poor experiencing the same method of execution.

The contraption was essentially L shaped, with a sharpened blade at the top of the higher portion. The bound prisoner was laid face down on a plank with his or her head placed through a hole. The triggered blade swiftly flew down, decapitating the person, whose head fell into a basket, often cushioned with sawdust.

While beheading machines had been around for hundreds of years, France popularized and exclusively utilized it. In 1789, in a speech before the French legislature, Dr. Joseph Ignace Guillotine, a death penalty opponent, called for its use as a more humanitarian form of execution. With the blessing and assistance of French King Louis XVI, a committee to design the device was created under Dr. Antoine Louis, Secretary of the Academy of Surgeons. On April 25, 1792, the "Louisette," named after the good doctor, came into use. Somehow, perhaps due to his prior speech, the device came to be called the guillotine. (After Dr. Guillotine's death in 1814, his children endeavored to get the name changed. Unsuccessful, they instead changed their own name.)

Right and *Below*: Two of the greatest baseball players of all time, Ted Williams (1939) and Joe DiMaggio (1941). (*DiMaggio image—Sporting News, Library of Congress; Williams—Apex Photo Company, Heritage Auctions*)

The father of modern-day psychiatry Sigmund Freud, whose theories were initially met with great skepticism.

The Roaring Lion, Winston Churchill. (*Yousuf Karsh. Library and Archives Canada*)

When German U-30 torpedoed the SS *Athenia*, a passenger ship carrying 1,103 passengers, Hitler, fearful of inflaming American sentiment, blamed it on the British. Thanks to safety features implemented after the *Titanic*, nearly 90 percent of those on board survived. (*Imperial War Museum*)

Fiorello LaGuardia, small in stature but a giant, was one of the greatest Mayors in American history. (*Courtesy of New York World-Telegram and Sun collection at the Library of Congress*)

Above: Jimmy Stewart and Claude Rains starred, among others, in *Mr. Smith Goes to Washington*. Initially it drew howls of protests. Quickly though, it became a classic.

Left: The Consul Aristides de Sousa Mendes disobeyed orders and issued countless visas saving countless people. In the end, he paid a heavy price.

One of the people saved by the actions of Mendes was the noted artist Salvador Dali. (*New York World-Telegram and Sun collection at the Library of Congress*)

Mobster Bugsy Siegel's lover, the married Countess Dorothy Di Frasso with Marlene Dietrich and Charles Boyer in Hollywood, 1935. (*Sueddeutsche Zeitung Photo/Alamy Stock Photo*)

When Stalin invaded Finland, he expected a quick Blitzkrieg-type result. What he got though was a humiliating victory.

The Finns, accustomed to winter fighting and camouflage, initially stymied the much larger Soviet forces. (*Military Museum of Finland; licensed under the Creative Commons Attribution 4.0 International license*)

Wishing to save the lives of his crew of the *Admiral Graf Spee*, German Captain Langsdorff scuttled his ship. (*Imperial War Museums*)

Another reason for the appeal of *Gone With the Wind* was an impeccable supporting cast including Olivia de Havilland and Hattie McDaniel, both of whom were nominated for Best Supporting Actress Awards, McDaniel winning it.

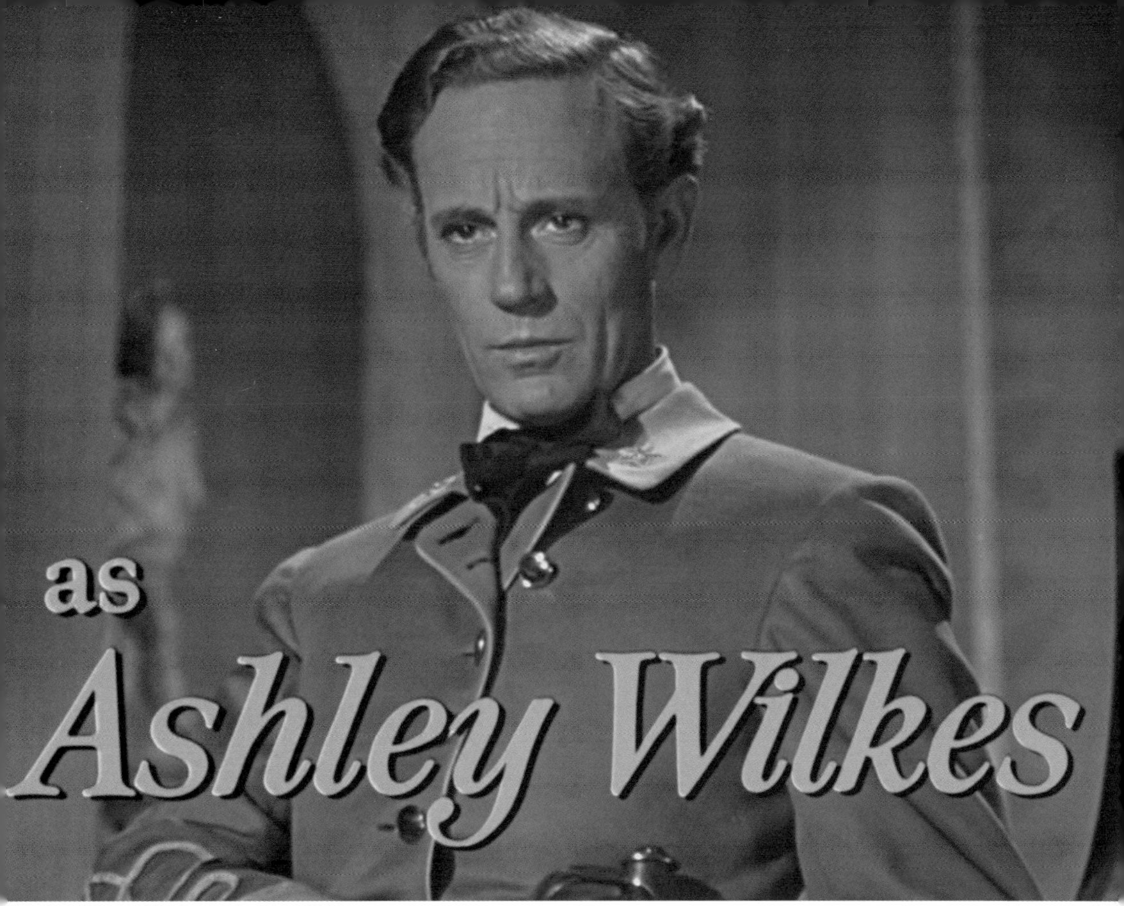

Above: Leslie Howard added to the firepower of the performers.

Right: David O. Selznick, the brilliant mind behind the brilliant movie. (*Library of Congress. New York World-Telegram & Sun Collection*)

Left: The 19-year-old Maureen O'Hara, who played the alluring Esmeralda Esmeralda in *The Hunchback of Notre Dame*.

Below: Rudolph the Red Nosed Reindeer, the creation of Robert May who looked out a window and came up with a legend. (*Max Fleischer, 1948, Library of Congress*)

On January 21, 1793, with the advent of the French Revolution, the 38-year-old King Louis was himself guillotined, as was his 37-year-old wife, Marie Antoinette, ten months later. During the time period of the 1793–1794 Reign of Terror, approximately 17,000 people met the same fate.

As was often the case with public executions, the word went out, the masses eagerly gathered, refreshments and souvenirs were sold as the convicted slowly traveled to death. Often the doomed arrived in great numbers in carts. In one instance, twelve prisoners were guillotined in thirteen minutes. Given the notoriety of Weidmann, he appeared alone, escorted by guards. Despite the morning hour, approximately a thousand people attended.

Weidmann said nothing as "Uncle Leopold" Desfourneaux, the black-garbed executioner, as reported by the *New York Times*, "placed the prisoner's head on the block and arranged his apparatus. Then the blade fell."

Given the "hysterical behavior" of the spectators, some of whom rushed forward to dip their handkerchiefs or scarves in Weidmann's blood, as well as the unauthorized filming of the spectacle, President Albert Lebrun banned all future public executions. Privately though they continued, the last one occurring in France in 1977.

As for the humanity and swiftness of the practice, a doctor witnessed the guillotining of Henri Languille in 1905:

> Here, then, is what I was able to note immediately after the decapitation: the eyelids and lips of the guillotined man worked in irregularly rhythmic contractions for about five or six seconds....
>
> I waited for several seconds. The spasmodic movements ceased. [I loudly called] "Languille!" I saw the eyelids slowly lift up ... with an even movement, quite distinct and normal, such as happens in everyday life, with people awakened or torn from their thoughts.
>
> Next Languille's eyes very definitely fixed themselves on mine and the pupils focused themselves. I was not, then, dealing with the sort of vague dull look without any expression, that can be observed any day in dying people to whom one speaks: I was dealing with undeniably living eyes which were looking at me. After several seconds, the eyelids closed again.
>
> It was at that point that I called out again and, once more, without any spasm, slowly, the eyelids lifted and undeniably living eyes fixed themselves on mine with perhaps even more penetration than the first time. Then there was a further closing of the eyelids, but now less complete. I attempted the effect of a third call; there was no further movement—and the eyes took on the glazed look which they have in the dead.

11

Gehrig, Riggs, Marble, and Gandhi Writes Hitler

Lou Gehrig

"The luckiest man on the face of the earth."

On July 4, 1939, in a ceremony before 61,808 fans, "without doubt," as the *New York Times* reported, "one of the most touching scenes ever witnessed on a ball field and one that even made case-hardened ball players and chroniclers of the game swallow hard," a weakened Lou Gehrig slowly and eloquently delivered what would become Baseball's Gettysburg Address. The Iron Horse, who played in 2,130 consecutive games, would play no more. In two years he would be dead, struck down by amyotrophic lateral sclerosis (ALS)—the disease that now carries his name.

Born Heinrich Ludwig Gehrig in 1903 in New York City, he weighed 14 lbs. He would be the only one of his parents' four children to survive childhood. His mother, a maid, became the center of his life as his father, whom he loved, suffered from alcoholism and a patchy work history, perhaps due to his epilepsy. With his German name anglicized, he went by Lou to set him apart from his similarly named father.

In a high school exhibition game, Lou hit a towering home run out of a major league stadium, a feat rarely, if ever, accomplished by one so young. After graduating in 1921, he attended Columbia University, playing both baseball and football, while majoring in engineering. On the day Yankee Stadium opened in 1923, Babe Ruth hit a home run while Gehrig, pitching elsewhere for Columbia, struck out seventeen as he continued to dazzle a New York Yankee scout who had been following the athletic prodigy. More dazzled with Gehrig's gargantuan hitting than his pitching, the Yankees signed the left-handed 19-year-old "next Babe Ruth," thus prematurely ending both his collegiate and pitching careers.

A first baseman, Gehrig played behind a power-hitting and supportive Wally Pipp. Pipp helped lead the Yankees to winning the World Series in 1923 and a second place finish the next year while leading the league in RBIs and triples. In 1925, the Yankees and Pipp dipped in production and success. As the legend goes, on June 2, Pipp, suffering from a bad headache took two aspirin and sat out the game. He was replaced by Gehrig, whose stint at first base would end fourteen years later in 1939. As Pipp later observed, "I took the two most expensive aspirin in history."

Many consider the "Murderers Row" 1927 Yankees the best team ever, with six future Hall of Famers compiling a 110–44 record, winning the American League Pennant by nineteen games, and sweeping the Pittsburgh Pirates 4–0 in the World Series. In that season, Gehrig hit .373 with an astonishing 218 hits, including forty-seven home runs and a then record of 175 runs batted in. He won the American League MVP despite his equally ferocious teammate Babe Ruth smacking sixty home runs.

Over the course of his career, his hitting prowess was legendary, batting .350 or higher six seasons and leading the league in home runs three times, runs scored four times, and RBIs five times (while garnering over a hundred or more RBIs for thirteen straight seasons). He won the triple crown once. Batting clean-up after Ruth, they made up the greatest 3–4 tandem in the game's history. In 1929, the Yankees became the first team to wear numbers on their uniform. Gehrig, hitting fourth, wore four, while Ruth, hitting before him, wore three. Of all the retired numbers in baseball today, Gehrig's number was the first.

Gehrig's fearsome play on the field was matched by his dignified behavior off it as evidenced by the annual Lou Gehrig Memorial Award that recognizes players for "both [their] community and philanthropy." A monument to Gehrig stands in Yankee Stadium celebrating his remarkable achievements.

When Gehrig was honored on July 4, the effects of his disease had already taken a toll on his once formidable strength. "If Lou starts to fall, catch him," manager Joe McCarthy signaled one of his players. Despite the weakness he felt, he summoned up his reserves to give his celebrated speech. While there was no known contemporaneous recording or transcription of the full talk, this is the accepted version:

> Fans, for the past two weeks you have been reading about the bad break I got. Yet today I consider myself the luckiest man on the face of this

earth. I have been in ballparks for seventeen years and have never received anything but kindness and encouragement from you fans.

Look at these grand men. Which of you wouldn't consider it the highlight of his career just to associate with them for even one day? Sure, I'm lucky. Who wouldn't consider it an honor to have known Jacob Ruppert? Also, the builder of baseball's greatest empire, Ed Barrow? To have spent six years with that wonderful little fellow, Miller Huggins? Then to have spent the next nine years with that outstanding leader, that smart student of psychology, the best manager in baseball today, Joe McCarthy? Sure, I'm lucky.

When the New York Giants, a team you would give your right arm to beat, and vice versa, sends you a gift—that's something. When everybody down to the groundskeepers and those boys in white coats remember you with trophies—that's something. When you have a wonderful mother-in-law who takes sides with you in squabbles with her own daughter—that's something. When you have a father and a mother who work all their lives so you can have an education and build your body—it's a blessing. When you have a wife who has been a tower of strength and shown more courage than you dreamed existed—that's the finest I know.

So I close in saying that I may have had a tough break, but I have an awful lot to live for.

Lou Gehrig died on June 2, 1941. He was 37 years old. His wife never remarried and they had no children.

Bobby Riggs

"When I can't play for big money, I play for little money.
And if I can't play for little money, I stay in bed that day."

On July 7, 1939, Bobby Riggs won Wimbledon. Later fame would come in 1973 when he battled and lost to Billie Jean King in the acclaimed Battle of the Sexes tennis match. King was fortunate she did not have to play the Bobby Riggs of 1939. If she had, she would have undoubtedly lost as that 21-year-old Bobby Riggs was the best tennis player in the world. Not only did he win his singles match at Wimbledon, he also won the Men's Doubles and the Mixed Doubles. By hitting the trifecta, he also, as the tale told by him goes, secretly won over a million dollars by betting on himself. Of course, he also later admitted having occasional lapses separating fact from fiction.

Born in 1918 in Los Angeles, Riggs was one of six children. His father was a minister. Starting to play tennis before even entering his teenage years, he benefited greatly from the teaching of a female coach, Esther Bartosh, and quickly rose through the ranks. Considered too small to compete with the taller, stronger, and heavier tennis greats at the time, the 5-foot-7-inch, 140-pound Riggs made up for his physical shortcomings by speed and agility, mixed with ball control and a heavy dose of court savvy and moxie, both on and off the court. His lob and drop shot may have been the best in the game. Tennis legend Jack Kramer described Riggs as a "kid hustler," who never gave an opponent a break.

During high school he never lost a match and was the first person ever to win three consecutive California state singles titles. Despite his busy high school schedule, he found time to compete around the country, winning consistently. A junior at 16, he was nationally ranked fourth. In 1938, he won fourteen tournaments and was a key cog in America's Davis Cup victory (then called the International Lawn Tennis Challenge), which was played in early September in Philadelphia.

Still an amateur, as many of the great players were at the time, Riggs hit 1939 running. He was runner-up in the French Open before playing in the oldest, and arguably most prestigious, tennis tournament in the world—still true even today–England's Wimbledon. There he won the singles match against Elwood Cooke in five sets; the men's double match, now teaming with Cooke; and the mixed doubles match with the dazzling and charismatic Alice Marble. After Wimbledon, he won a host of other tournaments, launching him to the number one ranked tennis player in the world.

Leaving the glory of competing in the amateur's well-known and well-regarded Grand Slams, he turned professional in 1941 and continued his winning ways. Even in his later years he won senior titles and acclaim.

Ever the hustler, he made bets that he could beat one while lugging a bucket of water or suitcase around the court, or by wearing weights on his ankles, waist or wrists; he allowed an opponent to use the doubles alleys, or played with chairs obstructing his side of the court. No bet was too small or outlandish. With yet another angle towards making a score, Riggs recognized a golden opportunity to exploit the feminist movement. Taking a page from the self-promotion handbook of wrestler Gorgeous George and boxer Muhammad Ali, Riggs, now in his fifties, claimed that no woman, even those decades younger, could beat him on the tennis court and dared anyone foolish enough to try. Margaret Court, a superb tennis player, indeed the #1 female in the world at the time, ill-advisedly took him up on his challenge. What would come to be known as the Mother's Day Massacre,

Riggs, using an array of junk shots and gumption, handily defeated her, 6-2, 6-1. So national was his exploit that *Time* and *Sports Illustrated* featured him on their covers. Riggs pocketed thousands for his efforts and basked in the spotlight, with an even larger spectacle looming on the horizon.

Billie Jean King, another highly ranked female star, earlier rejected what she viewed as the childish gimmick of playing Riggs. Given Court's ignominious defeat, however, she reversed course, feeling that she had to take on the braggart. And thus, the super-hyped Battle of the Sexes, held on Thursday night, September 20, 1973. Over 30,000 spectators filled the Houston Astrodome while circa 90 million people from America and around the world watched it. Carrying a great weight on her shoulders, she "thought it would set us back 50 years if I didn't win that match. It would ruin the women's tour and affect all women's self-esteem." King rose to the occasion, winning convincingly, 6-4, 6-3, and 6-3.

Even in defeat, Riggs profited, including making $50,000 (worth $330,000 today) for merely wearing a yellow Sugar Daddy jacket at the match. Perhaps even more importantly, he gained, despite what many might have thought at the time, the enduring friendship of his opponent, later teaming with her to raise money for AIDS research. He died in 1977 of prostate cancer. In his final conversation with King, she kindly told him, "I love you."

Alice Marble

"A smashing type of game."

On July 8, 1939, Alice Marble, in a match lasting less than half an hour, won the Wimbledon singles women's tournament. She also successfully defended her women's doubles victory from the year before and won the mixed doubles with her partner, the aforementioned, irrepressible, Bobby Riggs. The first female Triple Crown winner of the century, she duplicated that feat two months later at the US Open in Forest Hills, New York. Indeed, she would go undefeated for the entire year. Along with being an excellent all-around athlete, she was also a writer, singer, coach (one of her students being a young Billie Jean King), clothing designer, and lecturer who hobnobbed with Hollywood's elite.

And she may also have been a spy who was shot in the line of duty during World War II.

Marble was born in 1913, joining three siblings, Dan, George, and Hazel. Tim would come later, being the last child. They all lived on a ranch, which a few years later their father Harry sold and moved everyone to San Francisco, perhaps satisfying the wishes of his wife, Jessie, who originally came from that area. In 1919, tragedy struck when the hard-working Harry, recovering from a serious car accident, contracted pneumonia (perhaps exacerbated by the flu that was decimating millions around the globe at the time), and passed away. With the breadwinner gone, 6-year-old Alice and her family teetered on the line of poverty.

A tomboy and superb athlete, at 13 she started shagging fly balls and serving as the all-around mascot for the popular local ball club, the San Francisco Seals. During warm-ups she dazzled the ballplayers, and soon the press, marveling at her strong arm and talent, chasing down fly balls and "with a lusty heave [firing the ball] toward home, truly remarkable for a girl of 13." In time, she came to be the Seals's second most revered alum, only behind one destined for baseball immortality, Joe DiMaggio. DiMaggio, fourteen months younger than Alice, remembered her as one who "had a pretty good arm." Marble later proved that by joining her high school baseball team where she was its star pitcher, captain, and only female on the team. She also played basketball and ran track and, with the encouragement of the now head of the family, her brother Dan, tennis. She won her first tournament, a low-level one, in 1928, and quickly propelled herself, with a booming serve and superb net play, to the 8th ranked female under 18 in the state.

One evening, while leaving the darkened tennis courts, she was raped; a tragedy which seared her soul and stayed with her throughout her life. "It made me tough and made me turn all the more to tennis to counteract my low self-esteem.... Later, tennis became a substitute for sex (though a poor one), the physical activity giving a measure of release."

With brains and a photographic memory, she was accepted at Berkeley but opted not to attend, deciding to concentrate on tennis. Although already an excellent player she realized that to make it to the ultimate level, she needed help. She soon found it with "the person that would change my whole life," Eleanor Tennant. Tennant, a solid player in her own right, turned to coaching, where she found great success. With Alice, the 35-year-old Eleanor quickly became far more than a mentor, and was a constant presence involved in all aspects of her young student's life, including, perhaps, that of a lover.

Amateur tennis players had a difficult lot. While widely acclaimed and playing in the most prestigious tennis matches in the world, they rarely made any money. While the United States Lawn Tennis Association (the USLTA) fronted the expenses needed to travel and play, all money not spent had to be returned. As such, the unwealthy amateurs, including Alice, had to take odd and often mundane jobs along the way just to survive economically.

Even later in her career, although a sporting goods company provided free tennis rackets, Marble had to pay for their restringing. Some of the more successful amateurs had sponsors, which made life far more bearable.

Living and coaching in Los Angles, Tennant attracted an ardent following of the rich and famous, many of whom considered tennis life's calling. Not only did they play, but they eagerly attended local matches. Soon the likes of Clark Gable, Carole Lombard (who nicknamed Tennant "Teach"), Marlene Dietrich, Bette Davis, Charlie Chaplin, Myrna Loy, and others became enthralled with the attractive, talented, and friendly Alice Marble, who returned the adoration. And with their tennis coach Eleanor making the formal introductions, they were marriages made in heaven.

Eleanor and Alice were frequent guests in San Simeon where they played tennis and socialized with William Randolph Hearst and his bubbly girlfriend, actress Marion Davis, who nicknamed Alice "Pinky," and Eleanor "Becky." Despite staying in a mansion with scores of rooms, Marble and Tennant shared a large single one.

The tennis world was hers for the taking. Until it wasn't. In 1934, she collapsed during a match in Paris. Diagnosed with pleurisy and tuberculosis, she was told she'd never play again. A thoughtful note from Carole Lombard, who had been involved in an earlier serious car accident, buoyed her spirits. "For six months I lay on a hospital bed, just like you are today. Doctors told me I was through, but then I began to think I had nothing to lose by fighting, so I began to fight. Well, I proved the doctors wrong. I made my career come true, just as you can—if you'll fight. If I can do it, so can you."

And Alice did. Spectacularly successful in tennis, she also conquered other fields—singing in nightclubs, designing clothes, raising large amounts of money for the military, speaking, and writing. When William Moulton Marston created Wonder Woman—a female counterpoint to Superman—and worked with comic book pioneer Max Gaines to create the comic book, Marble shared with Gaines her belief that real life "wonder women" stories should also be told. In the very first issue of *Wonder Woman*, one of its newly anointed associate editors, Alice Marble, wrote a four-page story of real-life hero Florence Nightingale. And Alice would do it for nineteen more issues, ending with abolitionist Lucretia Mott.

During World War II, while singing and entertaining soldiers and sailors in a New York nightclub, Alice met Army Air Corps Captain Joseph Norman Crowley of Kansas, a graduate of Ohio State, and soon to be Mr. Alice Marble. After a whirlwind romance, a navy chaplain married them aboard a ship moored in a New York harbor and witnessed by "a hundred sailors."

And soon Alice was pregnant.

Or was she?

And Crowley was killed when his plane was shot down over Germany.

Or was he?

There is no record of a Joe Crowley ever serving, or even registering to serve, in the military; no record of his being killed in action; no record of his attendance at Ohio State; and no marriage certificate.

In August 1944, while allegedly five months pregnant, yet not showing any baby bump and playing in a tennis match, Alice was on the way home from a party when she was run off the road by "a drunk driver" and miscarried. No mention of the mishap appeared in any news accounts. One month later, Alice was playing in another tennis match and appearing on Milton Berle's radio program.

The most mysterious aspect of Alice's life involved one whose name she would not reveal, settling on calling him Hans Steinmetz, a Swiss banker. He watched her at Wimbledon in 1938 and became her first male lover. Their affair was torrid and brief. Seven years later, Alice volunteered to travel the nation, raising money for the war effort. As the war was ending, those in military intelligence, asked her to go to Geneva under the guise of playing tennis and giving lectures. Once there she would reconnect with Steinmetz, who "[didn't] worry where the money comes from," as he dealt with the Nazis secreting their stolen loot and valuables in Switzerland.

She underwent vigorous training. Her mission—finding out what Hans knew and photographing any incriminating evidence in his possession. Once secured she was to deliver the information to her contact in Geneva, Franz Regenbogen, who to the world was a quiet local goldsmith. Overseen by her handlers—Captain Al Jones and Colonel Linden—Marble was given a firearm and spy camera, trained in hand-to-hand combat, map reading, and safe cracking and provided with the layout of Hans's over 300-year-old palatial living quarters.

Given her fame, Marble arrived in Geneva to a hearty reception. Within a few days Hans had reached out to his former lover. Soon they rekindled their relationship and she moved in with him. One evening while he was away, despite the wait staff hovering around and about, she struck, sneaking downstairs, breaking into a vault, which contained paintings, gold bars, jewelry, and a ledger detailing who owned what. Pictures taken and job completed, she quickly left to meet Franz.

Conveniently, Hans had recently returned, leaving his Mercedes, with the keys still inside. Jumping into the car, she sped off. As she motored away she peered at her rear-view mirror where she saw, to her great dismay, a car's headlights quickly gaining on her. As it got closer, Marble recognized its driver, Captain Jones, and breathed a sigh of relief. As she pulled over and opened the car door, she yelled, "Al, thank God it's you. I was frightened to death. I have the film!"

Jones left his vehicle and approached, asking for the film and saying there had been a change of plan. As this went against her orders to turn it over to her contact in Geneva, she hesitated. A voice from inside Jones's car yelled out, "Stop wasting time on that bitch! Get the camera! Someone's coming!" A struggle broke out and the camera fell to the ground. Jones's partner again shouted. "C'mon fool! Kill her! Hurry!"

As Jones reached for the camera, he pulled out a gun and pointed it at her. Marble turned and ran. She heard the squeal of brakes and doors flung open. Shouts and shots rang out. A bullet found her back. Blackness followed.

Alice awoke in the hospital to the soothing face of Colonel Linden, who told her that the now deceased Captain Jones and his partner were Russian agents and traitors, shot by a team sent to assist her—but not before Jones shot her in the back, a wound that would heal. Unfortunately, Jones exposed the film as he lay dying. Fortunately, however, Alice possessed a photographic memory and was able to largely resurrect what was lost.

Once again, no corroborating evidence exists, although that should not be surprising in a top-secret mission.

There is little question that Marble was bisexual (observing "who knew how to please a woman better than another woman"). Being labeled gay in that era, however, was akin to a career death sentence. People were often fired from their jobs on a mere suspicion of homosexuality. Thus, any gay person, especially one in the public eye, had to be vigilant.

One long-term friendship (there is no concrete evidence that it was sexual) she had was with Will du Pont—he of the ultra-wealthy DuPont family—who asked her to marry him on several occasions. She never did and despite her numerous rejections, du Pont generously financially supported her, even setting up a small trust fund. He also built and allowed her to stay in a house on one of his large estates, which Alice and her fellow tennis player, friend, and roommate Mary Browne, twenty-two years her senior, moved into. Two days later du Pont died, at which point his daughter Jean, who blamed Alice for the break-up of her parents' marriage, had them evicted. Alice allegedly also had a long-term affair with a fellow tennis aficionado, the married Rod Serling, the gifted writer and creator of the eternally beloved *Twilight Zone* television series.

As with many as we age, Alice suffered from many physical ailments including the removal of a cancerous lung and some ribs, as well as her teeth due to gum disease. She also continued to suffer financially despite her many accomplishments, which bought recognition and respect but little money. Invited to attend Wimbledon at one point, she initially lacked the funds to make the trip. She even drove a beat-up old car.

When she died at 77 in 1990, relatively few people remembered her. They should have. She deserved more. Alice Marble revolutionized tennis as noted by Hall of Fame tennis great Jack Kramer. "[She was a] lady who most changed the style of play for women. She introduced the aggressive and athletic style that has led down to the female stars of today."

A giant in other areas, including fighting for the equality of women, Alice was also instrumental in breaking down the segregation of tennis when she took on the establishment, which soon bowed, allowing budding tennis great Althea Gibson to competitively play. If people knew what she achieved, the kindhearted, humble, and talented Alice Marble would not now reside in the ashes of obscurity.

Gandhi writes Hitler

"Dear Friend."

On July 23, 1939, Mahatma Gandhi penned a letter to Adolf Hitler, addressing him as "Dear Friend." In his short missive, he appeals, "for whatever it may be worth. It is quite clear that you are today the one person in the world who can prevent a war which may reduce humanity to a savage state." While prescient, it never reached its intended recipient as the colonial government would not allow it to be sent.

Gandhi, like nearly many at the time, knew what the future held: war and destruction. The machinations as to who would be fighting the war, and on what side, however, was in doubt. It would be addressed shortly.

12

The Home Front

In 1939, costs varied depending on where one lived; someone residing in New York City typically paid more than someone living on a farm in Iowa. At all times consumers, still feeling the effects of a weakened economy, had to be wary of spending. Generally, though, it cost approximately $750 to buy a car, 10 to 19 cents a gallon for gas to fill it, and between $3,800 and $6,400 for a house to drive it to. For those who could not afford the high costs of home ownership, rents went for around $28 a month. One either drove or walked to the local grocer or butcher to buy a loaf of bread (9 cents), a gallon of milk (23 cents), sliced ham (39 cents a pound), ketchup (9 cents a bottle), peanut butter (23 cents), and a dozen eggs (18 cents). Despite these seemingly low costs, people didn't earn very much, with an average yearly salary of $1,368 (or $1,730 per another source), or a little over a hundred dollars a month. If a couple were married, typically only the husband worked outside the house while the wife took care of home and family, greatly assisted by ovens, washers, and fans, assuming they could be afforded.

If one were musically inclined and wished to purchase a guitar, it cost approximately $9; the more athletic, wishing to buy a pair of roller skates, shelled out around $2. A movie ticket cost 23 or so cents, but, again, varied depending upon where one lived, the time of the showing, and whether the ticket purchased was for an adult or child. If for a child, he would most likely be named Robert, James, John, William, Richard, Charles, David, Donald, Thomas, or Ronald. The top names for girls included Mary, Barbara, Patricia, Betty, Shirley, Carol, Nancy, Judith, Dorothy, and Margaret.

Like many glued to television today, the golden age of radio served as the adhesive for the masses in 1939. Around 44 million sets existed, with the larger and heavier versions, more like pieces of furniture, costing $19.99. Smaller types might weigh a low of 4 lbs. A wide variety of broadcasts provided entertainment across the spectrum, something for everyone, including, as now, comedy, drama, westerns, detectives and crime, music (often in the form of big bands and swing), gossip, news, and audience participation. The shows listeners often set their dials to included those featuring Jack Benny, Bob Hope (who introduced what would be his signature tune, *Thanks for the Memory*), Bing Crosby, Fibber Magee and Molly, Eddie Cantor, Al Jolson, Fanny Brice, Kate Smith, Edgar Bergin and his wisecracking wooden counterpart Charlie McCarthy, and a host of other well-known figures at the time.

Demonstrating radio's power and influence, at eight o'clock on Sunday evening, October 30, 1938, *The Mercury Theatre on the Air* came on, starring and narrated by the velvety voice of 23-year-old Orson Welles. Influenced by other shows at the time, Welles simulated a live newscast, complete with convincing sound effects, of events as they unfolded. One listening heard what appeared to be a normal evening broadcast, complete with a weather report and music provided by "Ramon Raquello and His Orchestra" from a local hotel ballroom. Suddenly, news flashes interrupt the presentation talking of strange gas explosions on Mars. A reporter, Carl Phillips, interviews a Princeton astronomy professor who calmly assures all that there is no life on the red planet. As the show returns to Ramon's melodious music, it is again, and more urgently, interrupted with another news flash. A landing in Grovers Mill, New Jersey. Phillips races to the scene where he finds chaos created by a foreign and strange-looking closed cylindrical object. As it slowly unwinds, the police on the scene carefully approach, waving a flag of truce. A space monster emerges, firing a heat ray. Everything and everyone nearby are burned and sizzled. Screams fill the air. Phillips shouts out what's happening. And then silence. An announcer comes on the air explaining "some difficulty with [their] field transmission." A shaken Phillips returns, struggling to bring developing tragic news to its listeners. Martial law is declared. The militia responds. Martians destroy it. Thousands hearing the reports flee the area, clogging the highways. More Martians come. Power stations, bridges, and railroads are destroyed. And then a friendly gun crew hits a Martian ship which immediately spews poisonous black smoke. Five other Martian ships expand the attack to New York City. People dive into the East River "like rats!" And soon the entire nation is under siege. In the end, New York City is destroyed, but so too are the invaders, falling ill to earth's pathogenic germs.

At the end, Welles tells his stunned audience that what they just heard was a "holiday offering. ... If your doorbell rings and there's nobody there, that was no Martian; it's Halloween."

Unfortunately, many who heard the broadcast thought it was real, that Martians had indeed invaded and wreaked havoc. Telephone lines jammed as people tried to call neighbors, loved ones, the police. Highways grew crowded with people trying to flee the area. Some listeners thought the invaders were Germans. Cooler heads soon thankfully prevailed. The *New York Times* building flashed "ORSON WELLES CAUSES PANIC," while the paper led with the story front and center on page one. Many thanked the popularity of the Edgar Bergen show, which ran at the same time, for diminishing the effect of the far less popular and listened-to Welles program. For three weeks, over 12,000 news reports described the farce. Hitler thundered from afar that the incident showed "the corrupt condition and decadent state of affairs in democracy." While the story faded in time, it never disappeared. More notably, Welles's career took off, as well as the exaggeration the panic caused that grew with the years, much like a fisherman's tale of the whooper he either caught or got away.

In April of 1939, with some Americans listening to CBS's coverage of a Hitler speech dedicating a German battleship, the sound mysteriously cut off in mid-speech, quickly propelling a rumor that Hitler had died.

While many focused on the radio to bring them news from around the world, probably an equal, if not greater, number resorted to the radio purely for entertainment purposes. Thus, the popularity of gossip columnists Hedda Hopper and Walter Winchell, sending out often lascivious stories of the rich and famous. Not much has changed. The 1990s had Paris Hilton and Nicole Richie controlling the airways and magazine covers, joined by Jennifer Aniston who on a nearly weekly basis was falsely rumored to be pregnant, often with twins. Soon these "stars" grew older and out of view, only to be replaced by the Kardashians and others. Such persons forever populate our culture, coming and going through the turnstile of America's endless quest for celebrity and gossip.

Lisa Fonssagrives, meanwhile, paved the way for all supermodels following her. She was arguably the first. Born in Sweden in 1911, she studied painting, sculpture, and dance before finding herself in—where else—the most cosmopolitan of all cities, Paris, where she trained for the ballet. While riding an elevator of all places, photographer Willy Maywald spotted her. Drawn by her charm, looks, and charisma, he asked to photograph her. Fame quickly followed with spreads in such popular magazines as *Vogue*, *Der Stern*, and beyond. In July 1939, she came to America, already a top model, if not *the* top model. Through the next decades, to the fifties, her image graced the front covers of many major magazines, including *Life*, *Time*, *Vogue*, *Vanity Fair*, and *Town and Country*. Reported to be "the highest paid, highest praised, high fashion model in the business," she modestly described herself as "[merely] a good clothes hanger."

Those grasping for celebrity sightings zeroed in on where the rich and famous romped—Hollywood, New York, and Newport, where the even more fabulously and obscenely wealthy went about their business. Debutante balls and coming-out parties were THE thing. When Brenda Diana Duff Frazier came out as "Debutante of the Year" on December 27, 1938, *Life* featured the teenager on its cover, as did many papers and magazines throughout the nation. Propelled by the writings of columnists Walter Winchell and Cholly Knickerbocker (real name Maury Henry Biddle Paul), who earlier wrote of the then 14 or so year old: "It may seem a bit early, but I—here and now—predict Brenda Frazier will be one of the belles—if not *the* Belle—of her season." Labeled "Glamour Girl #1" she joined fellow "Poor Little Rich Girls" and "Glamour Girls" Gloria Vanderbilt, Doris Duke, and Barbara Hutton in vying for the public's attention. She even popularized a look—white face, red lipstick, powdered white skin, and perfectly and stylized dark coiffed hair. Despite the positive attention tossed her way, she did have her detractors, many observing her obvious lack of talent and noting that she was famous for merely being famous, a common rebuke hurled through the ages to this day. Sadly, she later joked that she also "invented anorexia." Frazier married twice to men with names more suited to a novel or movie—Shipwreck Kelly and Robert Chatfield-Taylor. While not married, she engaged in many other turbulent romances, including one with Howard Hughes, all of which the tabloids and its readers devoured.

Another source of entertainment included books, magazines, and newspapers including the comic variety. *The University of North Carolina Buccaneer*, a student humor magazine lived on the university's campus for twenty years, from 1920 to 1940. In 1939, selling for 15 cents, it published its controversial. "*Sex Issue*." Often printing cartoons of scantily clad women and risqué stories, the November issue crossed the line for many and set off a firestorm with, of all people, student leaders pushing for its suppression and destruction. "[S]uch an issue would seriously and permanently damage the reputation and lessen the prestige of the University in general," opined its concerned student body president. The cover featured a barely dressed made-up tootsie wearing only a revealing and amply filled light colored bra, and dark fishnet stockings adorning her spread-apart legs as she blew smoke rings while sitting on a couch. The student newspaper reported its fate. "4,000 'Over-Sexed' Bucs Meet Fiery End in Local Incinerator." Somehow the university survived the ordeal.

As America grew, housing approximately 131,000,000 people, its transition from a rural (44 percent) to an urban (56 percent) society continued. Women with an average age of 65, then as now, outlived men, whose average age was 61. Long-distance travel was accomplished via the railroad. No interstate highways existed and those that did were often not optimal for long-distance driving. Those living in urban areas experienced better transportation, shopping, and the other amenities of life, along with the disadvantages of overcrowding and crime. Rural America came into the twentieth century as we know it with the introduction of electricity in 1939, thanks in large part to FDR's New Deal. At the start of the decade, 90 percent of rural homes used kerosene lamps. Electricity opened a world hitherto dark and unknown, bringing in light, electric-powered appliances, and powered pumping stations providing running water and indoor bathrooms.

Americans overwhelmingly wanted to steer clear of any entanglement in a European War, as shown by the Neutrality Acts of 1935 and 1937, preventing any aid to any belligerent countries. When the war started, however, FDR, prophetically knowing what the future held, proposed the Neutrality Act of 1939, which permitted aid to certain nations, e.g., France and England. Despite strong opposition by the isolationists in Congress, the Act passed and arguably saved the Allies. While the mainland proclaimed, "Stay out of War," it also wanted to "Help England and France." That general sentiment of non-involvement prevailed until Japan bombed Pearl Harbor, which in a flash changed everything.

Two years before Pearl Harbor, on December 7, 1939, American novelist and child prodigy, Barbara Newhall Follet, who published her first two novels at 12 in 1927 and 14 in 1928, walked out of her Brookline, Massachusetts, home, leaving an unhappy marriage behind. Like Judge Crater, she was never heard from again. As Barbara's husband made little effort to find her, suspicion fell on him, but nothing came of it. Since she went by her married name, Rogers, newspapers in America remained in the dark as to her disappearance, only learning and publicizing it in 1966.

Thanksgiving, an American mainstay since Abe Lincoln's less famous proclamation in 1863, finally adopted President Washington's 1789 suggestion that we celebrate a ("Day of Publick Thanksgivin"). It fell on the fourth Thursday of November. That was until 1939, when FDR, wishing to boost the economy, added an additional week of shopping between Thanksgiving and Christmas, and moved it back a week.

As with any change to an event to which people have become acclimated, a firestorm erupted. Former Republican Kansas Governor Alf Landon intoned that the move was yet

> [a]nother illustration of the confusion which [FDR's] impulsiveness has caused so frequently during his administration. If the change has any merit at all, more time should have been taken in working it out ... instead of springing it upon an unprepared country with the omnipotence of a Hitler.

Moving from the far right of Hitler to the far left of Stalin, another citizen, from South Dakota, more directly wrote to the president that "we are not running a Russia[n] or communistic government." Like the people, the states were also equally split, with twenty-two following the new edict while twenty-three stuck with the original date and rejected "Franksgiving." Texas and Colorado observed both dates while Mississippi never quite formally decided. Seeing the error of his ways and recognizing that the added week added little to boost the country's buying habits, in 1941 FDR rescinded his order. Like the University of North Carolina and its *Sex Issue*, the country also survived.

Former House Speaker Tip O'Neill once observed that "all politics is local." The same could be said for life. While people read with interest the news of the nation and world, they were often far more interested in their children, family and friends, community events, the start of deer hunting season, and other routine, if not mundane, daily occurrences. Thus, the major stories of Indiana's *Carlisle News* involved "Grass Fires Menace Farms," the state conservation clubs, and the Halloween carnival being held in the "old gymnasium." Also competing for front page coverage was its "Movement of People" column telling of the local comings and goings of its citizenry. There, readers learned of French Willis's business trip to Vincennes, the Gibbs' family spending the weekend with an aunt, and the Finches of Boonville visiting local relatives.

Near the small town of Carlisle stood the city of Sullivan, home to three newspapers and a population of 5,000 people. The *Sullivan Daily Times* covered world events and kept a close watch on how involved, if at all, the nation should be with those in Europe. Being a rather staunchly Republican area, the paper disfavored any foreign involvement, as evidenced by its opposition to any revisions to the Neutrality Act. By a nearly two to one margin, a local poll had 914 citizens in favor of continuing the embargo of arms, while 403 wanted it lifted. Along with the news of the world, the paper still found sufficient time and space to cover local happenings, such as the start of duck hunting season.

As with people today drawn to a lurid crime story, wherever it might occur, the paper covered those also, including that of 26-year-old Winnie Ruth Judd, who in 1931 shot and killed two female friends—Agnes Anne LeRoi (27) and Hedvig "Sammy" Samuelson (24)—over, what else, the affections of a man. In this case, the man was a scoundrel, playboy John J. "Happy Jack" Halloran a 44-year-old well-known and respected businessman who was sleeping with Judd. After being killed, with one dismembered, the victims were placed in trunks, thus giving the crime a catchy title, "the Trunk Murders." Although Judd committed the crime, Happy Jack, who was never charged, was thought to have assisted her in disposing of the bodies and covering up the murder scene, which added mystery to the already jazzed-up tale. Convicted, she served decades in jail, escaping numerous times thus pumping new life into an old story.

After reading items such as these the locals often turned to the radio for an evening of entertainment. They also occasionally added zest to their daily existence by adopting the medieval tradition of waking (assuming they were sleeping) newlyweds from their bedrooms and dragging them off to a joyous public celebration.

America in 1939 was for the most part a quiet and conservative nation, on the cusp of unimaginable expansion and influence. Little could those living at the time imagine what the near future held.

13

The World on the Brink and the Wicked Witch of the West

The Birth of the Atomic Bomb—Einstein's Letter to FDR

On August 2, 1939, Albert Einstein reviewed, edited, and signed a letter written by Hungarian physicist Leo Szilard that was sent to President Roosevelt, warning of Germany's endeavors to build an atomic bomb and suggest that America should do likewise. FDR took their advice.

The year 1939 was an active one for nuclear development. In January and February, uranium fission barreled to the forefront, propelled by German scientists, that set physicists around the world atwitter. Theories raised met confirmation via experiments conducted by Enrico Fermi, Professor John R. Dunning, and others in Columbia University's Pupin Hall physics building.

One at the forefront of theory and practice was Leo Szilard, who in 1933 conceived the idea of a nuclear chain reaction, and a year later patented a nuclear fission reactor. Born in Budapest, Hungary, in 1898 he joined its military during World War I. As his unit was being sent to the front, he contracted the Spanish flu and was held back, a fortuitous chain of events that probably saved his life as his unit was soon nearly decimated in battle.

Returning to civilian life after the war, he met intolerance for being a Jew, and relocated to Germany to continue his studies. In 1922, his dissertation on thermodynamics captured noteworthy honors and recognition, including that of Albert Einstein with whom he would later work. In 1930 he gained German citizenship but was wise enough to foresee a perilous future when Hitler gained power. Fleeing to London, he helped set up an organization to assist refugee scholars, who in the end numbered over 2,000.

In 1938, after he arrived in America, he briefly led a nomadic life, working and researching at colleges in Illinois, Chicago, Michigan, and Rochester, before settling in New York City, where he also used the Pupin Hall facilities. There he conducted a fateful nuclear experiment. "That night, there was very little doubt in my mind that the world was headed for grief."

Knowing the potential catastrophic destruction if made available to Hitler he drafted a letter to Roosevelt explaining the ramifications of nuclear power. Further aware that he needed star power to get Roosevelt's attention, he and a colleague drove out to the north fork of Long Island, where the world's foremost scientist, Albert Einstein, vacationed. There they talked with Szilard, telling his friend of the great effect H.G. Wells and his book *The World Set Free* had on him. The book spoke of uncontrollable and highly destructive "atomic bombs," of which Einstein offered, "I did not even think about that." After he did, Einstein discussed, revised, and dictated a new draft dealing with very powerful bombs that Germany might be developing. Szilard reviewed and gave the outline to his secretary to type. She later observed that at the time she "was sure she was working for a nut," notwithstanding Einstein's involvement.

Given the quickly changing events at the time, FDR could not schedule a meeting for a few months to discuss the matter with the representative for Einstein and Szilard, Alexander Sachs. Sachs, born in Lithuania, moved to the United States and went to school at Columbia. Working for a bank in bonds in Boston, he left to return to school, going to Harvard as a grad student studying social sciences, philosophy, and law. He then served as an aide to Supreme Court Justice Louis Brandeis—known earlier as "the people's lawyer" who fought for social justice—and the Zionist cause. Returning to business and banking, Sachs worked for Lehman Brothers, and later the government fighting the effects of the Depression. Along the way, he got to know Roosevelt.

On October 11, Sachs met with the president, his secretary, and scientific representatives from the army and navy and laid out the urgent contents of the letter. At the meeting's conclusion, FDR remarked: "Alex, what you are after is to see that the Nazis don't blow us up," and told an aide: "This requires action."

And thus, the birth of the top-secret Manhattan Project, a collaboration between the military and America's most highly regarded scientific experts to beat Germany in developing nuclear weaponry. In the end, two bombs were developed, one uranium—Little Boy—and the other plutonium—Fat Man. With the initial target being Germany, its surrender revised thinking and attention turned to Japan. Believing that the Japanese would not countenance surrender and would fight to the very end, the devastating bombs were dropped, thus confirming Szilard's prediction of bringing grief to mankind.

Despite Einstein's earlier involvement, he was deemed a left-leaning pacifist and security risk. He later deplored the use of the bombs on Japan and opined: "had I known that the Germans would not succeed in developing an atomic bomb, I would have done nothing."

Howard Hughes

"I don't think Howard could love anything that did not have a motor in it."

On August 7, 1939, Howard Hughes was awarded the Congressional Gold Medal "in recognition of [his] achievements in advancing the science of aviation and thus bringing great credit to his country throughout the world."

In 1905, Hughes was born in Houston, Texas, to a successful inventor/businessman father Howard Sr., and mother, Allene Stone Gano. Folklore has it that an ancestor, Minister John Gano, baptized George Washington. Howard Sr. founded the Hughes Tool Company and invented a drilling bit that Howard Jr. later commented upon, "We don't have a monopoly. Anyone who wants to dig a well without a Hughes bit can always use a pick and shovel."

A science whiz at age 11, Howard Jr. built Houston's first wireless radio transmitter and became its first licensed ham-radio operator. One year later he invented a motorized bicycle. Both his parents died at an early age, his mother in 1922, his father two years later. Orphaned in his late teens and inheriting his father's wealth, he established a medical research laboratory to honor his parents.

Hughes, an excellent golfer, attended two schools: Rice University and Cal Tech. In 1925, he married Ella Botts Rice, after whose uncle, William Marsh Rice, the university is named. Shortly after marrying, they moved to Los Angeles to make movies. Soon, after divorcing in 1929, his entrepreneurial spirit led him to other ventures, including air travel, which he also mastered, opening the Hughes Aircraft Company in 1932. As movie actress Gene Tierney later opined: "I don't think Howard could love anything that did not have a motor in it." Hughes unsuccessfully wooed Tierney on several occasions but did not hold a grudge after her rejections. When she later married fashion designer extraordinaire Oleg Cassini, she gave birth to a severely handicapped daughter, to whom Hughes made available, and paid for, the best medical care available.

At the time the 33-year-old Hughes was recognized by Congress, he had designed, built, and test flown airplanes for the company he founded, set several speed records (including a record flight around the world for which he won the 1938 Collier Trophy and celebrated in a ticker-tape parade in New York City), pioneered imaginative designs including retractable landing gears and rivets, and joints flush with the plane's body to reduce drag and increase speed, produced major motion pictures, including two Best Picture nominees *The Racket* (1928) and *The Front Page* (1931), and dated some of the most noteworthy and attractive actresses of the time. Another movie he produced, *Scarface* (1932), along with *The Front Page*, later gained recognition by the National Film Registry as being "culturally, historically or aesthetically" significant. *Hell's Angels* (1930), which Hughes produced and co-directed, starred the "Blonde Bombshell" Jean Harlow, featured daring aerial scenes during which three stunt pilots and a mechanic died while filming. Hughes, who replaced another stunt pilot who complained of the dangerousness of the endeavor, took over and, proving the stuntman's opinion correct, crashed, fracturing his skull and requiring facial surgery. The movie turned out to be one of the highest grossing films of its era.

In time he owned Trans World Airlines (of which he started purchasing shares in 1939), RKO Pictures Film Studio, and several Las Vegas hotels. In 2004, Leonardo DiCaprio portrayed him in the well-received movie, *The Aviator*. Hughes was also the inspiration for characters in several television shows and movies, including Willard Whyte, played by Jimmy Dean in James Bond's *Diamonds Are Forever*, and Tony Stark, portrayed by Robert Downey Jr. in *Iron Man*. Marvel comic book maven and *Iron Man* co-creator Stan Lee named Tony Stark's father Howard Stark, and based Tony on "one of the most colorful characters of our time ... an inventor, adventurer, a ladies' man."

After Hughes was nearly fatally injured in a plane crash—destroying three houses and much of Hughes's body, including a crushed chest, broken collarbone and ribs, and severe burns—he designed a hospital bed for people similarly hurt. Earlier, he invented and designed a push-up bra for Jane Russell, whom he signed to star in *The Outlaw* (1943), an acclaimed movie directed and produced by Hughes which made Russell a pin-up favorite of GIs throughout the world.

The plane mishap, combined with his growing eccentricities and OCD, took a severe toll on Hughes as he aged. He morphed into a recluse, not cutting his hair or fingernails, storing his urine, and acting, in Stan Lee's assessment, as "a nutcase." His second marriage to actress Jean Peters had long ago fizzled out. When he died in 1976, his 6-foot-4-inch frame had withered down to barely 90 lbs. He left behind an estate worth well over $2 billion, much of which went to his medical institute.

Hedy Lamarr

"The less you know the more you remember."

On August 11, the movie *Lady of the Tropics*, was released starring Hedy Lamarr. Dubbed "the world's most beautiful woman" by MGM's Louis B. Mayer, he changed her name and made her a star. In time he would reject her, as she rejected his many sexual advances. Not only was Lamarr sultry, sexy, alluring and every other word to describe such a woman, but she also possessed a brilliant scientific mind; so much so that when she was having an affair with Howard Hughes, he not only encouraged her endeavors but made his extensive technical team available to her. She, in turn, recommended to her lover that he streamline the design of his aircraft. She also helped develop technology today used in Bluetooth and Wi-FI, as well as the means for Allied submarines to evade German detection. Dissatisfied with the workings of traffic lights and soft drinks, she created alternative designs for them. Not only does Hedy have a Walk of Fame on the sidewalks of Hollywood, but also membership in the National Inventors Hall of Fame.

Born Hedwig Eva Maria Kielser in Vienna in 1914 to a bank director father and concert pianist mother, she lived an upscale life attending private school where her classes included ballet, music, and language. She also studied acting and, given her charisma, quickly gained recognition. Still a teenager and under the name Hedy Kielser, she landed the lead role in the movie *Ecstasy* (1933), which would bring her great notoriety, despite her later claim that she was duped into the scenes showing her nude and depicting sexual intercourse and orgasm. Needless to say, it was condemned and banned in America while being embraced in Europe—except Germany, as it featured a Jewish star.

At roughly the same time, Kielser met and married a wealthy arms merchant, Friedrich Mandl. She was 18, he 33. Despite his father being Jewish, Mandl insisted that his new wife convert to Catholicism, the religion of his mother. He also insisted that she give up acting and live in his isolated castle. Finding him overbearing, controlling, and unacceptably dealing with German and Italian fascists, Hedy fled both the marriage—literally in the middle of the night—and her country, given the rise of Nazism.

While searching for new talent, Studio czar Mayer met and signed Hedy. He also wanted her to change her name, in part to escape her association with *Ecstasy*. At the suggestion of Mayer's wife, the surname Lamarr was selected in homage to the woman labelled by some as "too beautiful for Hollywood," the hard-partying and now-dead silent film star, Barbara Lamarr.

When Hedy came on the screen in her first movie in America, *Algiers*, one viewer exclaimed, "everyone gasped ... Lamarr's beauty literally took one's breath away." One year later, she starred in *Lady of the Tropics*, in which she plays Manon DeVargnes, a local woman of mixed race—half French, half Vietnamese—living in Saigon and aching to move to France. Pursued by a very wealthy but rather sleazy, businessman Pierre Delaroch, whom she rejects in favor of the smooth-talking American Bill Carey, who gets by with his good looks and charm. Indeed at the opening of the movie, he is a guest on a yacht in the company of an attractive and wealthy young woman and her generous family. When Manon meets Bill and they talk, a smitten Bill notes her a mystery, to which she coyly replies, "The less you know the more you remember."

Suffice it to say, Manon marries Bill while Pierre plots his revenge by using his connections and money to ensure that she can't leave the country and Bill can't find employment. Cunning as well as comely, she secures a job requiring travel for Bill through, unknown to Bill, Pierre's company. While Bill is away, Manon is with Pierre doing who knows what. With the Hays Commission and censorship hovering over and about, nothing is particularly clear, including how the seemingly poor Manon manages to dress like a model from Paris throughout the film. In the Hollywood style of endings, upon Bill's return he learns of Manon's behavior, she professes her continuing love for him, they fight, Bill leaves to shoot Pierre, Manon beats him to the punch and, to save her husband from killing Pierre and going to Devil's Island, she shoots and kills Pierre, returns to her apartment and shoots herself. Bill comes home, confesses his love for her as she ever so slowly dies in his arms. Fade out.

Not the best of films and not aging particularly well, but noteworthy for those starring in it. Perhaps most significant was the one who authored the script, the legendary (although few remember him today), multi-talented Ben Hecht, who wrote or co-wrote many classic movies, including Howard Hughes's *The Front Page* and *Scarface*; 1939's *Gunga Din*, *Wuthering Heights* and *It's a Wonderful World*; Alfred Hitchcock's *Spellbound* and *Notorious*; and the Marx Brothers' *Monkey Business*. He also helped write numerous other films without receiving credit—*Gone With the Wind*, *The Shop Around the Corner*, *Mutiny on the Bounty*, *His Girl Friday*, *Foreign Correspondent*, and *The Greatest Show on Earth* to name but a few.

Lamarr went on to make nearly two dozen more movies, with perhaps *Samson and Delilah* (1949) being her crowning achievement. Demonstrating great beauty and intelligence, her sense of humor might have been somewhat lacking when she sued Mel Brooks for improperly using the name "Hedley" Lamarr in his classic movie *Blazing Saddles*. Brooks, admiring Lamarr for all the years of cinematic pleasure she gave him, told his lawyers to settle "within reason" and to please "send her my love and tell her where I live."

As for her looks, she did not see what others saw. "My face has been my misfortune. It has attracted six unsuccessful marriage partners. It has attracted [both men and women and] all the wrong people into my boudoir and brought me tragedy and heartache for five decades. My face is a mask I cannot remove. I must always live with it. I curse it."

The Molotov-Ribbentrop Pact

"Fascism is a matter of taste."

On August 23, 1939, Germany and the Soviet Union shocked the world when their foreign ministers, Joachim von Ribbentrop and Vyacheslav Molotov (better known for the "Cocktail" named after him), negotiated a non-aggression pact between the two thought to be mortal enemies. Russia's concurrent dealings with Britain and France proved so unworkable that Stalin thought he had no option other than to do the unthinkable and deal with Hitler. Although the pact was to last for ten years, all concerned knew at the time that war between the two was inevitable. To that end, the can was kicked down the road with both preparing for the coming conflict. Meanwhile, France and Britain (along with Poland) were again left on the sidelines, once again taking the wrong path when they came to the proverbial fork in the road.

The agreement contained a Secret Protocol that not only set their borders but established spheres of influence and how to divvy up the assets upon conquest. Little did the over 20 million residents of Poland, Bessarabia, Finland, Lithuania, Estonia, and Latvia realize that they were in the crosshairs of Russia, domination, and destruction.

So happy at the turn of events, Stalin himself, in a break from practice, personally greeted von Ribbentrop and his delegation when they arrived in Moscow. Stalin was on a high at the time, with military successes against Japan in the battle of Khalkhin Gol, which deescalated Japan's threat against Russia. The defeat also caused Japan to reconsider its Northern land-war strategy in favor of a Southern conquering-islands approach that culminated in the attack on Pearl Harbor.

From the time Hitler came to power, Stalin saw him as a threat. The feelings were mutual with Hitler characterizing Russia as "the greatest danger for the culture and civilization of mankind which has ever threatened it." In turn, Stalin opined that with Germany's dismantling of Czechoslovakia, "Aggressor states are waging a war, violating the interests of non-aggressive states, particularly England, France, and the U.S... We support nations who fell victims to aggression and fight for the independence of their homelands."

Knowing Hitler's views on Lebensraum ("living space") and expanding eastward, Stalin had good cause to be concerned, so much so that he was willing to turn to his other perceived enemies—the Western democracies—as an alliance with Britain and France made for a formidable two-front coalition.

Dealing with Neville Chamberlain, who despised communism, proved to be a fatal hurdle. "I must confess," Chamberlain wrote a friend, "to the most profound distrust of Russia. I have no belief whatever in her ability to maintain an effective offensive, even if she wanted to. And I distrust her motives, which seem to me to have little connection with our ideas of liberty." The New York Times, in an article about British feelings toward the Russian leaders, characterized those leaders as "tricky negotiators and unreliable partners."

Chamberlain had good reason to distrust Stalin. Indeed, if there had been no Adolf Hitler and his top ranking as the most evil tyrant in modern history, Joseph Stalin would assume the mantle, brutally eliminating far more of his countrymen than Hitler. He sent millions to the Gulags, wherein an untold number died; forcibly moved and resettled entire towns and villages; starved millions to death (notably in Ukraine) through inept policy decisions and as a means to control and intimidate; and initiated "The Great Purge," in which those thought to be rivals and detractors were killed, including 81 of the 103 highest ranking members of the Communist Party, and later, in 1937–1938, decimating senior military figures.

Chamberlain also knew that if Russia were to confront Germany it would have to pass through hostile nations—Poland and Romania. Serious territorial disagreements existed between those nations. Seeking an alliance permitting such movement was a non-starter as Poland and Romania feared that if Stalin entered their countries he would never leave. Believing that Britain and France could pressure Poland as they had pressured Czechoslovakia, Stalin was taken aback when that did not occur. Further exacerbating the negotiations was the failure of Britain and France to send officials who were authorized to make significant decisions, in contrast to the Russian delegation that was empowered to act quickly.

In the end each distrusted the other, often with good cause. Stalin needed an ally and when talks irrevocably broke down on August 21, von Ribbentrop was in Moscow two days later making a deal that the Allies should have made.

Like Stalin, Hitler similarly needed a partner. He had gained large swathes of property and control in Austria and Czechoslovakia and now had his sights on Poland, having planned its invasion to start on August 25. That task would be far easier with Russia out of the picture. With such urgency, a pact was agreed upon at warp speed. A further advantage for the two involved a trade deal, with raw materials going to Germany in exchange for technology and industrial equipment.

With the pact sealed, both governments needed to reverse course in its condemnation of the other. No longer were they enemies. To assuage Hitler, Molotov told reporters that "fascism is a matter of taste." Stalin toasted his newfound allies, "I know how much the German Nation loves its Führer. I should therefore like to drink to his health."

In the end, the appeasement deals Chamberlain and Daladier made with Hitler came to naught, with Britain and France gaining nothing. In contrast, Stalin's dealings with Hitler soon gave Russia half of Poland and other valuable lands and properties, along with industrial and technological assistance. Each nation got what it wanted and needed, despite the certainty that it was doomed to tumble, which it did less than two years later when Germany invaded Russia in 1941. At the outset of the invasion, much of the populace of the quickly conquered Russian lands rejoiced at having the tyranny of Stalin lifted. Quickly, however, they learned that Hitler's methods were even far more severe and brutal.

Public Enemy #1 Surrenders

"Mr. Hoover, this is Lepke."

At 10:15 pm on August 24, 1939, notorious gangster and fugitive Louis Lepke Buchalter got into a car driven by nationally syndicated columnist Walter Winchell, and in five short minutes slowly drove to New York's 5th Avenue and either 28th or 29th Street, where they exited the car and ambled over to a black limousine. Winchell opened the rear door and spoke to the man seated alone in its back seat. "Mr. Hoover, this is Lepke."

The head of the FBI, replied, "How do you do?"

As Lepke got in, he responded, "Glad to meet you. Let's go."

And thus ended a two-year worldwide manhunt for the man who ran the rackets, made millions, and helped foster Murder Incorporated, which killed the hundreds that the mob wanted rubbed out. Perhaps fitting for one of his ilk, Lepke didn't get the deal he bargained for. Instead, he got the chair.

Born in 1897, Louis Buchalter followed a far different path than his siblings—one sister and three brothers who grew to be a dentist, pharmacist, and college professor/rabbi. His mother Rose called him *lepkeleh*—a Yiddish term translating to little Louis—which eventually transformed into Lepke.

His father, a Russian immigrant who operated a hardware store on the lower east side of New York, died when Lepke was 12. For health reasons Rose soon moved to Arizona, leaving Lepke behind in the care of his soon-to-be totally overwhelmed sister Sarah. Before long the soft-spoken, physically unintimidating young man entered a life of lawlessness, ping-ponging between crimes and incarcerations.

His criminal career blossomed upon his release from jail in 1922, teaming with a childhood friend, Jacob "Gurrah" Shapiro—a brutish ying to Lepke's seemingly mellow yang, slowly infiltrating the labor unions of the thriving garment industry where the now dubbed "Gorilla Boys" pilfered union dues and shook down businesses, offering protection and promises not to strike. From garments, they moved onto the trucking and baking industries. Rivals who stood in their way were murdered.

Despite his brutal tactics, Lepke was the antithesis of the perceived view of gangsters. He listened while others spoke; when he did speak he did so quietly; and, unlike many, he generously took care of his underlings. In 1931 he married a 27-year-old widow, Betty Wasserman, and adopted her 8-year-old son, while still remaining close and loyal to his family. He didn't drink, smoke, gamble, or cheat on his wife, and lived in a lavish Central Park West apartment. Adopting a business approach to the big business of organized crime, he simply did not look like the gangster that he was.

Whether they started Murder, Incorporated or merely greatly enhanced its presence is of no import. Wishing to avoid the bloody gang wars of the 1920s, Charles "Lucky" Luciano and Meyer Lansky formed the National Crime Syndicate, aka The Commission, a coalition of crime families to calm and resolve gang disputes and mete out punishment to those who did not toe the line. Enforcement fell to, as known to the world, Murder, Incorporated; insiders called it the "Combination." Under the leadership of Lepke, Gurrah Shapiro, and Albert "The Mad Hatter"/"Lord High Executioner" Anastasia, the killing machine flourished, carrying out assassinations near and far.

Of its hundreds of hits, the most famous involved noted gangster Dutch Schultz, who, in October 1935, sought to take out the racket-busting crusading prosecutor Thomas E. Dewey, who was assembling a strong case against Schultz. The Commission, after hearing Schultz plead his case, decided that the heat generated by such a killing promised to turn atomic and vetoed the request, a decision in which Lepke concurred. Schultz, foolishly and fatally, did not take the news well and vowed to kill Dewey anyway. In turn the Commission took another vote, this one authorizing the immediate removal of Schultz. On October 23, Dutch and three of his associates were shot in the aptly named Palace Chop House in Newark,

New Jersey. They all died shortly thereafter. On his deathbed, Schultz, born Jewish and named Arthur Simon Flegenheimer, converted to Catholicism.

With his crime empire soaring, Lepke soon felt the searing attention of law enforcement. First, in 1936, the feds moved in, charging him and Shapiro with violating the anti-trust laws in the rabbit fur industry. Convicted, but out on bail pending sentencing, the two defendants dropped out of sight. Meanwhile, in the same year, Lepke decided that Joseph Rosen had to go. Believing, perhaps falsely, that Rosen (who had earlier worked in the garment industry but now owned a candy store in Brooklyn) was cooperating with Dewey, Lepke gave the order.

A year later Lepke was federally indicted for conspiracy to smuggle heroin. While Shapiro surrendered in April 1938, Lepke remained hidden, resulting in a continuing worldwide manhunt for, as J. Edgar Hoover proclaimed, "the most dangerous criminal in the U.S." Still running his criminal empire, the noose started to tighten. Fearing that one-time allies might turn on him, he ordered them eliminated, resulting in an estimated sixty to one hundred deaths over a two-year period. It has been observed that actions taken to avoid a certain outcome often result in the dreaded outcome being realized. Such was the case with Lepke, as his decisions—perhaps fueled by a dash of paranoia—drove targeted comrades into the arms, and hoped-for protection, of law enforcement. Soon they were testifying and hitmen and gangsters were going to jail, if not the chair.

As the bodies piled up in 1939, Lepke ordered another hit on a union official, Philip Orlovsky, with whom he was once affiliated. Three killers—Seymour "Blue Jaw" Magoon, Abe "Pretty" Levine, and Martin "Buggsy" Goldstein—stole a car a few days prior to the attack, planned for July 25. At 6 am that morning, they planted themselves outside of Orlovsky's apartment and waited. Fifteen minutes later, they saw him exit the building. As he walked by their stolen car, Goldstein jumped out and fired six shots ... at Irving Penn, an innocent businessman who resembled Orlovsky.

As mobsters fell violently by the wayside, the public grew weary and angry. Its anger turned to outrage though with the brazen murder of a law-abiding and sympathetic bystander. The mob was in a quandary. Thanks to Dewey, indictments and convictions were flying in. Even Charles "Lucky' Luciano, the head of the Commission, suffered from Dewey's wrath, receiving a hefty prison sentence for his involvement in the widespread prostitution industry throughout the city. With further crackdowns in the offing—the police no longer turning a blind eye to mob criminality—and money drying up, something had to be done. A sacrificial lamb was needed. Lepke fit the bill. If he resisted though, another gang war loomed.

Word came quickly to Lepke—it's time to surrender—or else. Lepke was indecisive until he received further news. A deal had been struck. In exchange for turning himself into the feds, Lepke wouldn't have to face Dewey and the state of New York. It was a lie. No deal had been made. As Luciano later related: "Of course, we didn't make no deal at all with Hoover, but it had to look damn sure to Lepke that we did."

Lepke went to prison and then Dewey hung the Rosen rap on him, thanks to the now cooperating Abe Reles, who, while facing the chair for his prolific work with Murder, Incorporated, decided he'd rather squeal than fry. The testifying Reles and other cooperating hoodlums sent a half dozen or so killers to the electric chair. Before he could do any further harm to Anastasia and others, however, Reles found himself, while under heavy police protection, tossed from the sixth-floor hotel window in which he was housed and closely watched.

As for the Irvin Penn killing, Blue Jaw Magoon also cut a deal and testified against his one-time friend and partner, Buggsy Goldstein, who got the chair in 1941. Three years later, Lepke, the first major crime boss to be given the death sentence, joined him, prosecuted by Dewey, whose life Lepke helped save years earlier when he nixed Dutch Schultz's assassination plan. Looking back, Lepke opined that perhaps he had made the wrong decision. While the mob continued to murder and maim, Murder, Incorporated was out of business.

The Wizard of Oz

"There's no place like home."

On August 25, 1939, *The Wizard of Oz* was officially released to mixed and, at times, horrid reviews by those who should have known better.[2] *The New Republic* wrote, in part, that the movie "weighs like a pound of fruitcake soaking wet ... The story of course has some lovely and wild ideas [with interesting characters] but the picture doesn't know what to do with them." As for Judy Garland, she "[thumps and romps with] everyone get[ting] wet when she is forlorn." *The New Yorker* piled on, calling the movie a "stinkeroo," with "Bert Lahr, as the Cowardly Lion, funny but out of place." Continuing, the clueless reviewer wrote that he "sat cringing before MGM's Technicolor production ... which displays no trace of imagination, good taste or ingenuity."

The highly influential *New York Times* was far more charitable, saying what all came to believe: "[A]ny reviewer who would look down his nose at the fun-making should be spanked and sent off, supperless, to bed."

In time, *Oz* grew to mythical proportions, starting with its re-release in 1949 with far more generous reviews. Seven years later, in 1956, CBS tried to purchase the rights to air *Gone With the Wind* for a million dollars, MGM refused but offered *Oz* for $225,000 plus an option to air it annually. With that, the "stinkeroo" became, according to the Library of Congress, the most watched film in viewing history.

As with most, if not all movies, the making of *Oz* involved numerous people entering, exiting, staying, and leaving. In all, there were ten writers, of which only three received credit, and four directors, with only Victor Fleming being named. Fleming did not even hang around long enough to finish it as he rushed off to rescue *Gone With the Wind*, replacing director George Cukor, who Fleming had earlier replaced on *Oz*. King Vidor jumped in and brought it to the finish line. With MGM having eighty-one writers, 120 actors, and a host of directors under contract, all worked on its various movies, often simultaneously and interchangeably. While some did not like being passed over, others took it in their stride. When the very first *Oz* writer, the brilliant, heavy-drinking, gambling Herman Mankiewicz was tossed aside, he too took it in his stride. As he earlier told a friend: "Go ahead and write me out and then find someone to write you out." Of course, even he at times found it tiresome. On one occasion, he, when irked, wrote a script wherein the heroic dog Rin-Tin-Tin carried a baby into a burning building.

Often so little regarded, writers routinely were not even invited to view the newly released movies they had written. The ones at the top of the heap were the producers, who like many in different professions, ranged from brilliant to inept, and often maddingly arrogant. When one such clueless producer told a talented songwriter that the song he'd written wasn't any good, the writer challenged him, asking him how he knew. "Because you're standing in front of the desk and I'm sitting behind it," came the bigheaded reply.

The underlings, however, did occasionally prevail, as when they convinced the powers to be to keep "Over the Rainbow" in the movie. The producers sought to delete what would become one of the greatest Oscar winning songs in film history as it was too long, thought to be above the heads of the children watching, and, of all things, sung in a barnyard.

The shuffling of talent included those appearing in the movie. When Louie B. Mayer could not secure a deal with another studio to get Shirley Temple to play Dorothy, Judy Garland filled the red ruby shoes. The gangly Ray Bolger, who played the Scarecrow, was initially cast as The Tin Man. Dancer and songbird Buddy Ebsen, destined for later television immortality as Jed Clampett on *The Beverly Hillbillies*, switched from his role as the Scarecrow to that of The Tin Man, singing all his songs and going all the way through rehearsal prior to filming. When he had a near fatal reaction to his toxic make-up, he was hospitalized and left the movie, replaced by Jack Haley. Comic actor Ed Wynn didn't play the Wizard as the role was "too small," while the brilliant W.C. Fields passed due to money issues. Finally, Frank Morgan came aboard. The ragtag coat he wore in the movie came from a second-hand store. Rumor had it that a label in the coat ironically indicated that it had once belonged to Frank Baum, the author of the *Oz* books, written decades before. Too good to be true, the tale was likely put out by MGM's creative PR Department.

The Scarecrow's search for a brain, the Tin Man a heart, and The Cowardly Lion, courage, strangely mirrored those playing the roles. Ray Bolger, although not getting past high school, was thoughtful and creative with a sharp brain; Jack Haley, a very religious Catholic, lived by the tenets of charity, love, and philanthropy; Bert Lahr, meanwhile, personified anxiety and nervousness. Being deeply in love with another woman while caring and paying nearly a quarter of a million dollars for his institutionalized wife added to his misery. Shortly after his annulment, he married the other woman not long after the release of *Oz* and remained with her until his death in 1967.

In sharp contrast to those similarities, a single mother raising a young son, Margaret Hamilton was the polar opposite of the evil character she played. One wonders how a movie with the terrifying Wicked Witch of the West (not to mention the frightening bike pedaling Almira Gulch) could be called a children's one when it scared, and scarred, the living begeebees out of every one of us, despite her appearing for only twelve minutes. When Hamilton reprised the role on *Sesame Street* in 1976, her character so upset the young and old alike that the episode disappeared and went into hibernation for forty years.

Hamilton, a former schoolteacher, worked as a character actor throughout her career while promoting education and support for children and pets. In the 1950s she taught Sunday school. She even served on the Board of Education for the Beverly Hills school system from 1948–1951. A gentle soul off-stage she, like some of the others, found the rigors of her role difficult during the six or so months of shooting. Whether it was Jack Haley sitting in a chair having his make-up applied for nearly two hours a day, six days a week, and then confined to a unbending tin-like casket that would not permit him to sit ("I could only lean against a reclining board"), or Ray Bolger enduring a plastic bag-like mold being cemented onto his entire head (save his eyes), which ultimately partially permanently scarred part of his face, was often torturous. "The mask wasn't porous, so you couldn't sweat. You couldn't breathe through your skin." Compounding the ordeal, mammoth lights needed to film the newish color process emitted skin numbing heat. "We felt like we were suffocating." Bolger observed. At the end of the day, it took an hour to peel his mask off.

Bert Lahr joined their club of misery, having to live in a heavy, cumbersome, and unforgiving lion's outfit, that he often shed after every shot. Dripping wet from sweat, he could not even open his mouth, given the lion's nose and mouth glued to his face. Hydration and nourishment came through a straw. While the lunch hour offered some respite for the ravenous Haley and Bolger, it didn't for Lahr, who was jealous of his fellow thespians. "Look at you. I can't eat anything and you guys are eating up everything in the whole world. Besides, I had gas all night."

True suffering, however, laid with Hamilton. Like the others, her costume and make-up, green in her case, were highly uncomfortable and constricting, which not only made eating difficult but also required the assistance of an aide when using the bathroom. Long after filming, her skin carried the green tinge of her make-up, only dissipating after several months. During filming, she had few with whom to confide, much less talk. She rarely worked with anyone other than Garland and the Winged Monkeys and was never on set the same day as the Wizard, Frank Morgan. Given a canvas tent with a dirty rug with "one chair and a card table with a light over it" as her dressing room, she didn't complain at the luxury afforded her fellow witch Billie Burke, who enjoyed a pink satin dressing room "and the little fur rug next to the [pink] chaise-lounge which she could step onto when she was through taking her rest." Perhaps the studio felt that good witches like Glinda the Good Witch of the North deserved it; more likely, though, the fact that Burke was the wife of the late famed Flo Ziegfeld formed the decision.

All of these indignities paled, however, to the events of December 23, 1938. When filming Hamilton's fiery exit from Munchkinland, a trapdoor was supposed to open and whisk Hamilton from danger. It didn't. Fire engulfed Hamilton, severely burning her face and hand, obliterating her skin. Her toxic make-up added to her injuries. Patched up at the scene, she called a friend to drive her to a doctor. As the doctor tended to her, the studio called asking when she could return to work. She was out six weeks. While recovering, her co-star Burke sprained her ankle, at which point MGM called both an ambulance and a photographer to memorialize her being whisked away. No mention was made of Hamilton. As before, Hamilton took it in her stride. "I was very much amused."

Upon her return, the studio wanted to shoot the scene in which she screams and screeches while riding her broomstick with smoke billowing out. Given her past experiences with heated special effects—and giving special meaning to the idiom "once burned, twice shy"—Hamilton demurred rather vehemently, proclaiming that she wasn't going anywhere near fire again. She stood her ground, even when threatened. Finally, her stunt double Betty Danko was called in. The asbestos covered pipe spewing smoke exploded, landing Betty in the hospital for eleven days. A studio worker called her in the hospital, greatly concerned about what had happened to the hat Danko was wearing when she was blown up.

As the players in the movie were older, and veterans of the ways of Hollywood, they long ago learned to cope with whatever was thrust upon them. Thus, Hamilton and Danko could weather the adversity and thoughtlessness, while Haley accepted having to give back $1,000 of his $3,000 salary he made each week in return for being allowed to continue working on his weekly radio show. All managed though except for one, Judy Garland. Much has been written about a forty-seven-year life that in the end could only be called sad. Suffice it to say, the talented teenager who played Dorothy was introduced to drugs and generally mistreated, even by some of the Munchkins, who allegedly sexually harassed her. Told she was too ugly and too fat—Mayer called her his "little hunchback"—surely permanently wounded her young psyche. Becoming a mega star came at an exorbitant price.

While thousands of children and their parents saw the movie upon its release, the studio lost money that would not be recouped until its re-release a decade later. For the actors playing their roles, it was merely another job. When the Wizard, Frank Morgan, died in 1949, his obituaries carried no mention of his *Oz* appearance. Hamilton gained no fame for two decades until she started appearing on television.

Nominated for six Academy Awards, including Best Picture, it won for best score, which comes as no surprise as it was one of the first movies in which songs advanced the plot, setting the standard for future movies and shows; best song, the one MGM wanted to delete, "Over the Rainbow"; and Best Juvenile Performer, Judy Garland.

Given its warming themes—

"There's no place like home."

"A heart is not judged by how much you love, but by how much you are loved."

Its snappy dialogue that we quote and use to this day—

"I'll get you, my pretty, and your little dog too!"

"Are you a good witch or a bad witch?"

"Toto, I've got a feeling we're not in Kansas anymore."

"Lions and tigers and bears! Oh my."

"Put 'em up! Put 'em up!"

"That, my dear, is a horse of a different color."

"I'm melting! melting!"
"I think I'll miss you most of all."
"Now I know I've got a heart, cause it's breaking."
And perhaps the one still most relevant, "Some people without brains do an awful lot of talking, don't they?"
And fabulous music that we all know and sing—
"Ding Dong! The Witch is Dead"
"If I Only Had a Brain [Heart; the Nerve]"
"If I Were King of the Forest"
"We're Off to See the Wizard," among others.

And loveable characters we can relate to, in search of attributes they already have, a brain, heart, and courage, all of which makes *The Wizard of Oz* an immortal movie that remains to this day one of the very best ever made.

The Gleiwitz Incident

"The victor will not be asked whether he told the truth."

On August 31, 1939, a radio announcement at 10:30 pm breathlessly announced a Polish assault on German soil:

> There have been reports of an attack on a radio station in [Gleiwitz], which is just across the Polish border in Germany. The German News Agency reports the attack came at about 8 pm this evening when the Poles forced their way into the studio and began broadcasting a statement in Polish. Within a quarter of an hour, say reports, the Poles were overpowered by German police who opened fire on them. Several of the Poles were reported killed but the numbers are not yet known.

None of this was true. As before, whether it was the attack on the Reichstag or German propaganda falsely complaining that Germans were being horribly mistreated in the Sudetenland and elsewhere, they were all lies, told to justify yet another invasion. Indeed, the Poles had nothing to do with the operation. As Gestapo chief Reinhard Heydrich told his underlings, "An actual proof of Polish encroachment is necessary for the foreign press and for German propaganda." The Gestapo planned the incidents in Gleiwitz and other locations, dubbing the operation "Grandmother has died." German operatives dressed in Polish uniforms seized the station and broadcast a brief anti-German message.

At the Dachau concentration camp, the Gestapo took and murdered Franciszek Honiok, who was known to be sympathetic to the Polish cause, along with a handful of other inmates, dressed them in Polish army uniforms, and dumped their bodies by the station to demonstrate that the broadcast was in fact accurate.

Along with Gleiwitz, other "false flag operations" took place on the border. Hitler had been stirring up false accusations for months, planning to justify his invasion as merely a defensive action taken against a belligerent and hostile enemy. He earlier informed his generals that, "I will provide a propagandistic *casus belli* [an event that brings about a declaration of war]. Its credibility doesn't matter. The victor will not be asked whether he told the truth."

Six hours after the broadcast Germany invaded Poland.

14

The War Starts, the Yankees Clinch the Pennant, and a Mobster Heads to Hollywood

Germany invades Poland

"What now?"

At 4:45 am on September 1, 1939, the German gun ship *Schleswig Holstein* fired on a Polish fort in Danzig, followed by its military, using many weapons seized from Czechoslovakia, swarming in and over Poland in what was clearly a mismatch.

As they did so, Hitler hoped that Britain and France would stand down. That they didn't surprised, if not shocked, him. In the lead-up to the invasion, he repeatedly sought to isolate Poland. He argued, persuasively to some, that all he wanted was for Poland to return Danzig and some other land, which had been ceded to Poland in the Versailles Treaty. Despite the transfer, Danzig remained German in population and allegiance.

At first, Hitler tried to reach an accommodation with the Polish leaders, even envisioning Poland joining the German-Italian-Japanese Axis. In 1934 Poland had signed a Non-Aggression Pact with Germany, mirroring a similar pact signed two years earlier with Russia. In 1938 Poland not only supported the break-up of Czechoslovakia in the hope of becoming a regional power, but it helped itself to some of its land.

Hitler, though, underestimated Polish pride and determination, emboldened by its surprising earlier victory in 1920 over an invading Russia bent on taking over the newly formed state and spreading communism. Following its triumph, the Poles built up their country and military, remaining all the while wary of its hungry neighbors. Seeing how Hitler acted with those he bullied, Poland's leader Józef Beck refused to engage, declaring, if need be, that "we will fight." By so doing, Poland became the only state in Europe to stand up to Hitler.

With the rare failure of intimidation, plans were laid for invasion. Concomitantly, diplomacy continued, with the governments of Chamberlain and Daladier fervently working to strengthen the fraying string of peace. Despite cables and meetings flying back and forth at dizzying speed, Hitler gave the order to invade on August 26, a not-so-secret date ascertained by Allied intelligence. On that early morning, 1.5 million men massed and marched and eagerly awaited the final okay. Hitler, who authorized the attack, suddenly pulled back and called it off.

To those on the other side, the sign was well-received. Perhaps Hitler had come to his senses. Perhaps the united British-French stance of drawing a line in the sand worked. When news of an Anglo-Polish Agreement of Mutual Assistance reached Hitler, it struck like a "bombshell." Or perhaps it was the reluctance of Mussolini to join in that gave Hitler pause; not only was Italy militarily compromised, but Italian public opinion lagged and so Italy announced its neutrality in the matter. Still, though, Hitler believed if push came to shove, the British and French would not risk a world war over Poland. The British and French conversely believed that if they held firm Hitler would back down.

On September 1, Germany invaded in what it deemed a defensive war, given Poland's hostile acts to its German population in Gleiwitz and other nearby areas. While Germany awaited a response, the United States was preparing its call for restraint and peace, reflecting that its population overwhelmingly wanted America to stay neutral.

Britain and France demanded that Germany withdraw and come to the bargaining table but initially gave no ultimatum. Italy floated the idea of a conference. Hitler thanked Mussolini but could not withdraw given "the blood sacrifice" of his German soldiers. Mussolini, wishing to not appear weak and unsupportive of the Führer, portrayed himself as heroically trying to quell the matter, only to be thwarted by British intransience. In the end, on September 3, Chamberlain and Daladier declared a war that neither wanted. When Hitler learned of the resolve of the Allies, he sat in silence before turning to Ribbentrop and asking, "What now?"

As Germany advanced, it arrested and eliminated officials, teachers, priests and religious figures, artists and all those essential to a cohesive and functioning society. Brutal and mindless acts of atrocity were implemented to beat the Poles into subservience and acquiescence. As Hitler told his generals a week earlier, "The object of the war is [to] physically destroy the enemy. That is why I have prepared … orders to kill without pity or mercy all men, women, and children of Polish descent or language. Only in this way can we obtain the living space we need.

As Poland wishfully looked to its allies for quick assistance and involvement, none came. Instead, two weeks later, on September 17, Russia attacked from the east as "Poland was falling apart [making it] necessary for the Soviet Union, in consequence, to come to the aid of the [oppressed] Ukrainians and the White Russians." On October 6, Poland was no more, carved up like a turkey on Thanksgiving, as per the Molotov-Ribbentrop Pact signed in late August.

Civilian Polish losses initially numbered between 150,000 and 200,000. When all was said and done, over 5.5 million Poles would perish, approximately 3 million of whom were Jews. Meanwhile, in Germany, a euthanasia program was announced to kill its physically and mentally challenged citizens, thus freeing the nation of all inferiors.

A Mobster Heads to Hollywood

"Come on Gangy! Come back!"

On September 5, 1939, the movie *Golden Boy* was released, featuring Barbara Stanwyck, Adolph Menjou, Lee J. Cobb, and, in his first major role for one destined for Hollywood greatness, a barely recognizable William Holden. Billed as a drama, one today cannot quite hold back some well-deserved snickering.

Holden plays Joe Bonaparte, a young, headstrong boxer, who, to get ahead, gives up playing the violin and in so doing breaks the heart of his Italian father, played by Lee J. Cobb. That Holden at the time was 21 to Cobb's 27 starts the giggling. Barbara Stanwyck, as a cynical and weary Lorna Moon, propels it along, playing first the too-young girlfriend of an obviously much older fight promoter, who she leaves to be the too-old girlfriend of young Holden. For good measure, offensive insensitivity is also thrown in, portraying Cobb as a dark and greasy Italian.

Bonaparte starts winning his fights regularly, drawing the attention of mobster Eddie Fuseli, who takes over after buying a piece of him. Falling under the clutches of the mob, as we all know about movies made back then, can only lead to disaster. Joe goes from a sweet and talented violin player to a hard-boiled and successful boxer. In his biggest match to date, one leading to a shot at the crown, he knocks out his opponent, Chocolate

Drop, who promptly dies, causing Joe and Lorna to re-evaluate their lives. Joe gives up boxing, returns to his beloved violin, and presumably lives happily ever after with his still way-too-old girlfriend.

Even a forgettable film may be notable and *Golden Boy* is no exception. At the outset of filming, the producers grew disenchanted with Holden and sought to fire him. With Stanwyck's strong support, they backed down. Holden remained ever grateful. When they were reunited at the 1978 Academy Awards, Holden paused their reading of the nominees to thank Stanwyck for saving his career. Four years later, shortly after Holden died, Stanwyck received an Honorary Oscar. In her acceptance speech she returned Holden's respect, "I loved him very much, and I miss him. He always wished that I would get an Oscar. And so tonight, my golden boy, you got your wish."

When the movie was released, many New York boxing fans eagerly attended, anxious to see the pivotal fight scene taking place in Madison Square Garden. One such attendee was Murder, Incorporated killer Abe "Pretty" Levine, who, while viewing the fight, saw its brief shots of the screaming crowd, cheering on either Bonaparte or Chocolate Drop. His mouth opened in shock when he spotted one particular ringside fan. What in God's name was Irving "Big Gangy" Cohen doing there? When Albert last saw him two years earlier, they were murdering Walter Sage.

Walter Sage, before his demise, cut an impressive figure. Attractive and nattily attired, the 32-year-old one-time taxicab driver left that business to sign on with the far more lucrative and dangerous Murder, Inc. Joining forces with "Kid Twist" Reles, Harry "Pittsburgh Phil" Strauss, "Buggsy" Goldstein, and "Blue Jaw" Magoon, they killed when hired to do so. They also ran the rackets. Illegal slot machines comprised one such criminal enterprise and when they were placed 75 miles away from New York, in Sullivan County, Sage was named overlord. Unfortunately, his fingers were sticky and violated a sacred rule—Thou shalt not steal from the Mob. Those who did were taught a violent and, in his case, fatal lesson.

Commonly, when the Mob wished to eliminate one of their own a close friend who the victim implicitly trusted was selected to do the deed. The one named had little choice for if he balked he'd find himself next on the hit parade. The Sage assignment went to his best friend, Irving "Big Gangy (or Gangi)" Cohen, a well-liked (by his friends) giant of a man who weighed in the mid-200s, spoke in a rat-tat-tat manner, and was handy with a gun and icepick.

As killers ordinarily don't make contemporaneous notes of their encounters, what transpired is somewhat unclear. It appears though that the plan concocted was a common one involving two cars—the kill car, with Cohen seated behind Sage who was seated in the front passenger seat (think Clemenza seated behind Carlo on the day Carlo's newborn son was earlier christened in *The Godfather*). Joining them was killer Jack Drucker. The trailing car followed with "Pretty" Levine driving, joined with "Pittsburgh Phil" Strauss and Allie "Tick-Tock" Tannenbaum.

Early on the Tuesday evening of July 27, 1937, an unsuspecting well-dressed Walter Sage, wearing a grey striped suit with an accompanying purple pocket handkerchief and a similarly colored shirt, joined his friends. The leisurely drive on a quiet and dark country road ended abruptly when the mammoth Cohen grabbed Sage's neck from behind, choking and immobilizing him. Drucker quickly pulled out his handy icepick and repeatedly plunged it into Sage, stabbing him over thirty times. During the melee, the icepick found Cohen's arm once as the car careened off the road, landing in a ditch. As Levine's crew quickly arrived, Drucker emerged wiping his bloody weapon as Cohen shot out of the rear seat "as if fired from a cannon," screaming incoherently, and running wildly into the woods. Levine yelled out to him, "Come on Gangy! Come back!" He didn't.

Four days later, Sage's hogtied body with a slot machine tethered to his back, was found bobbing in a lake. Missing a shoe, a single penny was found in his pocket.

Whether an epiphany, along with the icepick, hit Gangy, or guilt at offing his best friend, or the realization that sometime down the line his number would be called, he disappeared. When Pittsburgh Phil somehow heard rumblings that Cohen had landed in California, he sent hitman Sholem Bernstein to pay him a murderous visit. According to the somewhat improbable tale Bernstein later weaved: "I went to California to kill Big Gangy. But I didn't kill him. I got Big Gangy a job as an extra in the movies. I had connections out there."

Whether a fanciful tale or not, Big Gangy indeed found himself in Hollywood. While the wisdom of someone on the run wishing to keep a low profile appearing in movies is rather questionable, that is precisely what happened. Changing his name to Jack Gordon, Big Gangy entered show business. After being outed by his appearance in *Golden Boy* and with Pretty and Tick Tock flipping and joining others available to testify, Gangy was arrested on the set of an Errol Flynn movie in which he was appearing.

Whisked back to New York to stand trial, the witnesses against him consisted primarily of his former cronies. At one point, with Levine on the stand, Cohen broke down, wailing and sobbing and so loudly proclaiming his innocence that a recess had to be called. After an eight-day trial, the jury barely deliberated before shockingly finding him not guilty. Apparently he had learned much about acting.

With his acquittal behind him, Gangy returned to the big screen and appeared in a number of films. He ended his career on a high note as the stand-in for Dan Blocker's Hoss Cartwright on the hit tv show *Bonanza*. He even appeared in numerous background crowd scenes. In the end, he traveled far from Walter Sage and Sullivan County.

Yankees Clinch Pennant

"The Yankee Clipper"

On September 16, 1939, the New York Yankees clinched their fourth consecutive American League Pennant, finishing seventeen games in front of the runner-up, Boston Red Sox, who also had a good season, finishing at a respectable 89–62. In a month New York would go on to win its fourth consecutive World Series, becoming the first time in the history of baseball to do so, sweeping the Cincinnati Reds in four straight games.

When all-time great baseball teams are discussed, the Yankees often dominate the conversation, with the teams of 1927 (110–44–1), 1961 (109–53), and 1998 (114–48) leading the way. Rarely mentioned are the 1939 Yankees, which might have been the best team ever. In that season, not only did they win 106 games while losing forty-five, for a .702 winning percentage (joining the 1927 and 1998 teams), but their run differential over their opponents was an astounding never-to-be-duplicated, plus 411 (967–556). No team has ever outscored their opponents over a season by that many runs.

In the three previous years, the Yankees captured the pennant by an average of fourteen games, while averaging 101 wins against fifty-two losses, for a jaw-dropping .660 winning percentage. In their three World Series wins they won twelve games while dropping only three.

In a 1939 season overshadowed by the tragic illness of the thought-to-be immortal Lou Gehrig, Joe DiMaggio was in the process of joining him on the Mount Rushmore of Yankee and Baseball Greats. DiMaggio joined the Yankees on May 3, 1936, just as they were starting their four-year streak. In his rookie year, he set a then franchise record by hitting twenty-nine home runs, which stood for decades until Aaron Judge hit fifty-two in 2017. One year later, in 1937, DiMaggio continued his brilliance, hitting forty-six home runs and accounting for 151 RBIs, and finishing second in the Most Valuable Player race. Detroit second baseman, one of the best of all time, Charlie "The Mechanical Man" Gehringer won the MVP that year. Earning his nickname due to his robotic consistency as both a hitter and fielder, a more apt moniker might have been "The Quiet Man." As his player-manager Mickey Cochrane kidded, "Charlie says 'hello' on Opening Day, 'goodbye' on closing day, and in between hits .350." Some attribute the quote to Tiger great Ty Cobb.

In 1939, DiMaggio won the MVP along with the batting title, hitting .381, despite missing over forty games early in the season due to an injury. Upon his return he netted over an RBI per game. In August alone he was responsible for fifty-three, tying Hack Wilson for most RBIs in a single month. DiMaggio, however, did not win the RBI race, that honor going to Boston Red Sox rookie sensation Ted Williams, who knocked in 145 runs (to DiMaggio's 126) and was the first rookie to do so. Williams made his major league debut on April 20, going 1–4 against star Red Ruffing's Yankees. Three days later Williams recorded his first home run. In his rookie season, Williams hit .327 with thirty-one home runs to accompany his league leading 107 walks, another rookie record. *Boston Globe* sportswriter Gerry Moore wrote of the birth of the battle of continuing brilliance between the two, "Not since Joe DiMaggio broke in with the Yankees ... in 1936 has any baseball rookie received the nationwide publicity that has been accorded ... [Ted] Williams."

During a season featuring the first night games and daily radio broadcasts, Yankee announcer Arch McDonald marveled at DiMaggio's talent, comparing his speed and range to that of a Pan American airplane. Arch went on, stamping DiMaggio with a still familiar name, "The Yankee Clipper," joining those of "Joltin' Joe" and "Joe D." Williams, meanwhile, out dubbed him with, "The Splendid Splinter," "Teddy Ballgame," "The Kid," and "The Thumper."

No single athlete, no matter how great, can do it all himself, and DiMaggio was no exception. Five of the starting eight Yankee fielders hit over .300; all eight hit double-digit home runs; and four had over 100 RBIs while three others had over eighty. While only one pitcher, Red Ruffing, won twenty-one games, six others also had double-digit wins. The most losses by a pitcher was eight. Ten Yankees were named to, although they didn't all play in, the All-Star team—pitchers Red Ruffing, Lefty Gomez, and Johnny Murphy (who led the league in saves) joining outfielders Joe DiMaggio and George Selkirk, catcher Bill Dickey, first baseman Lou Gehrig, second baseman Joe Gordon, shortstop Frankie Crosetti, and third baseman Red Rolfe.

So dominant were the Yankees in 1939 that they, in single games, beat the Detroit Tigers 22–2, the Philadelphia Athletics 23–2 and 10–0 in a double header, scored in every inning to beat the St. Louis Browns 14–1, and had a rookie pitcher Atley Donald win his first twelve starts. Ivy Leaguer third baseman Red Rolfe scored at least one run in eighteen straight games (scoring thirty in total during the streak), hit .329 for the season, led the AL in runs (139), hits (213), and doubles (46). Their star pitcher, Red Ruffing, who became a pitcher after losing four toes in a mining accident, hit .307 with a home run and twenty RBIs. The Yankees led the American League with 166 home runs, over 900 runs batted in, and a .451 slugging percentage. Six players from the team were destined for Hall of Fame immortality: Lou Gehrig, Joe DiMaggio, Bill Dickey, Lefty Gomez, Joe Gordon, Red Ruffing—along with their manager, Joe McCarthy, and owner Jacob Ruppert (1867–1939), who was also a four-term Congressman (1899–1907), who didn't live to see his team's continued success, dying in January.

The 1939 Yankees were ranked the greatest of all time in the book *Baseball Dynasties: The Greatest Teams of All Time*, and on Bill Simmons respected website, *FiveThirtyEight*. Sadly, the baseball public at large has not as yet come around.

Sigmund Freud dies

"My golden Sigi."

On September 23, 1939, Sigmund Freud, the famed doctor who created psychoanalysis by studying and writing about the inner workings of the mind, died. While some considered him one of the greatest thinkers and innovators of the time, others ridiculed his new-fangled ideas. Despite the controversy he stirred, his impact was nonetheless great.

Born in 1856 in Moravia to poor Jewish parents, Freud and his family moved to Germany for a year and then to his future home of Vienna when he was just 4. His father Jacob was a twice-divorced wool merchant when he married his third wife, Amalia Nathansohn, who was twenty years his junior and barely older than Jacob's two sons from his first marriage. Eight children would be born of the union, with one dying in infancy.

Amalia doted on her firstborn, originally named Sigismund Schlomo Freud, "my golden Sigi," who at a young age showed signs of brilliance as later evidenced by his proficiency in eight different languages—English, German, French, Spanish, Greek, Italian, Latin, and Hebrew. That closeness between mother and child—"the most perfect, the most free from ambivalence of all human relationships"—influenced Freud throughout his career. As close as he was to his mother, he remained somewhat aloof from his much older father whom he viewed as meek and passive, albeit lighthearted and optimistic about life.

Freud attended medical school in Vienna and gravitated toward psychiatry and nervous diseases. In 1886, he married Martha Bernays of Hamburg, who would give birth to six children. Along the way he may also have had an affair with his wife's younger sister, Minna. When Minna's fiancé died of tuberculosis in the same year as her sister and Sigmund married, she came to live with the Freuds. Described as "intelligent [and] caustic," she stayed with them for forty-two years. Dr. Carl Jung, a once close friend and later disliked rival, claimed that Minna told him of the intimacy. Given the toxic relationship between Freud and Jung, many discredited his account. In 2005, however, hotel records from August 13, 1898, came to light, indicating that Freud, 42 at the time, and 33-year-old Minna spent a two-week vacation in the Swiss Alps, sharing a room and signing in as husband and wife. Adding an additional layer of mystery, in 1900, Freud and Minna traveled to Meran, Austria, where some believe she had an abortion. The debate remains to this day. So, too, the truthfulness of his remark: "I stand for a much freer sexual life. However I have made little use of such freedom." The one vice of which we are certain was his indulgence in smoking twenty cigars a day.

Using hypnosis to get to the root of one's problems started Freud's journey into psychoanalysis. Initially basing his findings on subconscious sexual motives as the root of one's problems found little support. With time, his methods gained worldwide recognition, albeit not universal acceptance.

In books and articles, he grew his seed of psychoanalysis—"the assumption that there are unconscious mental processes, the recognition of the theory of repression and resistance, the appreciation of the importance of sexuality and of the Oedipus complex [where a young boy hates, or desires to eliminate his father and have sex with his mother]."

The clash between the conscious and unconscious often leads to mental anguish. The unconscious determines behavior and perception owing to drives and can be found in, among other areas, dreams, mannerisms, and Freudian slips. The awareness of such hitherto unconscious thoughts triggers resistance and repression, the result of which is suffering. In psychoanalytic sessions, the patient relates dreams, fantasies, and memories (the unconscious), from which the doctor can relate to the mental health issues of which the patient complains. By confronting resistance and repression, patients can better understand themselves.

Freud treated, and wrote on, a host of psychological subjects—of how social restrictions on unconscious sexual desires led to anxiety and physical problems; sexual masochism; narcissism; self-destructive behavior; the father complex; identification with a group influencing individual behavior; and the Oedipus complex at the center of phobias. He developed concepts of the id (seeking pleasure), superego (seeking perfection), and ego (the mediator between the two—one's impulses vs. inhibitions) and the anxieties created due to unresolved conflicts between the id and superego.

Along the way, he opined that the only objectionable aspect of male homosexuality existed in cruel laws making its practice illegal. Conversely, he thought lesbianism a gateway to mental illness (despite his beloved youngest daughter Anna, an innovative and renowned child psychoanalyst in her own right, who remained with her partner Dorothy Burlingham for over a half a century). Freud also championed the use of cocaine, legal at the time, to treat various ailments. When a friend, Ernst von Fleischl-Marxow, a noted doctor, physiologist, and inventor, suffered a serious injury and great pain, he became addicted to morphine and heroin. Freud counseled cocaine as a treatment option, resulting in Fleischl-Marxow becoming addicted to it. Returning to morphine, he prematurely died at 45.

In 1925, Samuel Goodwyn of MGM offered Freud, "the greatest love specialist in the world," a sizable contract to consult on, and even write, scripts involving noted historical love stories, including Cleopatra and Mark Antony. Having no interest in either the movies or the United States, Freud declined.

Being Jewish, more secular than religious, near the end of his life Freud was forced to flee his beloved Austria when Germany annexed it in 1938. Other family members were not as fortunate as four of Freud's five sisters were later murdered in concentration camps. He moved to his new home in Hampstead, England, where he passed a year later at 83. Of the theories he espoused, some found acceptance, others rejection. He, though, along with a few colleagues and other influential thinkers, started the juggernaut, creating new attitudes on mental health and treatment, and indeed on human thought processes in general. While his death marked an end to his life, his influence remains to this day.

15

Germany Pummels Poland as Mr. Smith Goes to Washington

The War in October

"The Phoney War."

Needless to say, the war dominated the news in October as it would for the months and years that followed. On the first day of October, Winston Churchill—still on the outside looking in, as Neville Chamberlain continued his reign as Prime Minister—famously observed Russia to be "a riddle wrapped in a mystery inside an enigma." He continued on and elaborated upon the riddle, "but perhaps there is a key. That key is Russian national interest."

And with self-interest at its center, Russia wrapped up its conflict with Japan and then declared war on Poland in mid-September. Three weeks later Poland was no more, split between Germany and Russia. Immediately, both countries imposed a brutal will over the newly conquered nation and its soon to be terrorized citizens.

The day Russia entered the war, German submarine U-29 torpedoed the HMS *Courageous*, which sunk in twenty minutes. Having the dubious distinction of being the first major warship sunk in World War II, 519 British sailors died, including its captain. The head of all German U-boats, Karl Donitz, deemed the action, "a wonderful success," that led to widespread elation in Germany. Donitz, a Hitler clone, would briefly lead Germany after Hitler committed suicide in 1945.

On October 8, Germany created the first Jewish ghetto in Poland. By the 25th, all Polish Jews were required to wear a yellow star on their clothing. One day later, those between the ages of 14 and 60 were essentially made slaves, ordered to engage in forced labor. Meanwhile, under the guidance of

Adolph Eichmann, Jews from Austria and Czechoslovakia were deported to Poland. By the end of the month, Britain released a report on concentration camps being built in Europe to house Jews and anti-Nazis.

After conquering Poland, Hitler offered to make peace with England and France, both of which, knowing of the duplicity of past offers, rebuffed the initiative as noted by PM Neville Chamberlain: "Past experience has shown that no reliance can be placed upon the promises of the present German Government." Despite the refusal of the Allies to engage in peace talks they did equally little on the battlefield, so much so that United States Senator William Borah opined that "There is something phoney about this war." He continued: "You would think that Britain and France would do what they are going to do now while Germany and Russia are still busy in the East, instead of waiting until they have cleaned up the eastern business." Indeed, as German General Alfred Jodl later stated, "during the Polish campaign, the approximately 110 French and British divisions in the West were held completely inactive against the 23 German divisions." Another general added to the assessment, recognizing that if the French had attacked in September when the war started, the German army "could only have held out for one or two weeks."

As it would turn out, the phoney war essentially lasted for eight months, ending when Germany attacked France and the low countries in May. This is not to say that there was no fighting at all. Indeed, early on the French launched the Saar Offensive, attacking Germany and initially making some progress, seizing approximately 5 miles of territory and a dozen or so villages. The offensive quickly fizzled, however, due to an outdated World War I strategy; a fear that Germany, thought to be militarily superior, would bomb Allied cities and towns; and the quick fall of Poland that allowed Germany to regroup and relocate its military forces. The French army quickly retreated to what it perceived to be the safety of the Maginot Line.

Far more action occurred on the waters where German U-boats continued to sow carnage. On October 14, U-47 sunk the British battleship HMS *Royal Oak*, resulting in 833 deaths, including that of a rear admiral. A month earlier, submarine U-30 sunk a passenger liner, the SS *Athenia* heading to Canada. The passengers included citizens, many of whom were women and children, from the US (311), Canada (469), and England (72) along with 315 crew members. Five hundred were Jewish refugees. Thanks to the safety features installed after the tragic sinking of the *Titanic* decades before, most survived the attack and were rescued by ships in the area, including the *Southern Cross* (a yacht once owned by Howard Hughes) and an American cargo ship, the *City of Flint*, soon to figure in a second incident. Despite the heroic and speedy efforts taken, 117 people died.

Realizing the sinking would inflame American sentiments, Germany denied its involvement. Instead, it blamed the incident on the First Lord of the Admiralty, Winston Churchill, who, it alleged, wished to turn public opinion against Germany. The lie was believed by some, including former President Herbert Hoover ("It is such poor tactics that I cannot believe that even the clumsy Germans would do such a thing.") and North Carolina's Democratic Senator Robert Rice Reynolds, an ardent isolationist and antisemite ("[England had a motive] to infuriate the American people."). Still, though, the majority of Americans held Germany accountable for the vile act.

On October 9, the *City of Flint* found itself on the receiving end of Nazi aggression. Carrying various items, including tractors, grain, fruit, leather, and wax, and headed to England, it was intercepted by a German ship. Taken to various locations as a prize of war, the act was condemned by the United States and the American public, which closely followed what turned out to be a 116-day long ordeal, which ended when the ship returned home. It was not so lucky on January 23, 1943, when it was sunk by German submarine U-575.

A failure of the German navy, perhaps its most significant, came on October 30, when the U-56 fired at the HMS *Nelson* off Orkney. None of the three torpedoes exploded, much to the relief of Winston Churchill, who was aboard the vessel.

While the American press closely reported, and the American public closely followed, news emanating from Europe, the war remained in the cloudy distance, thousands of miles away. While President Roosevelt essentially knew what was coming and what he had to do, the public was not yet ready to commit itself to active involvement. Indeed, the opposite was true. Despite a fascination with the growing tragedy from afar, Americans went on living their often routine, if not mundane, daily lives.

The New York City Municipal Airport Opens

"Name it LaGuardia Airport."

On October 15, 1939, the New York City Municipal Airport opened in Queens, with 325,000 people attending the festivities. Mayor La Guardia and the other speakers that day referred to it by a far more popular name, the North Beach Airport. It would be renamed again years later, this time to the man responsible for its creation.

Years earlier, in 1886, when the area stood barren, William Steinway, of the renowned Steinway & Sons piano company, developed the Bowery

Bay Beach, later called North Beach, into a summer resort complete with a bathing pavilion, lawns, a boathouse, and later the Gala Amusement Park. Compared to Brooklyn's Coney Island, the German-influenced area fell into disfavor with World War I, provoking antipathy to anyone and anything associated with Germany. With prohibition, a growing pollution problem, and the downside of industrial progress, the park closed in the 1920s.

Shortly thereafter, in 1929, nodding to a growing demand, a small private seaplane base opened. One year later it expanded and came to be called the Glenn H. Curtiss Airport, after a pioneer in aviation. While the facility catered to an expanding clientele, it was still too small to compete with New Jersey's Newark Airport, which handled the bulk of airline traffic, much to the chagrin of proud New Yorkers who gnashed their teeth at the lost business and prestige.

The mayoral election of 1934 changed all of that with the election of Fiorello La Guardia, who, as earlier noted, created many forward-looking and beneficial programs and projects, including the World's Fair. A man of integrity and vision, along with dashes of occasional belligerence and irascibility, he seemed to be everywhere at once. At the outbreak of World War I he left, but did not resign from, Congress and enlisted. Eschewing a cushy and safe job, he learned to fly and flew missions out of Italy. He was so successful that he was awarded medals for his valor. When some constituents signed a petition to remove him from Congress due to his absence, La Guardia retorted, "You might say that if any signers of the petition will take my seat in a Caproni bi plane, I shall be glad to resume my upholstered seat in the House."

Sadly, he had his share of tragedy. His first-born daughter Fioretta, sickly at birth, passed within a year. Six months later, in November 1921, his wife, Thea Almerigotti, succumbed to tuberculosis. Devastated and suffering, Fiorello took time off and travelled. Upon his return, he buried himself in his work.

Throughout his ordeal one steady rock anchored him. When a teenaged Maria Fisher started working for Fiorello, she never left, following him as he ascended the political ladder. When he went off to fight, Marie dealt with his constituents; when Fioretta and Thea grew ill, Marie took care of their home; when they died, she spoke for the family; when he ran for office she was front and center, ensuring the campaign ran smoothly. Calm and cool, she contrasted with the more volatile Fiorello, who recognized he could not live without her. When they married in 1929 she stopped working, to which La Guardia observed, "[I] lost a good secretary and gained a bum cook." They adopted two children, including the niece of his first wife.

Given his knowledge of flying from his war days, and the belief that New York needed a major airport, La Guardia, upon assuming office, quickly put his ideas into motion. After some setbacks, expanding the small North Beach Airport came into focus. With support from the WPA and others, a garbage dump on Rikers Island provided the landfill. In 1937, it started being moved to the waters and land surrounding Queens. Over the next two years the city spent over $20 million developing 550 acres. Looking to the future, La Guardia ensured that extra land was given to the airlines, including large and available hangars at affordable prices. In 1939, American Airlines opened the first private airline club in the world, calling it the Admirals Club.

Success immediately followed, with the new facility heralded as not only an aviation marvel but a tourist one as well, with people flocking in to watch planes take off and land. Nearly a million dollars came in annually from admission and parking fees, concessions, and other non-travel-related proceeds. *Time* magazine called it "the most pretentious land and seaplane base in the world," while the *New York Times* labelled it "the world's greatest airport."

During the dedication ceremony three skywriters flew overhead spelling out a mile-high message, "Name it LaGuardia Airport." Three months before La Guardia's death in 1947, it was.

Mr. Smith Goes to Washington

"[O]ne of the most disgraceful things I have ever seen."

On October 17, 1939, Columbia's *Mr. Smith Goes to Washington*, a dramedy about political corruption in the United States Senate, starring Jean Arthur, Jimmy Stewart, Claude Rains, and Thomas Mitchell among others, premiered in Washington, D.C. Thought to be a coup in arranging to open in Washington with 45 senators, 250 congressmen, justices, military personnel, and other luminaries joining 4,000 fellow attendees, it turned out to be a disaster. A movie depicting senators as corrupt, and members of the press as conniving bunglers is rarely a good idea when showing the movie to actual reporters and senators, many of whom shouted their disapproval before stomping out, joining nearly half the audience.

Condemnation came swiftly. Senator Alben Barkley, a liberal democrat from Kentucky, called the picture "a grotesque distortion of the way the Senate is run, as grotesque as anything I have ever seen." A fellow senator noted that "I speak for the whole body. The vote is 'no' and it is 96–0." Even Ambassador Joe Kennedy, serving in England, voiced his outrage from afar, wiring Will Hays, the head of the Production Code:

> I have just seen Mr. Smith Goes to Washington. STOP. I consider this one of the most disgraceful things I have ever seen done to our country. STOP. To permit this film to be shown in foreign countries and to give people the impression that anything like this could happen in the United States Senate is to me nothing short of criminal. STOP. I am sending a copy of this wire to the President of the United States.

The Production Code folks were already aware of the movie. Prior to even starting production, the studio sent the book, *The Gentleman from Montana*, upon which the script would be written, to Hays for review. What came back was problematic, the commission agreeing with the later audience unease. "The generally unflattering portrayal of our system of government might well lead to such a picture being considered here and, more particularly, abroad as a covert attack on the democratic form of government."

Notwithstanding the negativity, Columbia went forward. When the script was completed and again sent to the commission, its tune strangely changed, now calling it "a good yarn that will do a great deal of good for all those who see it [stressing] the importance of democracy."

The pessimists among us might say the commission's reversal came as the result of some nefarious backdoor back door dealing, ironically similar to those depicted in the movie, while we optimists might view the change of heart as demonstrating the earnestness and competence of all those involved. With the preview meeting substantial political blowback, studio head Harry Cohn and producer/director Frank Capra had a quandary on their hands. Some advised shelving the movie completely, fearful of a vindictive Congress passing harmful legislation, while others, confident in the film's quality, thought it prudent to release it as scheduled and letting the public decide its worth.

After much angst and argument the decision came—show the movie. Glowing reviews and public enthusiasm led to eleven Academy Award nominations. And contra to the concerns of the naysayers, the film garnered enthusiastic applause from overseas. Given the man responsible—Frank Capra—it came as no surprise.

Capra, the personification of the American dream, emigrated from Italy with his family to California at the age of 5. As their ship passed the Statue of Liberty, Capra's father emotionally and excitedly verbalized the thoughts of many immigrants, "Look at that! That's the greatest light since the star of Bethlehem! That's the light of freedom! Remember that!"

Capra worked many jobs, went to Caltech where he studied chemical engineering, and joined the military during World War I. Later, living in San Francisco and barely getting by, he happened upon a notice in a newspaper about a new movie studio opening in the area. Lacking any experience but awash with confidence and chutzpah, he called the studio head, fabricated a Hollywood background, and found a job. With talent and drive came success and soon he relocated to the movie capital where he continued to thrive, writing many "Our Gang" episodes along with other comedic short films as he continued to hone his notable skills. A big break awaited and it came via Columbia's vile boss, Harry Cohn.

Capra's first meeting with Cohn—apocryphal perhaps but certainly accurate in a general sense—came with the youngster entering the boss's office and coming face to face (or perhaps another part of one's anatomy) of casting couch ogre Cohn having sex with one of his young starlets. Cohn casually waved him away and told him to return shortly.

Capra—who wanted to write and direct—and Cohn—who wanted to make money and gain respect—quickly joined forces, notwithstanding the inevitability of their future divorce. Over the span of a decade both got what they craved, making movie history along the way. The trip though was rocky and bumpy, Capra referring to Cohn as a monster and Cohn calling Capra a dago.

Initially making silent movies, Capra quickly grasped, unlike many, the future of talkies upon the release of *The Jazz Singer*. Uniquely positioned, given his college education in engineering and his movie experience, Capra was off and running, making both talkies and money. In 1933, he directed *Lady for a Day*, which both the public and critics loved. Nominated for four Academy Awards, Capra was confident of winning Best Director. The ceremony, hosted by his friend Will Rogers, droned on until the seminal moment.

> [A]nd the award for best director of the year is ... the envelop please ... yes, here it is. Well, well, well, what do you know! I've watched this young man for a long time ... saw him come up from the bottom, and I mean the bottom. It couldn't happen to a nicer guy. Come up and get it, Frank!

Capra and his cohorts jumped for joy. As Capra raced to claim his well-deserved award Rogers continued. "Frank Lloyd!"

Being resilient, if not partially humiliated, Capra turned to his next project, *Night Bus*, on which he stumbled out of the gate. First he couldn't get any of the many actresses he wanted, until Claudette Colbert finally agreed to take the role. Then he encountered problems with the male lead, as Clark Gable was working for another studio. Finally, deals and concessions were made, the pieces came together, the title was changed, and *It Happened One Night* made movie history, sweeping the 1934 Oscars, winning, for the first time ever, all of the major Best Awards—Picture, Actor, Actress ("I owe Frank Capra for this!"), and, finally and fairly, Director.

So popular was Capra that in another unprecedented move his name was moved, going above the title of his movies: "Frank Capra's *Mr. Deeds Goes to Town*" (1936) (winning Best Director; nominated for Best Picture); "Frank Capra's *Lost Horizon*" (1937) (nominated for Best Picture); and "Frank Capra's *You Can't Take It with You*" (1938) (winning both Best Director and Best Picture).

Capra's seemingly unparalleled successes continued with *Mr. Smith Goes to Washington*, the story of a country bumpkin, Jefferson Smith, a youth Ranger Scout leader from an unnamed state who finds himself selected to fill the seat of a recently deceased senator. Governor Hubert "Happy" Hopper is torn between naming Horace Miller, the unpopular stooge of corrupt boss Jim Taylor, and Smith, a highly popular youth leader played by Jimmy Stewart. To decide, Happy flips a coin that lands on its edge against a newspaper article featuring Smith. Happy decides to go with him, reasoning that it will satisfy both the public and Taylor who would easily manipulate him.

The highly respected senior Senator Joseph Paine, played by the distinguished and eloquent Claude Rains, takes the naïve and overwhelmed Smith under his wing, sharing tales of a once close relationship with Smith's late father. Little does Smith suspect that Paine has been corrupted and is in the middle of a dirty lucrative land deal with Taylor involving the construction of a dam that would greatly enrich their holdings.

Smith travels to Washington, where he spontaneously embarks on a tour of the capitol. In awe of all the sights, he finds reverence when he sees a young boy reading the words on the Lincoln Memorial to his vision-impaired father. Capra actually witnessed this when touring Washington in preparation for making the movie and was so taken that he added the scene.

The task of keeping Smith in tow falls to his aide, the smart and attractive Clarissa Saunders, played by Jean Arthur. Her male friend, newspaperman "Diz" Moore (Thomas Mitchell), drinks too much, hungers for a woman he will never have, and like Clarissa has grown weary and cynical of the Washington ways.

Outside of Saunders's watchful eye, Jefferson is cornered by a gaggle of loud and overbearing reporters, who quickly tab him a country rube. Depressed, he turns to Senator Paine who recommends drafting a bill. Enthused by the prospect he returns to his office and with Saunders'sassistance works through the night on legislation to create a national boys' camp. The site he picks is the dam site. While Saunders knows of this, she says nothing as she is slowly drawn in by Jefferson's sincerity and earnestness.

When Jefferson brings his bill to the Senate, Paine realizes the conflict and in a pang of conscience tells Taylor he wants out. The boss does not take this lightly and threatens and cajoles Paine, who gives in. The next day Senator Paine rises and speaks against Jefferson's bill and falsely accuses the junior senator of owning the very land he seeks to sell to the government and produces falsified and forged documents in support of his allegation. Taylor's machine in their home state ratchets up a one-sided media offensive against Jefferson, accusing him of impropriety. The Senate moves to expel him.

A disillusioned Jefferson is fed up and ready to leave the hornet's nest of Washington when a now sympathetic, falling-in-love Saunders convinces him to filibuster the Appropriation bill containing the Paine-Taylor plan and defend himself against the scurrilous accusations. Jefferson rises to the occasion and for twenty-four hours, with Saunders supporting and coaching him from the gallery, pleads his case and exposes the graft of Paine and Taylor and their unholy and Un-American alliance. His words and pleas are not sent to his home state though, as Taylor has clamped down. The Ranger Scouts, upon hearing of the suppression, print their own papers and distribute them, only to be viciously attacked by Taylor's henchmen.

On the Senate floor, Paine dumps a pile of letters from their misguided home state constituents calling for Smith's ouster. Broken at the news, Smith, now hoarse and exhausted, attempts to soldier on, but collapses. Paine, overcome by guilt and remorse, rushes out of the chamber and attempts to shoot himself, only to be stopped by the gathering crowd around him. Thwarted, he quickly returns to the Senate floor where he confesses all.

Never-say-die resilience, the willingness of the little guy to fight for the truth against high odds and powerful foes, and just plain old-fashioned common decency resonated with the public. Capra himself later described it as:

> The more uncertain are the people of the world, the more their hard-won freedoms are scattered and lost in the winds of chance, the more they need a ringing statement of America's democratic ideals. The soul of our film would be anchored in Lincoln. Our Jefferson Smith would be a young Abe Lincoln, tailored to the rail-splitter's simplicity, compassion, ideals, humor, and unswerving moral courage under pressure.

And with that, what would be not only one of the highest grossing movies of 1939 but of the entire decade, *Mr. Smith Goes to Washington* achieved movie greatness.

16

Hitler Dodges a Bomb While Big Greenie Gets Clipped

Hitler Dodges a Bomb

"A man has to be lucky."

On November 8, 1939, Georg Elser planted a bomb near a platform on which Hitler was going to speak. When it exploded, eight people were killed and sixty-two wounded. Unfortunately, Hitler was not among them having left unexpectedly thirteen minutes earlier.

German-born Elser came into the world in 1903 to an alcoholic father and mother who married one year after Georg's birth. Five boys would join them over the years and were often cared for by Georg as his parents worked, his father in the timber industry, his mother on a farm. Georg was a good student and over the years worked a variety of jobs involving his hands: lathe operator, woodworker/carpenter, furniture maker, and clock worker. Along the way he moved about, roomed with a communist co-worker, and met a waitress who he impregnated. Separating from her, he could not afford support payments. For entertainment he played a variety of musical instruments including the accordion, bass, flute, and zither. Eventually he found work in an armament factory where he had access to detonators and fuses.

Although fairly apolitical, Elser leaned left, voting for the Communist Party which he felt most strongly favored his fellow workers. He disliked the Nazis and refused to listen to Hitler's broadcasts. He even eschewed the Nazi salute.

Fearing war and needless bloodshed, and wishing to improve the lot of ordinary Germans toiling away, he decided in the fall of 1938 that German leadership had to be removed. The only time they were all together, he learned, was at the annual November 8th anniversary of Munich's Beer Hall Putsch. He attended the 1938 festivities to get the lay of the land. Two days later, on November 10, the violence of Kristallnacht exploded, which probably incentivized his determination to act.

Throughout the following year he methodically planned his assault, surveying the hall and determining where best to place the bomb he was building to do optimum damage. At work, he slowly stole explosives and secreted them in his bedroom. Despite being fired after an altercation with a superior, he used his newfound free time to return to the beer hall to fine-tune his objective. He even took a camera with him and used the pictures taken to sketch out how to best proceed.

Temporarily finding another related job, he stole an arsenal. Knowing he only needed a few detonators, he took over a hundred as well as over a hundred blasting cartridges. "I knew two or three detonators were sufficient for my purposes, but I thought the surplus [would] increase the explosive effect." he later confessed. In July 1939 he went to a remote area and tested his prototypes. In August he returned to Munich, rented a room, and became a regular at the restaurant in the beer hall, staying late and hiding until it closed. Over the course of two months, he quietly and meticulously worked in darkened silence on the pillar in which the explosives would be placed, hollowing it out and adding sound insulation. In the morning, he snuck out as life returned to the area, carrying away the debris from the prior evening's work. During the day, he worked on what he hoped to be a powerful and fatal bomb. In early November he planted the explosives and returned a few days later to install the triggering device. After, he celebrated by going to a kiosk where he drank two cups of coffee.

On November 8, Hitler arrived with an army of dignitaries including Heinrich Himmler, Joseph Goebbels, Rudolph Hess, Reinhard Heydrich, Julius Streicher, and other high-ranking Nazis. The plan called for Hitler to speak for two hours, starting at 8:30. The bomb was set to go off midway through his speech.

All was set. Until there was a change of plan.

With the coming war with France, Hitler needed to return to Berlin. Ordinarily he would have flown but with fog predicted, travelling by train became the preferred option. When it was determined that a 9:30 departure was most prudent, Hitler moved the start time of his speech to 8:00 and decided to speak for only an hour.

Before an audience of 3,000 Hitler ranted, ending his talk at 9:07, and departing with his entourage. At 9:20 the bomb went off. The arena shook. Many of those who were slow in departing were blown apart.

When Hitler learned how close he came to death, he exclaimed, "A man has to be lucky." Soon though he changed his view to one of divine intervention, "Now I am completely at peace! My leaving the [beer hall] earlier than usual is proof to me that Providence wants me to reach my goal."

On the morning of the planned explosion Elser moved to escape, travelling first by train and then foot. Eighty feet from the Swiss border, two border guards intercepted him. With his pockets overflowing with incriminating evidence—suspicious at first, but deadly once the bomb went off—Elser was quickly identified as the culprit. Severely tortured, Elser confessed, but insisted, despite the beatings, that he had acted alone.

Hitler—who could not believe that a German would do him harm—and his propagandists insisted that the British were behind the murderous plot and desired a public trial to prove the allegation. Elser refused to implicate others. While the Gestapo marveled at the sophistication of the bomb's construction, its agents acted, as usual, brutally, and irrationally. They randomly murdered twenty-one Jews in a local concentration camp as retribution (despite Elser being Protestant) and withheld food from all of the imprisoned Jews for three days. They also interrogated and brutalized anyone remotely associated with Elser.

Elser was not immediately put to death; to the end, Hitler wished for a public trial. Instead, he was sent to a concentration camp where he surprisingly received preferential treatment, including a work area to make furniture and even visits to the camp's brothel. Such treatment later led to conspiracy theories that Elser was actually a Nazi, planted to support the theory that no force could kill Hitler, who knew of the bomb beforehand and thus left before its detonation.

A month before the end of World War II, Hitler, who assuredly had other things on his mind, ordered the murder of the man who tried to kill him. The Gestapo directive read in part:

> The question of our prisoner in special protective custody, [Elser], has also again been discussed at the highest level.... [I]t shall be pretended that [Elser] suffered fatal injuries [and be liquidated] as discreetly as possible. Please take steps that only a few people, who must be specially pledged to silence, hear about this.... After noting the contents and carrying out the orders contained in it, destroy this letter.

On April 9, 1945, Elser was shot, killed, and incinerated in the camp's crematorium. The war ended one month later.

The Venlo Incident

> "After a while it became boring to converse with such arrogant and foolish people."

On November 9, in a story worthy of John le Carré or Tom Clancy, two duped British agents were snatched by the Nazis in the parking lot of a quiet diner, the Café Backus. Located in Netherland's Venlo, a town by the German border, a Dutch agent was also killed. In the end the debacle would have wide-ranging consequences.

The British Players:

Born in 1885, Sigismund Payne Best looked the spy that he was. Tall, snobbish, regal and reflecting his upper-class education, he wore tweed suits, spats, a monocle, mustache, and an attitude. His mastery of four languages—English, German, French, and Dutch—made him a natural as an intelligence officer in Belgium during World War I, where he set up spy networks and worked with local resistance groups. Caught sleeping with the wife of a resistance fighter, he was sent back to London.

After the Great War, he returned to the Netherlands, married a Dutch painter, opened a British firm trading pharmaceutical products, and kept his hands and eyes in and on the intelligence pot. Living in a toney neighborhood of The Hague, he played golf at an upscale course and enjoyed excellent relations with Dutch royalty. With a new world war looming, in 1938 he eagerly joined the Z Organization, a new spy group running alongside that of MI6, Britain's Secret Intelligence Service (SIS).

Major Richard Henry Stevens came with less experience than Best, who was eight years his senior. Serving primarily as an Intelligence Officer in India, he also spoke several languages—Arabic, Malay, Hindustani, Greek, German, French, and Russian. Perhaps his superiors hoped that his past intelligence work would make up for his dearth of experience in European affairs. Named to head the Passport Control Office (PCO) in Britain's Dutch Embassy, in reality he was a high-ranking member of its SIS.

For the sake of Dutch neutrality, one of its nationals, Lieutenant Dirk Klop pretended to be British using the name Captain Coppens.

Admiral Hugh Sinclair, "C", was the head of MI6, and dying of cancer. Colonel Claude Majoribanks Dansey was the #2 man in MI6, who had earlier worked with his fellow fuddy duddy Best during World War I and recruited him to head up Holland's Z Organization. Other Z Organizations, set up throughout Europe and comprising mainly of English businessmen living and working in its cities, were created in case of an embassy being overrun or a PCO compromised, in which case Z would step in and fill the void.

In August 1939, Dansey, angling to replace Sinclair, foolishly ordered Best's Z Organization to merge with the MI6 PCO, thus negating Z's purpose. Unbeknownst to Dansey, Netherland's PCO had been totally compromised by Nazi counterintelligence, SD, short for Sicherheitsdienst. That its PCO was infiltrated should have come as no surprise given the ineptness of its leaders. One head, Major Dalton, embezzled funds and after being blackmailed by a double agent on his staff, shot himself. His successor got drunk at a social function, loudly outed Best as a spy, and threw up on a woman. A bungling Major Stevens, he of limited experience, fit right in. So thorough was German penetration that it secretly planted a camera that recorded every visitor to Stevens's office.

Sir Stewart Menzies was the new "C" who replaced Admiral Sinclair when he died on November 4, thus frustrating Dansey.

The German Team:

In 1933, Walter Schellenberg joined the German SS. A lawyer by trade, he hitched his wagon to Nazi higher-ups Heinrich Himmler and Reinhard Heydrich. Working counterintelligence, he headed up the SD operation against the British, calling himself Major Hauptman Schammel.

Dr. Franz Fischer, a trusted asset of the PCO, was in reality a German agent. Facing embezzlement charges in Germany, he fled to France where he contacted German operatives, offering to work for them by identifying German exiles. Soon sent to Holland, he convinced British intelligence that he had contacts within the German military hostile to Hitler.

Major Solms of the Luftwaffe, whose true name was Johannes Travaglio, served the Nazi regime as a German major in its Abwehr.

Alfred Naujocks was the creator and servant of fake incidents, first at Gleiwitz and then Venlo.

The Plot:

Just prior to the outbreak of war, Dansey learned of Dr. Fischer's contacts with disgruntled German generals and assigned Best to cultivate him. Best later wrote that he "had the damned fellow up to my office and spent a morning interrogating him." Perhaps as an after-the-fact justification for his later actions, Best wrote that he thought Fischer a German agent and recommended that he be lured to England and arrested. His suggestion was ignored.

With war now declared, appeaser Neville Chamberlain still sought a way out, notwithstanding his public exultations to the English people to fight. When he learned from the new head of MI6, Sir Stewart Menzies, that Best had channels to dissident German military members, Chamberlain pounced on the news. During his earlier Munich negotiations, Chamberlain heard about such internal discontents who wanted the Prime Minister to resist Hitler's demands. Chamberlain ignored their exultations. He was not about to make that mistake again.

The meetings between Best, Stevens, and Fischer progressed slowly, with Fischer finally offering to up the ante by putting them in contact with one involved in the plot, a Major Solms. Best met Solms in a hotel in Venlo and found him to be "a big, bluff, self-confident fellow, a Bavarian [who talked] as big as he looked." Solms told Best of "a big conspiracy to remove Hitler from power" but would not furnish any additional details as the ringleaders desired to deal directly with Best.

Solms questioned Best's authority to deal on behalf of the British government and wanted evidence of Best's power. To do so, Best was asked to have the BBC broadcast an agreed-upon news item during one of its programs, the German News Bulletin. When Heydrich heard the transmission, he jumped, knowing the British had fallen for the ruse. It was time to call in the head of the counterintelligence section, Walter Schellenberg, to seal the deal.

On October 20, Schellenberg sent two agents posing as disgruntled German officers—Captain von Seidlitz and Lieutenant Grosch—to meet with Best and Stevens in a house located in the city of Arnhem (later the locale of a military operation memorialized in the 1977 movie, *A Bridge Too Far*). Suspicious Dutch police intervened, only to be assuaged by a calming Dutch lieutenant, Dirk Klop, who had accompanied the British agents. While the meeting unceremoniously ended, it served as only a temporary roadblock as Best had been authorized to assure the Germans that if Hitler were deposed, peace would follow with Germany allowed to retain much of the territory taken prior to the Munich Conference.

Moving from Arnhem back to The Hague, essentially command and spy central for the nation, another meeting took place, this one on October 30. Once again, moving up the ladder of deception, Schellenberg, posing as Major Schammel, joined the negotiations along with Grosch and a Colonel Martini. The three had earlier been detained at the Dutch border but were released to Klop who was sent to retrieve them. Best eyed Schammel and saw a man with "a babyish sort of face, most of it ... obliterated by the numerous scars of those sabre cuts so dear to German students." Like Solms before him, Schammel demanded answers and assurances of peace from Best. After all, Schammel explained, "We are Germans and have to think of the interests of our own country first. Before we take any steps against Hitler we want to know whether England and France are ready to grant us peace which is both just and honourable." Before ending the meeting, the Germain trio were given a wireless radio to remain in touch and continue the negotiations, which as it turned out occurred on an almost daily basis.

Upon hearing what the Germans wanted, Chamberlain and his foreign secretary, Lord Halifax, dutifully sat down and composed a pacifying statement. While it might have proven satisfactory to Schammel, it first had to be presented to Chamberlain's cabinet. The proposal did not go well. Reflecting the feelings of the exasperated group, Lord of the Admiralty Winston Churchill damned it as not only dangerous but deceptive in misleading the very citizenry being publicly urged to sacrifice and fight. In the face of such opposition, Chamberlain retreated, drafting a new statement demanding Hitler's removal before proceeding any further.

On November 7, to address the alleged safety concerns of Schammel and Grosch, Klop arranged to gather closer to the border, just outside the city of Venlo in the Café Backus. There, Best and Stevens informed the two of Chamberlain's response. While short of German expectations, they promised to pass along the information to their "Chief," a general who would join the next meeting. Wishing to move along quickly, Schammel suggested meeting the next day where "secret papers" would be given to the British for safe keeping in case the plot against Hitler failed. From the British perspective, talks were progressing to action.

A day later, on November 8, again at the Café, only Schammel appeared, explaining that at the last minute Hitler had summoned the general to meet with him in Munich. As the claimed plot against Hitler was scheduled for Saturday, November 11, time was of the essence. Thus the decision to meet the next day, the 9th, at the same location, at 4:00 pm.

As Best slowly pulled into the quiet parking lot of the Café,

> a large open car [drove] up round the corner till our bumpers were touching. It seemed to be packed to overflowing with rough-looking men. Two were perched on top of the hood and were firing over our heads from sub-machine guns, others were standing up in the car and on the running-boards; all shouting and waving pistols. Four men jumped off almost before their car had stopped and rushed toward us shouting: "Hands up!"

Klop quickly responded, firing his pistol. Shot in the head, he soon died. Best and Stevens were hustled into Germany, prisoners of Alfred Naujocks's smooth and efficient operation.

Responding quickly to allegations of an unjustified attack in a neutral country, Goebbels justified the incursion on the grounds of English involvement on the assassination attempt on Hitler the night before. Additionally, he argued that Dutch neutrality was a myth given Klop's association with the British agents.

Hitler ordered Best and Stevens into Berlin for questioning and on November 21, falsely announced irrefutable proof that they had acted with Elser. Pictures of the three were plastered on the front pages of German newspapers with a trial promised. Perhaps with that in mind, the three were kept, isolated from one another, in the special prisoners' section of the same concentration camp. While Elser was ultimately murdered, Best and Stevens received a better outcome, surviving their years' long incarceration.

So complete the befuddlement of British intelligence that they continued for twenty-one days after the apprehension of their two agents to use the radio transmitter to continue communicating with those thought to be German rebels. In fact, they were dealing with the Gestapo, a point gleefully later reported by the German press. Himmler allegedly quipped, "After a while it became boring to converse with such arrogant and foolish people."

The aftermath of the debacle proved devastating. It didn't help that when apprehended Stevens foolishly carried a list of British agents, thus exposing them and temporarily crippling the spy network in Western Europe. Upon assuming power, Churchill revamped the intelligence community, turning it into a much more effective entity. Being burned in Venlo, Churchill refused to deal with those claiming to be German dissidents, which proved to be harmful as evidenced in the July Plot to kill Hitler in 1944, involving Claus von Stauffenberg. Hitler also used Klop and Dutch involvement as justification for invading their country in May 1940. From the British point of view, no good came from the Venlo Incident, arguably its greatest intelligence failure of the war.

Circular 14

> "I would rather stand with God and against man than with man and against God."

On November 11, the Portuguese government issued Circular 14 which restricted the granting of passports and visas. Knowing the horrors being suffered by fleeing refugees, Jews, and dissidents, a conscious-stricken Consul Aristides de Sousa Mendes ignored the order and illegally issued thousands of documents, thus saving a countless number of people. In the end, he paid a high price for his heroism.

Perhaps even at birth Mendes was destined to be different. Born on July 19, 1885, shortly after midnight, his older twin brother emerged shortly before, on July 18. From an aristocratic background he studied law, gaining his degree in 1908, the same year he wed his childhood sweetheart. Fourteen children came from the union, born in various countries as he worked in the foreign service and traveled the world. A bon vivant, he loved his family, country (the "land of dreams and poetry"), Catholic religion, and a good song along with a glass of aged wine accompanying a fine meal.

With Germany declaring war on its own Jews and others deemed unworthy, followed by its invasion of Poland, came a multitude of people desperately trying to escape. Mendes, stationed in Bordeaux, France, knew well of their peril, including the Polish scientists obliterated by Hitler, and the University of Prague students either killed or sent to concentration camps for protesting Nazi aggression. Portugal, with a population of just over 7.5 million people, feared the onslaught of refugees would undermine the stability of its economy and nation. With over 9,000 having already entered, often illegally, there seemed to be no letup. To stem the tide, the restrictive edict materialized. Fully aware of the future of those not being able to escape, Mendes, and others, quickly ignored it. While such disobedience of a clear-cut order jeopardized his career, he simply responded, "I'm saving innocent lives." Adding to what had to be enormous pressure, his mistress, Andrée Cibial, a flamboyant French musician twenty-three years his junior, announced during a church service that she was pregnant with his child.

The steady stream of refugees became a raging torrent when Germany invaded France, Belgium, the Netherlands, and Luxembourg on May 10, 1940, creating the largest mass exodus of European citizenry in modern history. Mendes, suffering "a moral crisis of incalculable proportions," was further exasperated when a very pregnant Cibial arrived at his consulate and made such a scene that she was arrested. Driven to despair, Mendes secreted himself in his room, turning to prayer for guidance and divine inspiration. He described his anguish in a letter to a son-in-law, writing "Here the situation is horrible and I am in bed because of a strong nervous breakdown."

When France surrendered in June, Mendes shook off his debilitating malaise, and as per one of his sons, "washed, shaved and got dressed ... strode out of his bedroom, flung open the door to the chancellery, and announced in a loud voice: 'From now on I'm giving everyone visas. There will be no more nationalities, races, or religions.'"

While some close advisers tried to dissuade him from a career-ending decision, he remained firm in his conviction. Declaring that, "I would rather stand with God and against man than with man and against God," he set up a soon-to-be-overwhelmed-visa-allowing-assembly-line, issuing hundreds in a week from his consul post. Still, though, it was not enough as thousands deluged him, further exhausting him in the process. Ignoring cablegrams from Lisbon to cease and desist, he ordered a subordinate in another consulate near the Spanish border to issue visas to all who applied. A neutral Spain, like a neutral Portugal, fearful that its status was being jeopardized, protested and soon all Mendes-issued visas were declared null and void.

Ordered to return to Portugal, Mendes did so—but ever so slowly, continuing to issue visas along the way. At one point, another son later shared that:

> As his diplomatic car reached the French border town of Hendaye, my father encountered a large group of stranded refugees for whom he had previously issued visa. Those people had been turned away because the Portuguese government had phoned the guards, commanding [them not to honor any visas signed by Mendes]. Ordering his driver to slow down, Father waved the group to follow him to a border checkpoint that had no telephones. In the official black limousine with its diplomatic license tags, Father led those refugees across the border toward freedom.

Upon returning to Portugal, Mendes was charged. In defense, he claimed that by "obeying the dictates of humanity" he acted to save both the innocent and eminent, "whose suffering was indescribable." Found to have disobeyed an order during service, he was essentially fired from his position and ostracized.

Allowed to practice law, he eked through, living mainly on what was essentially a small pension. A stroke in 1945 left him partially paralyzed and unable to work. In 1948, his wife died. A year later he married his mistress, who continued to cause him grief by clashing with his family and spending money they did not have. In 1954 he died in poverty, essentially alone.

After death and over the years justice slowly emerged with the world recognizing and honoring him for his heroic deeds. Among those he saved included the artist Salvador Dali and his wife Gala; Marcel Dalio (the croupier in the movie *Casablanca*) and his wife Madeleine Lebeau (the young woman infatuated with Bogart's Rick in the same movie); H.A. and Margret Rey, the authors of *Curious George*; Maurice de Rothschild; leaders of Luxembourg; and thousands more. In the end, he truly served God.

Big Greenie gets clipped

"I hope you guys are not forgetting me."

On November 22, Benjamin "Bugsy" Siegel, Whitey Krakow, and Frankie "aka Frank Russo, Frank Trucker, Jimmy the Wop, Mr. Gray, Mr. Fury" Carbo murdered fellow mobster Harry "Big Greenie" Greenberg in his Los Angeles driveway. The order earlier came from Louie Lepke Buchalter who didn't take kindly to Greenberg's threats to squawk if he wasn't paid to keep his mouth shut.

At the time he gave the order, Lepke was on the lam and whacking everyone who might testify against him and he didn't want to take a chance on Greenberg who was threatening to do something, talk to someone, if he wasn't given what he thought he was due, $5,000 in this case.

Greenberg was born in 1909 in Brooklyn, and like many similarly situated economically disadvantaged boys spent much time hanging out on the streets. In so doing he met such future crime luminaries Buchalter, Benjamin "Bugsy" Siegel, Charlie "Lucky" Luciano, Meyer Lansky, and a host of other up and coming criminals and murderers. Soon, Big Greenie was one of them, a thug used to break strikes, kill rival bootleggers, and convince others to do his bidding and that of his bosses.

In 1927, Joseph Lefkowitz, a 42-year-old con who neither drank nor smoked, convinced 17-year-old Greenberg and 18-year-old Irving Rubinzahl to murder friend and cohort Benjamin Goldstein. Four years earlier Lefkowitz and the dim-witted Goldstein had hatched an insurance scam, with Lefkowitz taking out two life insurance policies totaling $70,000 (worth approximately $1.2 million today) on Goldstein's life. To assuage suspicions, they waited some years before putting the plan into action. Goldstein would fake his drowning by falling out of a boat. Another boat would pick him up and put him on a ship to Honolulu. Lefkowitz would collect and later split the insurance proceeds. A straightforward and simple plot; devoid, however, of mobster logic. Why give away 50 percent of ill-gotten loot when you can keep it all?

Greenberg and Rubinzahl sat in the rowboat as a soon-to-be-dead Goldstein rowed away. When they got a good distance out, Goldstein, with a satchel containing four suits for his trip to Hawaii, stood up to change positions. Rubinzahl pushed him over and out, Greenberg rowed away, and Goldstein, who couldn't swim, vainly pleaded for help. Later that day, Lefkowitz paid Rubinzahl $250 and bought Greenberg a $27.50 suit.

When Goldberg's dead body washed ashore, a brief and successful police investigation ensued. Rubinzahl flipped after being promised a twenty-year

Sing-Sing prison sentence to a reduced charge if he testified against his two former partners. Lefkowitz, out of central casting for one looking guilty, was found guilty. Conversely, Greenberg, appearing docile, pleasant, and cooperative, with excellent legal representation, beat the rap.

Not coming remotely close to learning any lesson from his ordeal, Greenie celebrated by stealing $500 and a diamond ring from a gullible young woman. A year later he, along with a handful of others including Bugsy Siegel, were arrested while plotting how to deal with rival mobster Waxey Gordon.

With the heat coming down on Lepke, he ordered Greenberg to leave town, "or else." Wisely wishing to avoid the "or else," he fled to Montreal. As many criminals at the time did not save or wisely invest their money, Greenberg soon found himself running short on cash. Rather than simply wire and explain his predicament and ask for assistance, he instead sent a threatening missive. "I hope you guys are not forgetting me. You better not." The request did not go down well. As associate Joseph "Doc" Stacher observed, "We all liked Big Greenie, but this was disloyalty." Later he added, "Allie [Tick Tock] Tannenbaum was told to bump him off."

Perhaps Big Greenie realized the error of his request and fled Canada, staying at least one step ahead of a pursing Tick Tock. His luck ran out, however, when Siegel found him living in Los Angeles with his wife. Bugsy, a handsome and debonair sociopath, came west at the behest of the Mob to gain control of Los Angeles. He also moved from New York to escape mounting pressure from the police for his role in rubbing out some of Waxey Gordon's boys, the Fabrizzo brothers. Keeping with his affinity for killing brothers, he also hit rival loan sharks Louis "Pretty" and Joseph Amberg. With enemies on his tail, Siegel moved to sunny California.

Good at his job, Siegel soon learned the comings and goings of the thugs residing in the area and quickly established himself, earning massive amounts of money with his partners through bookmaking and gambling, drugs, and prostitution. He also ingratiated himself with the rich and the powerful, politicians and businessmen, and those in the movies, from studio heads to those who starred in their movies. He borrowed greedily, over $400,000, without any intention of ever repaying the loans, knowing no one would dare ask him to. He even went international, travelling to Italy with his lover, the Countess Dorothy di Frasso, a glamourous and partying American heiress, to pitch a new-fangled explosive to Italian dictator Mussolini. The countess was married to the Count Carlo Dentice di Frasso, who was active in Italy's social and political scenes; they led separate lives with him spending most of his time in Italy while his wife cavorted in America. Regardless, when the test of the device fizzled, Mussolini passed on the offer.

Not afraid to dirty his hands again, he gladly accepted the guns that Tick Tock brought from back east. Lepke had ordered the hit on Greenberg and Siegel was not one to turn down an assignment. He told his underling Whitey Krakow to drive to the local wise-guy hangout on the corner of Hollywood and Vine and find someone to clip a car for the hit. Among the boys there, Krakow found a visiting Sholem Bernstein and gave the job to him (one wonders whether, while in California, Sholem also got Big Gangy Cohen a Hollywood job). Being in unfamiliar surroundings, Bernstein initially demurred. A talk with some of his bosses changed his mind. A few days later he delivered an Oldsmobile—which Siegel deemed inadequate and ordered Bernstein to steal another. Bernstein listened quietly, left, and returned to New York. An enraged Siegel decided that after taking care of Greenberg, Bernstein was next. No one walks out on a job, especially one orchestrated by Ben Siegel. Siegel later even travelled to New York seeking permission from the bosses to kill Bernstein.

As it turned out, Bernstein skipped town to return to his beloved mother, who he just learned was dying. As murderer and future turncoat Abe "Kid Twist" Reles explained to the mob panel deciding Bernstein's fate:

> So Sholem does not even think about the contract. He don't think of nothing. He lams out of L.A. and hustles home to be with his mama when she checks out. He drives day and night. All he wants is to hold her hand. He is a good boy. And that, gentlemen, that is why Sholem left town. Not on account of ducking the contract. But on the account his mama is kicking off.

No mobster could resist a good mother tale. The request to hit Bernstein was rejected.

Greenberg was not so lucky. Siegel gathered his squad and drove to Big Greenie's house. There in the driveway, triggerman Carbo fired five shots into Big Greenie's head. While those holding lofty positions in the mob order hits, they don't personally carry them out. Bugsy was different though. He went along for the sport.

Tick Tock, who was driving the backup car, and Reles, who knew of the hit, flipped and soon Siegel, Carbo, and Krakow were charged with murder. Witnesses disappeared, Reles went out the window while under 24-7 police protection, Krakow was murdered, and Siegel and Carbo walked. From there Carbo became the underworld's Czar of Boxing and Siegel, with the aid of others, gave birth to modern day Las Vegas.

Russia invades Finland

> "[W]e have only to kick in the door and the whole rotten structure will come crashing down."

On November 30, 1939, Russia invaded Finland and started the Winter War, or more formally, the First Soviet-Finnish War. All thought the incursion would last a brief time; everyone, that is, but the Finns. The Soviets had nearly twice the number of soldiers, one hundred times the number of tanks, and nearly 4,000 more aircraft. Guided by Germany's Blitzkrieg strategy, Stalin thought he'd quickly overrun and overwhelm Finland. What he didn't take into account was a terrain far different than that surrounding Germany. Finland had few roads, many forests, little daylight, and debilitating cold challenging even to a nation used to it. The fight would last three bloody months, ending in March 1940 with Russia a marginal winner; the main victor being one that didn't even enter the fray, Germany.

As with Gleiwitz, Stalin needed a false excuse to invade and found it by Mainila, a Soviet town located on the border of Finland. There, on November 26, a guard post was shelled, killing four and injuring nine. Russia, which staged the attack, blamed Finland, and made several unacceptable demands. When Finland predictably rejected them, Stalin renounced past non-aggression pacts, severed diplomatic relations, and invaded.

Historically, hostilities between the two neighboring nations had never been very good. Finland had been controlled by Sweden until conquered in the Finnish War of 1809 by Alexander I of Russia. Finland entered the domain of Russia, where it remained until the Russian Revolution of 1917 at which point Finland disengaged itself, with Lenin's acquiescence. A brief civil war ensued between Finnish factions, conservative Whites vs. Socialist Reds. The former won and brutalized the Reds, creating unrest and uncertainty. A growing economy in the late 1930s smoothed over much of the hostilities. During the same time period relations between the two nations remained strained even with the 1920 Treaty of Tartu, which recognized their borders. Twelve years later they signed a non-aggression pact.

Stalin, emerging from the Great Purge of 1938, turned his attention to Finland, wishing to bring it back into its fold. Given a lengthy common border and the close proximity of Finland to Leningrad, Stalin wished to extend its territorial control to guard against an invasion by Germany. On October 5, Russian diplomats reached out to Finland about its concerns and requested either ceding or leasing some of its property. Finland considered the proposal in which Russia offered to exchange its own land that was double the size of the land Russia wanted in return. After much debate, the deal was rejected with a counter-offer, an exchange including the doubling of the distance from its nation to Leningrad, thus addressing Stalin's main concern. With the parties quibbling as to which lands were to be traded, the Finnish delegation, expecting the negotiations to continue after five weeks of talking, returned home and waited for the Soviet response. It came two weeks later with the shelling of Mainila.

Perhaps Stalin, after his successes in Khalkhin Gol and Poland, was tired of the back and forth and blinded by the belief that war with Finland would be a convincingly brief one easily won. Thus, on November 30, 450,000 Soviet troops poured into Finland and bombed its capital Helsinki, killing approximately a hundred civilians and leveling half that number of buildings. The Soviets denied, as they would throughout the conflict, targeting civilians, asserting that humanitarian aid was being dropped to aid a starving population. Diplomatically, the Finns asserted that as no declaration of war had been made, the Soviets were in violation of past pacts that they had signed. The League of Nations agreed and expelled the aggressors.

The initial Soviet advance proved to be disastrous, with heavy losses suffered. Despite being greatly outnumbered, the Finns had the benefit of a treacherous terrain hostile to movement, few roads, a skilled cross-country corps adept at skiing and moving quickly while dressed in white to mask its presence, an effective hit and run guerrilla strategy, dark and brutally cold weather, and inept Russian leadership brought on in part due to the decimation of the officer corps during Stalin's Purge. Initially the Russian soldiers wore olive drab uniforms which stood out against the white background during the day.

Even with these advantages, the Finns quickly withdrew to the defensive Mannerheim Line, which had been built for the very purpose of guarding against Russian incursion. Assembled in phases in the early 1920s and throughout the '30s, it was not yet complete and offered little protection in places. Despite this, both sides publicly lauded its effectiveness, comparing it to the thought-to-be impenetrable Maginot Line; the Soviets fibbing to cover up its ineptness and the Finns to bolster public opinion and confidence.

Still though, time was not on the side of an underdog that had neither an air force nor a navy to speak of, few if any anti-tank weapons, a decided disadvantage in artillery, and even a gross shortage of ammunition. Its courageous fighters quickly grew exhausted as the Soviets learned and adjusted, replaced ineffective officers, and threw in additional troops. At the start of an offensive in February, the invaders over the course of a single day hurled approximately a third of a million shells at the overwhelmed Finns.

The war ended in March with the Moscow Peace Treaty, which resulted in Finland losing approximately 9 percent of its land, 12 percent of its population, and 13 percent of its assets. It did, however, maintain its sovereignty. With little fighting in Europe during the Phoney War stage, the focus of many centered on the conflict, verbally supporting Finland but failing to provide essential and meaningful military aid.

Although it is difficult to ascertain with certainty, the Finns appeared to have suffered approximately 70,000 troops either killed, wounded, missing, or captured with 3,000 or more civilians also killed or wounded. Conversely, Russia suffered far greater casualties, between 126,000–168,000 dead or missing and 188,000–208,000 wounded or sick with over 5,500 captured.

Despite his "victory", Stalin suffered a military humiliation, witnessed by all. Britain and France, while muttering about what to do, did nothing, proving an inability to effectively work together. The League of Nations, formed to avoid conflict, continued to fail. Only Germany, looking on and not having to do much of anything, emerged the clear winner, basking in the ineptness of its enemies. It reached out to Finland and improved relations, which would come in handy. With Stalin exposed, Hitler grew more confident with his plans to move eastward. As he would later say, "we have only to kick in the door [of Russia] and the whole rotten structure will come crashing down."

And on June 22, 1941, Hitler did just that, invading Russia. Three days later Finland joined Germany, starting the Second Soviet-Finnish War, also known as the Continuation War. Once again it would lose, this time more convincingly.

17

"Frankly my dear, I don't give a hoot"

The Gettysburg Address of Heisman Award Speeches

"So hold your hats."

On December 6, 1939, Iowa's Nile Kinnick, who won college football's highest honor, the Heisman Trophy the week before, gave his acceptance speech in New York City's Downtown Athletic Club. After the traditional thanks to all those responsible for his athletic success, he veered into unchartered territory:

> Finally, if you'll permit me, I'd like to make a comment which in my mind is indicative perhaps of the greater significance of football, and sports emphasis in general in this country, and that is this; I thank God I was warring on the gridirons of the Midwest and not on the battlefields of Europe. I can speak confidently and positively that the players of this country would much more, much rather struggle and fight to win the Heisman award than the Croix de Guerre.

In 1943, the greatest college athlete/scholar of not only the Midwest but all America died when the plane he was flying crashed.

Nile, born in 1918 in Adel, Iowa, was the oldest of three boys to loving parents who stressed education and hard work. At an early age he worked, went to school, played sports, and engaged in stimulating talks over the dinner table with his family. His extended family made impressions wherever and whenever they lived. His grandfather served as the governor of Iowa from 1913–1917.

In his junior year in high school in Iowa, Nile played football, basketball, and baseball, leading his teams to unbounded success. Due to the Depression, his father took a job in Nebraska, where Nile entered his senior year and again demonstrated his athletic dominance. In both football and basketball he was named 1st Team All-State. In baseball he caught and helped lead his team to the city championship; when he was younger he caught for legendary future Hall of Fame pitcher Bob Feller. Despite his time-consuming commitments to different sports teams, he maintained a straight A average and participated in plays and oratory contests. Humble, if not shy, he was, as might be expected, immensely popular with his classmates.

After high school, he spent part of the summer on a road trip with his brother Ben, visiting various sites out west and occasionally sleeping under the stars. When it was time to attend a college he considered the University of Minnesota which at the time was, along with Notre Dame, a powerhouse in football. He chose instead lowly Iowa, a team at the bottom, achieving little. As Nile's high school coach observed, "Kinnick was determined to go to some school that was down.... He didn't want Minnesota because they were on top.... He finally went to Iowa as he figured they were at their lowest ebb." In his freshman year, he again played three sports.

Despite Kinnick's best efforts, the football team remained mediocre. In 1937, his sophomore year, his team won only one game. Nonetheless, Kinnick was named first team All-Big Ten and third team All-American. He also led the nation in punting. Basketball followed, with Kinnick becoming the Big-Ten's fifteenth leading scorer. In 1938, he sustained a severe ankle injury which nagged him the entire year. Despite that, he was named honorable mention All-Big Ten. Along the way he dropped baseball and then basketball as they interfered with his studies.

With a new coach, Eddie Anderson, arriving in 1939, Kinnick entered his senior year with an unbending will to excel. "For three years, nay for fifteen years, I have been preparing for this last year of football. I anticipate the roughest, toughest all-around back yet to hit this conference.... I'm looking forward to showing Anderson what a real football player looks like—so hold your hats."

And that he did, as a not-large 5 feet 8 inches and 170 lbs. The 1939 newly dubbed "Ironmen" developed into one of the greatest football teams in Iowa history. And Kinnick, as predicted, led the way. The team finished ranked ninth in the nation, compiling a 6-1-1 record. Nile threw for eleven touchdowns and 638 yards on only thirty-one pass attempts, accounted for sixteen of the nineteen touchdowns scored, played 402 minutes out of a possible 420, and set fourteen school records, many of which still stand today. He won nearly every major collegiate award, often by a wide, if not unanimous, margin. On November 28, he won college football's greatest honor, the Heisman Trophy.

His speech at the award ceremony was met with thunderous applause. As one scribe wrote, "You realized the ovation wasn't alone for Nile Kinnick, the outstanding college football player of the year. It was also for Nile Kinnick, typifying everything admirable in American youth." Another wrote that Nile's comments "tackled Demosthenes and threw Cicero for a 15-yard loss."

That same year, Kinnick graduated with a 3.4 GPA with a degree in economics. Honored, he was named, with thirty others, to that year's Phi Beta Kappa class, the oldest and most prestigious academic award in America. He was also elected class president and gave the commencement address. In the (at the time) annual post-season, college football All-Star game against the champion NFL Green Bay Packers, Kinnick scored two touchdowns and kicked four extra points in a losing effort. The collegians scored four times with Kinnick on the field; when he sat, they gained but a single first down.

Eschewing offers to play professional football, he instead opted for law school, once again at Iowa. After his first year, he was third in his class. He also served as an assistant football coach. Demonstrating his gift of oratory and perhaps eying a future in politics, he introduced and spoke on behalf of Wendell Willkie, the 1940 Republican presidential candidate facing FDR:

> When the members of any nation have come to regard their country as nothing more than the plot of ground on which they reside, and their government as a mere organization for providing police or contracting treaties; when they have ceased to entertain any warmer feelings for one another ..., the moral dissolution of that nation is at hand.

Three days before Pearl Harbor, Kinnick left law school and enlisted in the navy, explaining:

> There is no reason in the world why we shouldn't fight for the preservation of a chance to live freely, no reason why we shouldn't suffer to uphold that which we want to endure. May God give me the courage to do my duty and not falter... Every man whom I've admired in history has willingly and courageously served in his country's armed forces in times of danger. It is not only a duty but an honor to follow their example the best I know how. May God give me the courage and ability to so conduct myself in every situation that my country, my family, and my friends will be proud of me.

On June 2, 1943, Kinnick perished. He was five weeks short of his 25th birthday.

The Battle of the River Plate

"There's the fucking *Scheer*! Open fire at her!"

On December 13, the Battle of the River Plate, the only clash to occur in South America, started with Germany's heavy cruiser *Admiral Graf Spee* battling Britain's counterpart cruiser, the *Exeter*, and two smaller vessels, the *Ajax* and *Achilles* (of the New Zealand Division), in the first naval battle of World War II. Although the fronts were relatively quiet during the Phoney War, five days later, on December 18th, the first air battle occurred at the Battle of Heligoland Bight. Both encounters would be breathlessly covered on the front pages of the *New York Times* and other papers throughout the world. After the war, streets and towns in various countries were named for some of the people and ships who fought in the famed River Plate sea battle. In 1956, a movie about it came out.

At the start of the war, 45-year-old Captain Hans Langsdorff commanded the *Graf Spee* with an assignment of taking down merchant vessels, which proved highly successful, sinking eight merchant vessels and one oil tanker. To accomplish its goal, concealment and deception were utilized to keep the Allies confused and out of sync. Langsdorff excelled at using wood, canvas, and paint to disguise his vessel, sometimes making it look like its sister ship, the *Admiral Scheer*. Other times, he flew an Allied or neutral flag when approaching his unsuspecting prey, and then, as per international law, switching to the Nazi insignia prior to opening fire. The directions he and others received from Erich Raeder, the head of the Kriegsmarine, was to attack essentially defenseless merchant vessels, hit them quickly and then flee, avoid combat with Allied ships, and retreat to neutral ports only if absolutely necessary. Under no circumstances were the Allies to take control of the ship: "Rather death with honour than strike the Flag." Raeder also gave his commanders wide latitude in deciding how, when, and where to strike.

Langsdorff proved adept at carrying out his mission. At times so rapid the strike that set upon vessels did not have time to destroy confidential books and orders, thus providing valuable information as to the whereabouts of Allied ships in the area. A professional navy man, preferring the naval salute to the Nazi one, Langsdorff did not wish to take human life if at all possible. Thus, as per his orders, a merchant ship would be swiftly set upon, shots fired if need be, and overrun with *Graf Spee* crew boarding, taking control, and ascertaining the merchandise being transported. The seamen of the seized ship were taken off, along with any valuable cargo. The vessel was then sunk. Sometimes the sinking proved difficult as was the case with the *Doric Star*, which survived demolition charges and then bombardment, before finally succumbing to torpedoes. Often, Langsdorff congratulated those he captured for their gallantry. At some point the prisoners were handed over to other German ships for internment.

In the face of over 50,000 tons of goods taken—sugar, grain, gas and kerosene, meat and dairy, maize, tea, etc.—Allied action was mandated. Against this backdrop and needing to protect the very vessels that supplied the lifeblood of its island nation, Britain, after reinstituting the vigorous Winston Churchill as the First Lord of the Admiralty, assembled naval groups to take out those that threatened it. It was no easy task, given the vastness of the ocean. Guessing that the enemy might strike next in the heavily travelled and target-rich River Plate area between Argentina and Uruguay, a force was sent there. On the 13th, the combatants converged.

Leading the Allied trio of ships was the 51-year-old Henry Harwood, who was known for his intelligence, judgment, and meticulous preparation, as well as his strategy of coming at its enemy in different directions to force him to divide his firepower or focus on a single target rather than two or more. Thus, the *Exeter* came from the northwest while the *Ajax*, which carried Harwood, and *Achilles* approached from the northeast. As they closed, the Captain of the *Exeter*, understandably confusing the disguised enemy vessel, excitedly yelled, "There's the fucking Scheer! Open fire at her!"

With that, the battle. Fire exchanged. In the end, seventy Allied deaths (twenty-eight wounded) with thirty-six Germans killed (sixty wounded). Like two heavyweight boxers at the end of a particularly grueling bout, both the *Exeter* and *Graf Spee* suffered debilitating damages; the lighter vessels experienced moderate ones. As with many campaigns, the knowledge at the time of the fight is often at odds with the reality of the situation. Long after the encounter, Captain Parry of the *Achilles* observed, "To this day I do not know why the *Admiral Graf Spee* did not dispose of us in the *Ajax* and *Achilles* as soon as she had finished with the *Exeter*." That she didn't resulted in a British victory with the heavily damaged *Graf Spee* limping into the neutral port of Montevideo in Uruguay.

International law limited the brief time that a belligerent ship could remain in a neutral country, thus handcuffing Langsdorff's options. He did, however, order the release of sixty-one English merchant seamen who had earlier been captured, including Captain Patrick Dove, whose merchant ship, the *African Shell*, was sunk on November 15. During the month the two officers were together they developed a respect, if not a surprisingly close rapport, so much so that when the dead seamen of the *Graf Spee* were buried in a nearby German cemetery, Dove appeared and laid a wreath "To the Memory of the brave men of the sea from their comrades of the British Merchant Service."

As the *Graf Spee* licked its wounds, its captain sought guidance from Berlin as to what to do. The reply received proved unsurprising and unhelpful—don't stay in Uruguay and don't allow the ship to fall into enemy hands. Fatally compounding the advice was the acceptance of Allied propaganda that a large fleet awaited the departure of the severely wounded and limited German ship, waiting to obliterate it. In fact, no such armada existed. On the 17th, thinking one did and deciding to save his thousand-plus crew, he ordered the *Graf Spee* to slowly depart Uruguay, witnessed by thousands of locals who had gathered as if at a major sporting event, not knowing how the event would play out; would the *Graf Spee* battle it out or make a mad dash out of harm's way? As it sailed to the border, Langsdorff told his sailors to disembark onto waiting transports which then delivered them to three Argentine ships. He then ordered the ship scuttled. It sank where it remains today.

With Hitler infuriated at the turn of events—that Langsdorff had disobeyed orders by engaging the enemy in the first place, and when cornered he did not fight to the finish—the Allies celebrated its victory with Harwood knighted and promoted to rear admiral.

The German crew were interned in Buenos Aires and later moved to different locations. At the war's end, many decided to remain in what had been confinement but turned into home. As for Langsdorff, he sat in his room three days after the *Graf Spee* went down and wrote a series of letters. One went to the German Ambassador, recognizing that "a captain with a sense of honour cannot separate his own fate from that of his ship," and pledging his "firm faith in the cause and the future of the nation and of my Führer." Another to his parents, and a third to his wife, telling her "to be proud in her grief." He then placed himself on the flag of the ship he once commanded, took out a pistol, and killed himself.

Gone With the Wind

"Frankly my dear, I don't give a hoot."

On December 15, 1939, *Gone With the Wind* premiers at Loew's Grand Theater in Atlanta. At approximately four hours it remains the longest and most expensive movie to date. It is also one of the most successful and acclaimed films ever, despite racial criticisms.

In all imaginable ways, the making of the movie was a monumental task, thought initially to be insurmountable. Among the other, and you'll pardon the unintended pun, battles, the producers, writers, and director had to contend with the censors. A single word, "damn," threw all concerned into a tizzy.

So popular and well-known is the movie that a detailed synopsis is not really needed. A spoiled, manipulative, possessive, and jealous Scarlett O'Hara lives on Tara, her family's Georgia cotton plantation, with dad, mom, two sisters—Suellen and Carreen—and a host of slaves. On the cusp of the Civil War, Scarlett loves a rather weak-willed Ashley Wilkes who loves his sweet and saintly cousin Melanie Hamilton. Since Scarlett can't have Ashley, she decides to basically throw away her life by vindictively marrying Melanie's younger brother Charles, who does everyone a favor by dying in the war. Along the way, she meets the sexy and mischievous Rhett Butler, who falls in love with her. The war ends, the South is ravaged, her parents die, and a strong-willed Scarlett battles on. "As God is my witness, as God is my witness, they are not going to lick me. I'm going to live through this, and when it's over, I'll never be hungry again. No, nor any of my folk. If I have to lie, steal, cheat, or kill, as God is my witness I'll never be hungry again."

Still in love with Ashley and needing money, she stabs her sister Suellen in the back by stealing and marrying her wealthy fiancé, Frank Kennedy, who also conveniently dies in a raid on a shanty town containing people who earlier accosted Scarlett. With Frank barely in the ground, she reconnects with Rhett, who she has seen off and on throughout the years, and marries him. Soon she gives birth to Eugenia Victoria, quickly nicknamed Bonnie Blue, and shuns Rhett as she still yearns for Ashley and wishes to avoid getting pregnant again and losing her stylish figure. Rhett goes on a lengthy business trip to London with his beloved daughter and returns to a pregnant Scarlett. They argue, she falls down the stately stairs and miscarries. As she is recovering, Bonnie Blue, who is growing into a lovely young girl, dies after falling off her pony. Melanie, meanwhile, is succumbing to the complications of a difficult pregnancy, thus potentially freeing Ashley. After speaking with him though, Scarlett has an awakening and realizes that she loves Rhett. Given the irreparable damage to his marriage, however, Rhett is no longer in love and ignores her beseeching him to stay. As he's exiting the mansion into the evening fog, Scarlett tearfully pleads for him to stay, "Where shall I go? What shall I do?" In response, he utters one of the most famous lines in movie history, "Frankly my dear, I don't give a damn." Showing her resilience and strength and ability to bounce back and recover from whatever obstacle thrown her way, she gives her own memorable final line, "Tara! Home! I'll go home and think of some way to get him back! After all, tomorrow is another day!"

The story's melodrama is overshadowed not only by the sheer spectacle of the movie using the new process of technicolor resulting in Academy Award winning glorious sets and scenes, such as the burning of Atlanta forever etched in our memories, but by the brilliance of the performances, garnering Oscar nominations for best actor, actress, and two for best supporting actress.

The journey started nearly a decade earlier with Peggy Marsh laboring over her Civil War novel, named at different times *Bugles Rang True*, *Tote the Weary Load*, *Another Day*, and *Not in Our Stars*, about Pansy O'Hara living in Fontenoy Hall and Ashley having a cousin Permelia, renamed Melisande. With many stops and starts along the way, Peggy, at the urging of her husband John, travelled to a local hotel where Harold Latham, a book editor from New York's Macmillan Publishers, was in town looking for local southern authors. Peggy, who had earlier met Latham at a luncheon, handed him 1,200 sloppy and misshapen pages, some typewritten, others handwritten, with cross outs and edits, all placed in different manila envelopes. Latham took the lump and put it in a suitcase he had to purchase to lug back to New York, where he grew enchanted at the depth and grandeur of what he was reading. When he received a telegram from Peggy telling him to return the manuscript as she had changed her mind, he responded with a contract, complete with an advance of several hundred dollars, to finish the book. Initially hesitant, she acquiesced, once again with the encouragement of John.

Over the course of six months, she diligently sat, reworked, and rewrote. She renamed the work, inspired by a line in a poem she had recently read about a man pining over a lost love— "I have forgot much, Cynara. Gone with the wind." Pansy became Scarlett, the cousin renamed Melanie, and Fontenoy now Tara. And last of all, Peggy decided to use her formal first name, Margaret, along with her maiden one, Mitchell.

Prior to publication Hollywood was approached. MGM's Louis B. Mayer thought a movie about the Civil War with selfish and profiteering protagonists and an unhappy ending unappetizing. Jack Warner mulled lending Bette Davis and Errol Flynn to play the lead roles but passed when Davis didn't want to work with Flynn again. RKO thought the costs of production unacceptably high. David O. Selznick, who had recently created Selznick International Pictures, read the telegram his story editor Kay Brown sent from New York: "I beg, urge, coax, and plead with you to read this at once ... drop everything and buy it." His response, "[M]ost sorry to have to say no in face of your enthusiasm for the story."

Tunes changed when Macmillan released the 1,037-page tome, which immediately became a critically acclaimed bestseller, as evidenced both by the almost 2 million copies sold and the review of J. Donald Adams of the *New York Times*, "This is beyond a doubt one of the most remarkable first novels ever produced by an American writer." Mitchell soon won the National Book Award and Pulitzer Prize. (Notwithstanding legitimate criticism due to racial portrayals, *Gone With the Wind*, both the novel and movie, remain firmly embedded in popular culture.)

Along the way Selznick realized the error of his earlier judgment, reversed course, and offered more money than ever before to purchase the film rights, $50,000. A compulsive and reckless gambler, this would be his greatest wager. The young, mercurial Selznick, who as per his personality meticulously, painstakingly, and maddeningly oversaw every single aspect of the film, was off and running and assembled his team. Noted director George Cukor was named director with Clark "The King" Gable immediately pursued to play Rhett. Starring in dozens of movies that decade and winning an Oscar for his leading role in 1934's screwball comedy *It Happened One Night*, the handsome and dashing Gable was at the apex of his popularity. As Samuel Goldwyn observed, "When someone like Robert Montgomery comes on the screen, you know he has cojones. When Gable comes on, you can hear them clanging." While other leading men—Errol Flynn, Ronald Colman, Gary Cooper, Basil Rathbone—were briefly considered, the role was Gable's. That he was under contract to MGM proved to be a hill and not a mountain to conquer. Selznick went to his father-in-law Mayer and struck a deal. Gable and $1,250,000 in exchange for distribution rights and a cut of the profits. MGM was now in the mix. While Gable was initially resistant, he needed the money to move his divorce quickly along as he wanted to marry an impatient Carole Lombard. Mayer offered him a bonus and Gable jumped. Although he had other commitments to other movies and would not be available for two years, it was just another passable hill. Problem solved. It would not be so easy casting Scarlett.

The two years it took to cast the sexy, sassy, smart, selfish, self-reliant, and attractive female lead involved nearly every age-appropriate actress in Hollywood and beyond. Nearly 1,400 would be considered in one way or another, including Tallulah Bankhead, Jean Arthur, Joan Bennett, Susan Hayward, and Lana Turner. Bette Davis, who initially demurred, now coveted it. When she didn't get the role, she turned to another movie, playing another Southern heroine in 1938's *Jezebel* for which she won an Oscar. Katherine Hepburn was also very interested, only to be brutally rejected by Selznick, telling her, "I can't imagine Rhett Butler pursuing you for ten years." Considering casting a newcomer both widened the net and generated additional publicity and anticipation for a film years in the making. As Selznick became overwhelmed, he whittled down the list to about sixty and then decided to go with an established actress, the well-respected, attractive, and talented Paulette Goddard.

There was only one problem. Goddard was living with movie star Charlie Chaplin. Given his rather scandalous private life (his first two wives were 16 years old) and controversial left-wing leanings, Chaplin had baggage. Although claiming to be married in Singapore, they could not produce a marriage license. Given the times, the moralists and religious howled and Goddard was out.

Selznick's brother Myron later provided the solution. Myron, the head of Hollywood's most powerful talent agency, represented half of the industry's major movers and shakers both on and off the screen. One client, Vivian Leigh, came from Britain and was not well known in America. Folklore has it that on December 10, 1938, Myron brought Leigh, who like many, desperately wanted the role, to the set of the movie shooting its very first scene, the colossal burning of Atlanta. Repainted and reassembled old sets on the studio backlot, from *King Kong*, *The Last of the Mohicans*, *Little Lord Fauntleroy*, and *The Garden of Allah*, were set ablaze in what had to be one take. Nearly three-hundred police officers, firemen, and studio assistants nervously stood by to ensure that nothing went too astray.

After the shooting, and as the ruins of Atlanta smoldered late into the night, a rather inebriated Myron arrived with Leigh and introduced her to his brother, "Hey, Genius, here's your Scarlett O'Hara." Selznick was instantly taken, later exclaiming, "The dying flames were lighting up her face. I took one look and knew that she was right. It's a look I'll never forget." That she had a somewhat similar Chaplin-Goddard "sinful" relationship with her English boyfriend and fellow actor Laurence Olivier, for whom she left her husband and 5-year-old daughter, apparently served as little deterrence to her hiring.

The remaining cast, both before and after Leigh was brought on board, went more smoothly, although some bumps also appeared along the way. After some hemming and hawing and second-guessing, Leslie Howard signed to play Ashley Wilkes; Olivia de Havilland, after her sister Joan Fontaine reportedly turned down the role, as Melanie; the ever busy Thomas Mitchell as Scarlett's father; Evelyn Keyes, who, as one story goes, got the role despite refusing Selznick's sexual advances, as sister Suellen; Hattie McDaniel as Scarlett's Mammy; and squeaky voiced Butterfly McQueen in her first major movie, as Prissy, who would utter yet another memorable line, "Oh no, Miss Scarlett! ... We got to have a doctor! Ah don' know nothin' 'bout birthin' babies!"

After the Atlanta scene, filming started out slowly with the respected Cukor, whom Gable disliked and with whom Selznick had creative differences, fired and replaced by a friend of Gable, Victor Fleming, who was pulled away from directing *The Wizard of Oz*. Once hired, he complained, rightly, of there being no workable script, pithily observing, "David, you haven't got a fucking script." Like on *Oz*, many worked on the script—eleven paid, including F. Scott Fitzgerald, and six informally solicited—in a piecemeal and often brief fashion. Filming was shut down as yet another writer Ben Hecht was grabbed from the Marx Brothers' *At the Circus* and brought in. When filming resumed the two stars occasionally clashed: Leigh, the professional well-prepared and at times irritating perfectionist, at odds with the more laid-back, not as well-prepared, and less diligent Gable. They did get along well enough, however, for Leigh to confide in him regarding an all too rare weekend off with Olivier, "We just fucked and fucked and fucked."

Scenes shot were often hectic with obstacles that needed to be overcome. Twenty-seven different deteriorating versions of a dress worn by Leigh over a lengthy passage of time were required and assembled, as were 1,500 costumes for the dying and wounded Confederate soldiers lying on the grounds of the Atlanta railway. That half were dummies made no difference as they still had to be dressed. Additionally, hundreds of hoop dresses were created, 1,500 drawings sketched, and numerous sets and models built. Filming ended on June 27, with the reshooting of an early scene. Much work remained though, as the film ran for nearly five hours.

Faithful to Mitchell's book, changes nevertheless had to be made to satisfy the Hays Office. Kisses had to be relatively brief, sexual heat turned down, if not off, a woman's leg hidden unless dancing, neither man nor woman shown in bed even if married, only the bad smoked, soldiers never cursed, Belle the Madam could never be referred to as such, and the "n" word never used. And then, one final roadblock. The book, near the very end, contained "My dear, I don't give a damn." While three different writers claimed to have added "Frankly," Hays banned all cursing. Alternate lines such as "Frankly, I don't give a hoot," "Frankly my dear, I just don't care," "It has become of no concern to me," "My indifference is boundless," and, what had to be a favorite among the very few, "It makes my gorge rise," were considered and rejected as Selznick recognized the power of the line as currently written. After much dickering, Hays finally came around, whether due to his love of the book, his artistic admiration of the word's necessity, or perhaps money or other perks exchanged. Tales of his levying a $5,000 fine exist to this day.

On September 9, moviegoers in Riverside, California, bought tickets to see two movies, *Hawaiian Nights* and *Beau Geste*. After the first ended, they were told they would not be seeing the one they expected but screening and rating a different one. Almost five hours later they were on their feet yelling and applauding (despite having to sit through two movies and maybe a cartoon and newsreel). The 37-year-old Selznick and his cohorts seated in the rear knew they had a hit. Spending the most money ever to make a movie—over $4 million—it had to be. A grand budget required grand publicity and the city of Atlanta obliged with a grand three-day long celebration if not coronation involving hundreds of thousands of fans culminating in a state-wide holiday. Like conquering heroes, the stars arrived in splendor and admiration to raucous cheers. Future President Jimmy Carter, who was 15 at the time, later shared that the spectacle was "the biggest event to happen in the South in my lifetime." Over 2,000 people viewed the movie and eagerly embraced the story of their past with its "eye-arresting, pulse-quickening, heart-warming details" as reported by the *Atlantic Constitution*. Sadly, due to segregation, Hattie McDaniel could not attend despite Gable insisting she be allowed. Rather than create a distraction, McDaniel bowed out.

As in Atlanta, the nation flocked to and adored the epic, making it the number one movie ever up to that point. The 12th Academy Awards fell in line with thirteen nominations, winning ten, two of which being honorary. Emcee Bob Hope quipped, "Welcome to this benefit for David Selznick." The major awards won included Selznick for Outstanding Production (in addition to receiving the Irving G. Thalberg Memorial Award for his drive and brilliance in bringing the book to the screen); Leigh for Best Actress ("Leigh doesn't play Scarlett. She *is* Scarlett"—Hedda Hopper, who earlier predicted doom when she was cast); Fleming for Best Director (despite Cukor's contributions as well as those of Sam Wood, who stepped in when Fleming fell ill due to exhaustion and clashes with Leigh and William Cameron Menzies, who shot a few significant scenes and won one of the honorary Oscars for his use of color); Hattie McDaniel for Best Supporting Actress (beating out de Havilland among others); and, after he was tragically killed in an August tractor accident on his Massachusetts farm, Sidney Howard for Best Screenwriter (despite over a dozen others contributing). Only a disappointed Gable lost, to Robert Donat who starred in *Goodbye Mr. Chips*. As for McDaniel, *Daily Variety* wrote, "Not only was she the first of her race [to be nominated and] to receive an Award, but she was also the first Negro ever to sit at an Academy banquet."

Criticized by some for playing the role as she had, McDaniel reacted as Mammy would have, feistily retorting, "[I'd] rather make seven hundred dollars a week playing a maid than seven dollars being one."

And with that, the legend of *Gone With the Wind*. As for Mitchell, she never published another book.

The Year Ends

"It was a fabulous time."

On December 31, the year 1939 came to a merciful end, but not before thousands perished on the 27th in a devastating earthquake in Turkey. The numbers killed and wounded, approximately 33,000 and 100,000 respectively, would sadly pale to the numbers slaughtered in the coming years as World War II savagely progressed. Hitler laid the groundwork for much of that misery on the 19th, when he named a physically inoffensive bureaucrat, later termed "the banality of evil" by Hannah Arendt, to a key post, overseeing Jewish affairs and evacuation. Adolph Eichmann took the role with relish and propelled an already murderous machine to atmospheric heights.

Eichmann was born in 1906 in Germany to a bookkeeper father and a stay-at-home housewife who oversaw their five children. Eight years later the family moved to Austria. When of age, Eichman attended high school, ironically the same as Hitler seventeen years earlier. Due to poor grades, his father sent him to a different school where he fared no better. Taking a job in his father's latest endeavor, a mining company, he lasted several months before moving onto another mediocre position, that of a sales clerk in a radio company, where he stayed until moving to an oil company. During this time he grew enraptured with Nazi ideology and joined the party in 1932.

A few years in, his creation of a pro-Nazi exhibit brought him to the attention of some Nazi leaders, including Goering and Himmler. Soon he found himself working in Jewish affairs where he immersed himself, working on how best to expel German Jews. Over time, Nazi policy changed from Jewish emigration to deportation and finally extermination. Serving as SS-Obergruppenführer Reinhard Heydrich's "special expert," Eichmann ran with his new assignment, quickly setting up a highly efficient killing apparatus that rounded up tens of thousands, then hundreds of thousands of Jews, plus other undesirables, and moving them to death camps. Many perished under the horrific conditions in the ghettos where they were herded, while others died while being transported under equally horrific conditions. Those who survived were mostly murdered upon arrival. The "more fortunate" temporarily postponed death, working as laborers until broken.

"I didn't care about the Jews deported to Auschwitz, whether they lived or died. It was the Führer's order: Jews who were fit to work would work and those who weren't would be sent to the Final Solution." Of the millions who died, Eichmann would "leap laughing into [his own grave with a conviction] of extraordinary satisfaction."

Fleeing Germany after the war and aided by Austrian Nazi-lover Bishop Alois Hudal, Eichmann landed in Argentina, where he inconspicuously lived, until kidnapped by Jewish intelligence and spirited out of the county to Israel in 1960. There he stood trial, was found guilty, and hanged. Before meeting his end, he exclaimed, "Long live Germany. Long live Argentina. Long live Austria. These are the three countries with which I have been most connected and which I will not forget. I greet my wife, my family, and my friends. I am ready. We'll meet again soon, as is the fate of all men. I die believing in God."

While Nazi propagandist Goebbels was cautioning "[1940] will be a hard year, and we must be ready for it," Americans, as always, remained far more optimistic. As they did throughout 1939, they flocked to the movies. Released on December 29th, *The Hunchback of Notre Dame* proved to be popular with the public and critics, who dubbed it a "super thriller-chiller," "a Class A, super-plus picture," "compelling dynamic entertainment," and "Very good! Audiences should be thrilled anew by this lavish remake of Victor Hugo's famous novel." As with most film reviewers, a negative Nelly existed in the form of *New York Times*'s Frank Nugent who found it "a freak show ... that and little more ... a bit too coarse for our tastes now."

Set in Paris in the Middle Ages, it featured a huge cast including actors portraying King Louis XI; his devilish Chief Justice Jehan Frollo set on wiping out evil in such forms of the Romas and printing presses; the beautiful (of course) Roma maiden Esmeralda (the lovely 19-year-old Irish subject Maureen O'Hara); love interests Captain Phoebus and poor street poet Pierre Gringoire; the king of the Romas, Clopin (the ubiquitous Thomas Mitchell); and the hunchback himself, the physically grotesque Quasimodo, the bell ringer of Notre Dame (Charles Laughton), who, when being publicly humiliated, is treated kindly by Esmeralda.

A "bewitched" Frollo sees Esmeralda, whom he lusts after. When he spots her talking to Phoebus, he kills his perceived competition in a fit of jealousy. He then blames Esmeralda and sentences her to death. Just as she is about to be hanged Quasimodo heroically swoops in, rescues her, and retreats to the safety of the cathedral and its right of sanctuary. Not to be deterred, the nobles plan to revoke the right of sanctuary and capture Esmeralda. In protest, Gringoire writes a pamphlet as Clopin and his charges storm the cathedral. An unsettled king learns Esmeralda is innocent, confronts Frollo, who confesses and scoots off. A big battle ensues between Clopin's Romas and the palace guards. Quasimodo is caught in the middle and when set upon by a dagger-wielding Frollo, gains the upper hand and hurls Frollo from the top of the church, killing him. In the end, King Louis pardons Esmeralda and her fellow Romas. As she leaves the public square with her true love Gringoire, a far-above and love-stricken Quasimodo turns to a nearby gargoyle and utters, "Why was I not made of stone, like thee?"

The movie was directed by German-born William Dieterle who left Germany in 1930 due to worsening political and economic conditions. Already an experienced filmmaker when he departed, he gained even greater success in his new home. In 1937, his movie *The Life of Emile Zola* won best picture. Even Nugent of the *Times* was dazzled, breathlessly claiming it to be "the finest historical film ever made and the greatest screen biography."

Known for consulting with astrologers as to what day to start shooting, wearing large hats and white gloves (developed early in his career to cover his hands when he had to turn from directing to attacking dirty technical problems), Dieterle spoke English haltingly with a thick German accent. One day, when the cast and crew arrived for their daily shoot they were greeted by a menagerie of apes, baboons, gorillas, and monkeys. Apparently as aide mistook Dieterle's request for a host of monks for monkeys.

Screenwriter Sonya Levien, born Jewish in Russia, came to America with her family in 1896. Rising above abject poverty, she went to school, became a lawyer but never practiced, preferring writing to lawyering. A feminist, she wrote sympathetically of the struggles of immigrants, women, and the downtrodden. Gravitating to Hollywood, she rose to the very top as Fox's highest paid female screenwriter in the 1930s. In her co-written script, one cannot ignore her subtly equating France's persecution of the Romas with Germany's persecution of the Jews.

Meanwhile, in the same month that *Gone With the Wind* and *The Hunchback of Notre Dame* entertained millions, out of the public eye a patent for fluorescent lighting was granted, laying the groundwork for an invention that would affect far more with a new and improved form of lighting destined for worldwide use. At the same time, in Chicago, the large, popular, and well-known retailer Montgomery Ward, which earlier that year had decided that its annual distribution of coloring books for children was far too expensive, sought a way to cut costs for its 2 million customers. The task fell to a talented, suffering, store advertising copywriter, Robert May, who was tasked with writing a new Christmas tale.

May's young wife was dying, succumbing in July 1939, leaving behind a 4-year-old daughter and a mountain of medical bills. Adding to his distress were unfulfilled professional aspirations. "I was heavily in debt at age 35, still grinding out catalogue copy. Instead of writing the great American novel, as I'd always hoped, I was describing white shirts." Given the option of declining his assignment, May plowed on, dusting off a poem from 1823—"A Visit from St. Nicholas," better known for its first line, "'Twas the Night Before Christmas." Adopting his daughter's fondness for reindeer, he came up with first Rollo, then Reginald, and finally Rudolph—the Red-Nosed Reindeer. Now that he had a name, he needed a story.

Peering out of his office window, his eyes wandered over to a thick fog hovering from Lake Michigan. "Suddenly I had it! A nose! A bright red nose that would shine through thick fog like a spotlight." Looking back at his shy past, he wrote the poem about a young reindeer with "a very shiny nose" about whom "All the other reindeer used to laugh and call him names." Santa, however, recognized his value and asked Rudolph to lead his sleigh and in so doing he became a hero. And thus the birth of one of the most iconic Christmas holiday figures, who indeed went "down in history."

Montgomery Ward distributed nearly 2.5 million copies of the poem. A decade later, May's brother-in-law Johnny Marks, who wrote such Christmas ditties as "A Holly Jolly Christmas" and "Rockin' Around the Christmas Tree," set the story to music, which Bing Crosby and Dinah Shore turned down. At the behest of his wife, the Singing Cowboy Gene Autry recorded it. The record soared to the top of the charts during the Christmas week of 1949, with nearly as many copies as the original poem in 1939. With soaring numbers, it soon came to be recorded by different artists—Dean Martin, Perry Como, Mitch Miller, and even Bing finally getting into the act, to name a few. Next to Crosby's *White Christmas*, it ranks second in all-time holiday hits.

As May was an employee, he was not entitled to any of the monies generated by his creation. In a show of holiday spirit, corporate generosity, and aware of May's economic troubles, Ward's president Sewell Avery gifted him the copyright to his poem, allowing him a bright economic future. He also remarried, this time to a fellow employee with whom he had five more children.

On New Year's Eve, 1,250,000 million New Yorkers gathered in a frigid 22-degree Times Square to usher in the new year. The seconds ticked down. The age-old brightly lighted sphere slowly descended. The large festive crowd cheered. Young inebriated girls kissed cops. Josephine Russo temporarily passed out. Marion Connelly fainted and died. Fireworks blazed. Hotel parties spilled out onto the streets. A hotel employee marveled that he hadn't seen anything like this since 1928. Twelve nightclubs claimed 7,000 guests. Women's skirts were shorter than ever. All night parties rang out with new "Boogie-Woogie" music and dance.

As the *Times* concluded, "No, it was no ordinary year whose dying the multitude toasted last night. It was a fabulous time."

Little did they know what time had in store.

Endnotes

1. Interestingly the fictional title of a movie on the Jerry Seinfeld television show.
2. As is often the case, movies have previews prior to their official release to gauge the audience's reaction to it. As such, *Oz* was seen in Green Bay and Kenosha, Wisconsin; Dennis, Massachusetts; Los Angeles; and New York City prior to the 25th. In New York, Garland, Mickey Rooney, and others performed live shows for three weeks after the movie was shown.
3. *The Times*, needless to say, intensely reported the conflict, often placing the story front and center on page 1. The war was also reported on a daily basis in its "The International Situation" section. What follows are portions of that coverage.

Sources

When I asked a fellow history lover about his latest read and its length, he replied "Four hundred pages not including the forty with footnotes and endnotes that I never look at." This book is for those like my friend, history lovers but not stodgy academics (not, citing Jerry Seinfeld, that there's anything wrong with them). As with my last book, *Old Whiskey and Young Women, American True Crime Tales of Murder, Sex, and Scandal*, this also is one not of scholarly, intricate, and intimate research. Indeed, nearly all of the sources utilized were secondary in nature. Various books, online articles, and newspapers were used as well as Wikipedia, the Encyclopedia Brittanica, and the like.

Chapter 1 (The Lead-Up to World War II)

Books:

A Short History of World War II (DK, 2020)

Hitler, Adolph, *Mein Kampf*, trans. R. Manheim (Houghton Mifflin, 1999 [1943])

Moorhouse, Roger, *Poland 1939: The Outbreak of World War II* (Basic Books, 2020)

Taylor, Frederick, *1939: A People's History of the Coming of the Second World War* (Norton, 2019)

Wikipedia: 1938 New England hurricane; Adolph Hitler's rise to power; Austria; Beer Hall Putsch; Causes of World War II; Charles D. Dawes; Condor Legion; Czechoslovakia; David Lloyd George; Dawes Plan; Duke and Duchess of Windsor's 1937 tour of Germany; Edouard Daladier; Erich Ludendorff; Ernst Rohm; Events preceding World War II in Europe; Francisco Franco; George Clemenceau; German Revolution of 1918–1919; Haim Arlosoroff; Lida Baarová; Karl Hanke; It's All in the Game (song); Great Depression; Joseph Goebbels; Magna Goebbels; Goebbels children; Luftwaffe; Marinus van der Lubbe; Mein Kampf; Munich Agreement; Night of the Long Knives; Paul von Hindenburg; Peace for our time; Rhineland; Stab-in-the-back myth; Spartacist uprising [Communist revolt of 1919]; Stennes Revolt; 30 January 1939 Reichstag Speech; Treaty of Versailles; Weimer Republic; Wilhelm II, German Emperor.

Other:

"10 Events Leading Up To WW2," ESKIFY, January 12, 2021

"5,000 British Soldiers Will Guard Czech Areas," *New York Times*, October 1, 1938

Alchin, Linda. "Events leading up to WW2," *American Historama*, January 9, 2018

Boissoneault, Lorraine, "The True Story of the Reichstag Fire and the Nazi Rise to Power," *Smithsonian Magazine*, February 21, 2017

"Germans Begin Czech Occupation; Troops Cross Old Austrian Border," *New York Times*, October 1, 1938

"Hitler Answers Roosevelt: The German Leader's Reply to the American President's Challenge," *Institute For Historical Review*

Hughes, David, and Neal Baker, "A Version of Hitler's notorious autobiography has become a bestseller in Germany," *The Sun*, August 26, 2017

"Hurricane Devastates New England; September 21, 1938," *Mass Moments*

Kramer, Gabrielle, "What was the difference between the Nazi SA and SS?" *HistoryHit,* June 5, 2018

Mommsen, Hans, "Hitler's Reichstag Speech of 30 January 1939," *History and Memory*, vol. 9, no. 1-2 (1997), pp. 147-161

"Nazi control of Germany," BBC Bitesize History 5, April 13, 2026, https://www.bbc.co.uk/bitesize/guides/zn8sgk7/revision/1

"Nazi rise to power," BBC Bitesize History 5, January 26, 2023, https://www.bbc.co.uk/bitesize/guides/zpknb9q/revision/1

"Nazis test new air force, Luftwaffe, on Basque town of Guernica," *History.com,* April 23, 2021

Philpot, Robert, "An early Zionist's unsolved murder fuels a mystery novel ripped from the archives," *The Times of Israel*, February 23, 2023

"Poles Ready to Act; Prepare to Take Over Teschen Silesia on Terms Reich Got; Hungary Drafts Claims," *New York Times*, October 1, 1938

Rosen, Jeremy, "Magda Goebbels & Chaim Arlosoroff," January 26, 2017, https://jeremyrosen.com/2017/01/magda-goebbels.html

Setterfield, Ray, "I Have Heard The Voice of Adolf Hitler ...," *On This Day*, June 5, 2025

Simkin, John. "The Nazi Party: The Night of the Long Knives," *Spartacus Educational,* March 2021

"This Day In History: Spanish Civil War ends," *History.com*, May 27, 2025

"This Day In History: The Pact of Steel is Signed; the Axis is Formed," *History.com*, January 31, 2025

Vermaat, Emerson, "Hitler Predicted Holocaust As Early As January 30, 1939," *Militant Islam Monitor*, February 3, 2009

"Weimar Germany," BBC Bitesize History 5, January 27, 2023, https://www.bbc.co.uk/bitesize/guides/zh9p34j/revision/1

"World War II: Causes, Timeline, Key Battles, Facts & Legacy," *History.com*, June 4, 2026

Chapter 2 (Hollywood)

Books:

Adams, Charles F., *1939: The Making of Six Great Films From Hollywood's Greatest Year* (Craven Street Books, 2014)

Block, Alex Ben, and Lucy Autry Wilson eds., *George Lucas's Blockbusting: A Decade-by-Decade Survey of Timeless Movies Including Untold Secrets of Their Financial and Cultural Success* (Dey Street Books, 2010)

Bowers, Scotty, and Lionel Friedberg, *Full Service: My Adventures in Hollywood and the Secret Sex Lives of the Stars* (Grove Press, 2012)

Ebert, Roger, *The Great Movies* (Broadway, 2002)

Ebert, Roger, *The Great Movies II* (Broadway, 2005)

Fleming, E.J., *The Fixers: Eddie Mannix, Howard Strickling and the MGM Publicity Machine,* McFarland & Company, 2005)

Harmetz, Aljean, *On The Road To Tara: The Making of Gone With The Wind* (Harry N. Abrams, 1996)

Kantrowitz, R. Marc, *Old Whiskey and Young Women: American True Crime Tales of Murder, Sex, and Scandal* (Fonthill Media, 2015)

McBride, Joseph, *Billy Wilder: Dancing on the Edge* (Columbia University Press, 2021)

McLellan, Diana, *The Girls: Sappho Goes To Hollywood* (LA Weekly Books, 2000)

Russo, Vito, *The Celluloid Closet: Homosexuality in the Movies* (Harper/Colophon Books, 1981)

Sennett, Ted, *Hollywood's Golden Year, 1939: A Fiftieth Anniversary Celebration* (St. Martins' Press, 1989)

Vieira, Mark A., *Majestic Hollywood: The Greatest Films of 1939*, (Running Press, 2013)

Wikipedia: AFI's 100 Years . . . 100 Movies; Bette Davis; Beverly Hill, California; The Beverly Hills Hotel; Burton E. Green; Confessions of a Nazi Spy; Daughters Courageous; Dark Victory; Darryl F. Zanuck; Each Dawn I Die; Gottfried Reinhardt; Ernst Lubitsch; Frances Marian; George Brent; Greta Garbo; Harvey Henderson Wilcox; Howard Hughes; Jack L. Warner; Jack Pickford; Kenesaw Mountain Landis; Lina Basquett; List of American films in 1939; Louis B. Mayer; Lowell Sherman; Mary Pickford; Little Caesar; Louis B. Mayer; Martin Dies Jr.; Michael Curtiz; Motion Picture Production Code; 1939 in film; Ninotchka; Olive Thomas; *Only Angels Have Wings*; Patricia Morrison; Pre-Code Hollywood; Roscoe Arbuckle; Salka Viertel; Sam Warner; *Stagecoach*; *The Roaring Twenties*; *The Hunchback of Notre Dame* (1939 film); *The Jazz Singer*; *The Public Enemy*; *The Squaw Man* (1914 film); Thomas Mitchell; Wallace Reid; Warner Bros.; Will H. Hays

Other:

"AFI's 100 Years...100 movies - 10th anniversary edition," *AFI,* June 20, 2007

"AFI's 100 Years ... 100 Stars," *AFI,* June 16, 1999

Artsy, Avishay, "How Jewish émigrés impacted the birth of film noir" [last modified January 12, 2024], *KQED,* October 17, 2014

"Best Movies of 1939," *Films 101*

"Bette Davis," *IMDB*

Brown, Shane, "The Man Who Had Everything: The Curious Case of Jack Pickford and the *New York Times,*" *Bright Lights Film Journal*, January 28, 2014

Burr, Ty. "To the nines: 1939, Making the most of the studio system," *Boston Globe*, July 12, 2009

Casano, Ann, "12 Outrageous Abuses of Old Hollywood's Studio System, *Ranker*, July 3, 2024

Cavendish, Richard. "The Death of Louis B. Mayer: Richard Cavendish remembers the life of Louis B. Mayer, who died on October 29, 1957," *History Today*, Volume 57, Issue 10, October 2007

Chirico, Rob, "The Shirley Temple Story: Abuse, Sexual Predators, And More," *Ranker*, August 21, 2024

Copquin, Claudia Gryvatz, "Names of America: How Did Beverly Hills Gets Its Name? (And Who Was the First Real Housewife There)?" *Parade,* November 4, 2013

Dowling, Siobhan, "How Hitler helped make Hollywood," *Global Post*, February 14, 2013

Economou, Thane, "Old Hollywood Scandals that History Forgot," *Ranker*, June 11, 2024

Ellenberger, Allan R., "Daeida Wilcox Beveridge: the Mother of Hollywood," *Hollywoodland*, May 10, 2018

Farr, John, "Why 1939 was the Year of Thomas Mitchell," *Best Movies by Farr*, December 7, 2016

"Feature Film, Released 1939-01-01 and 1939-12-31 United States," *IMDb*

"Greatest Films of the 1930s: 1939," *AMC*

Gupta, Rohan, "John Wayne's illicit affair with the actress was investigated by FBI and ended his marriage," *Express,* August 20, 2022

Hamilton, Phillip, "Sinister Facts about Louis B. Mayer, the Monster of MGM," *The Shot,* June 26, 2024

"Howard Hughes's Wives, Girlfriends & Romances," *Ranker*, April 12, 2024

Hutchinson, Pamela. "Moguls and starlets: 100 years of Hollywood's corrosive, systemic sexism," *The Guardian*, October 19, 2017

Hyland, Jeffrey, "The Legendary Estates of Beverly Hills," *Haute Living,* September 28, 2009

"Jews who fled the Nazis to make films in Hollywood," *The Jewish News of Northern California*, November 27, 2014

Kantrowitz, R. Marc, "The Short and Tragic Life of Olive Thomas," *Massachusetts Lawyers Weekly*, May 29, 2021

"List of Seinfeld fictional films—*Prognosis Negative*," *WikiSein*

Longworth, Karina, "The Artist and the Millionaire: How Bette Davis made an affair with Howard Hughes work for her," *Slate*, November 12, 2018

"Louis B. Mayer," *Britannica*, June 13, 2026

Mathews, Jack. "1939: It was the greatest year in Hollywood history: 365 films were released and moviegoers were buying tickets at a rate of 80 million a week!" *Los Angeles Times*, January 1, 1989

Mayar, Alicia, "Three Things You Didn't Know About Louis B. Mayer," *The Film Colony*, October 29, 2013

"Movies of Bette Davis (Complete List)," *IMDB*

Nucilli, Ryleigh, "17 Incredible and Hilarious Pictures of Los Angeles from the Early 1900s," *Ranker*, July 3, 2024

"Paris Authorities Investigate Death of Olive Thomas," *New York Times*, September 11, 1920

"Prohibition," *History.com*, May 28, 2025

Rifkind, Donna, "Refugees Fleeing Nazi Germany Reshaped Hollywood: This Forgotten Woman Helped Make It Possible," *Time*, January 2, 2020

Rosenwald, Michael S., "'I'll ruin you': Judy Garland on being groped and harassed by powerful Hollywood men," *The Washington Post*, November 14, 2017

Schulberg, Budd, "Louis B. Mayer: Lion of Hollywood," *Time Magazine,* December 7, 1998

"The Emigration of Filmmakers under National-Socialism," *filmportal.de*

"The Flapper (1920)," *IMDb*

"The Public Enemy," *IMDb*

"This Day In History: First Academy Awards ceremony" [last modified May 27, 2025], *History.com*, November 24, 2009

Weiss, Antony, "Fleeing Europe's Darkness filmmakers took refuge in California sun," *Jewish Federation of Greater Orange County,* November 23, 2014

Chapter 3 (The Birth of Silicon Valley)

Wikipedia: American Graffiti; Bill Hewlett; Charles Litton, Sr.; Hewlett-Packard; HP Garage; David Packard; Fairchild Semiconductor; *Fantasia* (1940 film); 1969 New York Mets season; Frederick Terman; HP200A; Klystron; Litton Industries; Lockheed Corporation; Lockheed Martin Space; Mickey Mouse; Office of Scientific Research and Development; Operation Downfall; Pueblo, Colorado; Pueblo speech; Radio Research Laboratory (Harvard); Russell and Sigurd Varian; Stanford Research Park; Varian Associates; Walt Disney; William Shockley

Other:

Atkinson, Richard, Foreword to *Fred Terman at Stanford: Building a Discipline, a University, and Silicon Valley"* by C. Stewart Gillmor, Stanford University Press, 2004

Blank, Steve, *Secret History of Silicon Valley*, January 29, 2016, https://steveblank.com/secret-history/

Blank, Steve, "The Secret History of Silicon Valley" [lecture], *Lester Center for Entrepreneurship & Innovation*, February 24, 2011

"David Packard Net Worth," *Celebrity Net Worth*

DiBacco, Thomas V., "Tin cans helped U.S. win World War II—and kids cashed in" [last modified December 15, 2018], *Orlando Sentinel*, February 9, 2018

Hall, Mark, "Hewlett-Packard Company," *Britannica Money*, June 26, 2026

"How many Allied bomber crewmen were killed over Europe in World War II?" *Quora*, https://www.quora.com/How-many-Allied-bomber-crewmen-were-killed-over-Europe-in-World-War-II

"HP: About Us," https://www.hp.com/us-en/hp-information.html

"HP Computer Museum," https://www.hpmuseum.net/

"Klystron," *Britannica*, July 25, 2022

Sharpe, Ed, "Hewlett-Packard, The Early Years," *SMECC.org*

Chapter 4 (Earhart, Capone, and "an arm torn out by the roots")

Amelia Earhart

Wikipedia: Amelia Earhart; Neta Snook Southern; Fred Noonan; George P. Putnam; 20 Hrs., 40 Min.; "WE" (1927 book)

Other:

"Amelia Earhart" [last modified October 3, 2025], *History.com*, November 9, 2009

"Amelia Earhart: Quotes," *Goodreads,* https://www.goodreads.com/author/quotes/367092.Amelia_Earhart

Cohen, Jennie, "6 Mysterious Disappearances in U.S. History" [last modified February 7, 2025], *History.com*, August 14, 2012

Sartore, Melissa, "17 Historical Mysteries That Are Hopefully Solved In Our Lifetime," *Ranker*, May 6, 2025

Al Capone
Books:
Bergreen, Laurence, *Capone: The Man and The Era* (Simon & Schuster, 1994)
Eig, Jonathan,*Get Capone: The Secret Plot That Captured America's Most Wanted Gangster* (Simon & Schuster, 2010)
Kobler, John, *Capone: The Life and World of Al Capone* (Fawcett Publications, 1971)
Warren, George, *Gang Wars of the 30s* (Barclay House, 1974)
Wikipedia: Al Capone; Big Jim Colosimo; Bugs Moran; Johnny Torrio; Saint Valentine's Day Massacre
Other:
"7 Chicago Gangsters Slain by Firing Squad of Rivals, Some in Police uniform," *New York Times,* February 15, 1929
Daugherty, Greg, "How Al Capone Spent His Time in Alcatraz" [last modified May 28, 2025], *History.com*, October 29, 2021
Linder, Douglas O., "Al Capone Trial (1931): An Account," *Famous Trials*
"This Day In History: Al Capone convicted of tax evasion" [last modified May 26, 2025], *History.com*, November 24, 2009

The Super Stars of Horror
Wikipedia: Bela Lugosi; Bela Lugosi filmography; Deanna Durbin; *Destry Rides Again*; *Dracula*; Ed Wood; List of Universal Picture films (1930–1939); Marlene Dietrich; *Plan 9 from Outer Space*; *Son of Frankenstein*; Universal Pictures
Other:
Crumlish, Callum, "James Stewart's devastating "betrayal" of Marlene Dietrich after on-set romance, *Express*, June 6, 2022
Howe, Caroline, "John Wayne DID dodge the draft so he could continue his torrid affair with sexy German actress Marlene Dietrich, 'the best lay I've ever had,' new book reveals," *Daily Mail*, November 3, 2014
Preskar, Peter, "Love Affairs of John F. Kennedy," *Short History*, August 12, 2020
"Report: JFK, Marlene Dietrich trysted in 1962," *ABC News*, August 4, 2000
"Universal Studios," *Britannica*, June 6, 2026
"Upset Dietrich Started Abortion Rumour," *The Himalayan*, March 8, 2005

England's Difficulty—Ireland's Opportunity
Wikipedia: Coventry; Easter Rising; 1939 Coventry bombing; Proclamation of the Irish Republic; S Plan;
Other:
"75 Years Ago/1939—IRA Bombs in England," *Ulster Herald,* January 24, 2014
"Bomb Blasts Shake Cities in Britain; Irish Are Blamed," *New York Times*, January 17, 1939
"Easter Rising 1916: Who Signed the proclamation?" *BBC News*, March 23, 2016
Poole, Rebekah, and Jennifer Llewellyn, "The Provisional IRA's Mainland Campaign," *Alpha History*, 2018
"The long search for peace," *BBC News*, October 16, 1998

A Movie and an Earthquake
Wikipedia: *Gunga Din* (film); *Gunga Din* [poem]; *Indiana Jones and The temple of Doom*; 1939 Chillan earthquake; RKO Pictures, Thuggee

Other:
Griffin, Charles, "Quake Ruins 20 Chile Towns; Concepcion City Wiped Out; Loss of Life in Thousands," *New York Times*, January 26, 1939
"Sabu," *IMDb*

JOE LOUIS

Wikipedia: Enrico Fermi; Harlem Renaissance; Jack Johnson (boxer); James J. Braddock; John Henry Lewis; Joe Louis; Langston Hughes; Tony Galento.
Other:
Clarence, George. "Boxing History: Louis Kayos Pastor," September 20, 2016
"Jack Roper," *BoxRec*, https://boxrec.com/en/box-pro/10644
Roberts, James B., and Alexander G. Skutt, "John Henry Lewis," *The Boxing Register* (McBooks Press, 1999)
Rogers, Thomas, "Tony Galento, Brawling Heavyweight, Dies," *New York Times*, July 23, 1979
"Tony Galento," *IMDb*

HITLER'S STATE OF THE UNION

Wikipedia: 30 January 1939 Reichstag speech, Evian Conference; Federico Laredo Bru; *Voyage of the Damned*
Other:
Blakemore, Erin, "A Ship of Jewish Refugees Was Refused Landing in 1939. This Was Their Fate" [last modified May 28, 2025], *History.com*, June 4, 2019
Froomkin, Dan, "Talking to survivors of the SS St. Louis," *Medium*, January 27, 2027
"Hitler's Advice to Us," *New York Times,* January 31, 1939
Mommsen, Hans, "Hitler's Reichstag Speech of 30 January 1939," *History and Memory,* Vol 9, no.1/2, 1997
"MS St. Louis," *Brittanica*
"This Day In History: Ship carrying 937 Jewish refugees, fleeing Nazi Germany, is turned away in Cuba" [last modified May 28, 2025], *History.com*, May 21, 2019
Tolischus, Otto D., "Backs Rome in War; Indicated Issues in East Are Deferred in Favor of African Partition," *New York Times,* January 31, 1939

Chapter 5 (Sinatra, the Pope, and a Nazi Rally)

FRANK SINATRA

Books:
Kaplan, James, *Frank: The Voice* (Anchor Books, 2010)
Kaplan, James, *Sinatra: The Chairman* (Knopf Doubleday Publishing Group, 2015)
Kelley, Kitty, *His Way: The Unauthorized Biography of Frank Sinatra* (Bantam Books, 1986)
Taraborrelli, J. Randy, *Sinatra: Behind the Legend* (Grand Central Publishing, 2015)
Wikipedia: Frank Sinatra; Harry James; Major Bowes Amateur Hour; Tommy Dorsey.
Other:
Setterfield, Ray, "Voice Of The Century – 'And Not Even Close'" [last modified January 12, 2023], *On This Day*, July 1, 2016

Pope XI dies at 81

Wikipedia: Engelbert Dollfuss; Kurt Schuschnigg; Poland; Pope Pius XI; Pope Pius XII; Pope Pius XII and the Holocaust; Theodor Innitzer.

Other:

Harvey, Ian, "Pope Pius XII Ordered Death of Hitler during World War Two," *War History Online*, December 16, 2015

Hoeing, Paulina, "How Pius XII and the Church Saved Lives During WWII," *National Catholic Register*, September 1, 2019

Piper, Grant, "Hitler and the Two Popes: The close relationship of Pius XI and Pius XII with Hitler and the Third Reich," *Exploring History*, July 23, 2020

Wilde, Robert, "Hitler's Rise to Power: A Timeline," *ThoughtCo*, July 24, 2024

Stagecoach Opens

Books:

Sennett, Ted, *Hollywood's Golden Year, 1939: A Fiftieth Anniversary Celebration* (St. Martin's Press, 1989)

Vieira, Mark A., *Majestic Hollywood: The Greatest Films of 1939* (Running Press, 2013)

Yeck, Joanne L., and Tom McGreevey, *Movie Westerns* (Lerner Publications Company, 1994)

Wikipedia: *Stagecoach* (1939 film).

Other:

Nichols, Dudley, and Ben Hecht, *Stagecoach* [screenplay], *Daily Script,* 1939

Pfeiffer, Lee, "Stagecoach [1939]" [last modified June 24, 2026], *Britannica*, June 10, 2013

"Stagecoach (1939)," *IMDb*

Golden Gate International Expo

Books:

Cotter, Bill, *San Francisco's 1939–1940 World's Fair: The Golden Gate International Exposition* (Arcadia Publishing, 2021)

Wikipedia: Golden Gate Bridge; Golden Gate International Exposition; 1939 NCAA Basketball Tournament; Oregon Ducks men's basketball; Robert Louis Stevenson; San Francisco–Oakland Bay Bridge; Treasure Island.

Other:

Loney, Glen, "Pacifica in 1939: San Francisco's Own Version of World's Fair Art Deco," *Art Deco Society of New York News*, Vol. 2, No. 2, March-June 1982

"San Francisco World's Fair 1939: A Pageant of the Pacific," *Sleuth4Family*, June 17, 2020

"San Francisco World's Fair" [documentary], *News Parade*, 1939

"This Day in History: Golden Gate Bridge is born" [last modified January 2, 2021], *History.com*, November 24, 2009

Nazis Rally at Madison Square Garden

Wikipedia: 1939 Nazi rally at Madison Square Garden; Marshall Curry; Thomas E. Dewey.

Other:

"22,000 Nazis Hold Rally In Garden; Police Check Foes; Scenes as German-American Bund Held Its 'Washington Birthday' Rally Last Night," *New York Times*, February 21, 1939

A Night at the Garden [documentary], Dir. Marshall Curry (PBS Short Film Festival, 2019)
Chase, Andrea, "A Night at the Garden—Marshall Curry Interview," *PRX*, February 13, 2019
Dias, Nick, "The Pro-American Rally and The American Nazi Movement," *HistoryHub.info*, March 12, 2020
Diehl, Jeff, "Photos of San Francisco in 1939," *Spots Unknown*, September 3, 2010
Talbot, Margaret, "Revisiting the American Nazi Supporters of 'A Night at the Garden'," *The New Yorker*, February 22, 2019
"The Bund Meeting," *New York Times* Editorial, February 22, 1939
"The Pro-Nazi Rally at Madison Square Garden (1939)," *Jewish Virtual Library*
"This Day In History: Americans hold a Nazi rally in Madison Square Garden" [last modified June 30, 2025], *History.com*, February 20, 2019

Chapter 6 (Czechoslovakia, Nanchang, and Wives Killing Their Husbands in Philadelphia)

Bad Fad "Preserving (Gold)fish from Cruel and Wanton Consumption"

Wikipedia: Goldfish swallowing; Igor Sikorsky; Sikorsky Aircraft.
Other:
Bellis, Mary, "History of the Helicopter," *ThoughtCo*, October 4, 2019
Clark, Laura, "The Greatest Goldfish Swallowing Craze of 1939 Never Really Ended," *Smithsonian Magazine*, February 27, 2015
Connor, Tom, and Jim Downey, "What If We Tried This?" *Reminisce Extra*, January 2022
"Education: Goldfish Derby," *Time*, April 10, 1939
"Education: Gulpers," *Time*, April 24, 1939
"Goldfish Swallowing," *Bowling, Beatniks, and Bell-Bottoms: Pop Culture of 20th, Century America, Encyclopedia.com*, June 24, 2026
Heichelbech, Rose, "The Incredibly Strange Goldfish Swallowing Fad of 1939," *Dusty Old Thing*
Kruse, Colton, "College Bros In The 1930s Were The Champs Of Goldfish Swallowing," *Ripley's*, February 13, 2018
"Lothrop "Lofie" Withington" [obituary]," August 1, 2013, *Cartmell-Davis*
"Withington, Lothrop Jr.," *USAF Rotorheads*, August 1, 2013

Czechoslovakia Dies

Books: see Chapter 1 above
Wikipedia: Emil Hacha; Free City of Danzig; Lezaky; Lidice massacre; Munich Agreement; Occupation of Czechoslovakia (1938–1945); Reinhard Heydrich; Richard Bruno Heydrich.
Other:
"Armies On March, Reich Invades Slovakia and Czech Provinces Without Opposition, People Taken Unawares, But Czechs Keep Self-Control as State Is Snuffed Out," *The Associated Press*, March 15, 1939
"Bomb Blasts Rock Slovak Capital As Leaders Assert Independence, Six Reported Killed and Fifty Hurt During a Turbulent Metting," *The Associated Press*, March 14, 1939

Gedye, G.E.R., "Calls Slovak Diet, Premier Acts on Order From Hitler," *New York Times*, March 14, 1939
Gedye, G.E.R, "Czechs Taken By Surprise," *New York Times*, March 15, 1939
Kuhn, Ferdinand Jr., "Chamberlain Sees Munich Flouted; Cancels Trade Parlays in Berlin," *New York Times*, March 16, 1939
McEnchroe, Thomas, "March 15, 1939: The day Czechoslovakia ceased to exist," *Radio Prague International*, March 15, 2019
Naillon, Erin, "Lidice and Lezaky," *Prague Guide*
"On This Day: Hitler Invades Czechoslovakia, March 15, 1939," *Wikipedia Commons/German Federal Archive*
"The breakup of the republic (Czechoslovak history)," *Britannica*
"The Hitler Proclamation," *New York Times*, March 15, 1939
Tolischus, Otto D., "Hacha Sees Hitler, Czech Statesmen Agree to Loss of Freedom in Three-Hour Meeting, Autonomy Is Promised," *New York Times*, March 15, 1939
Vadney, Emil, "Czech Area Seized, Chancellor's Banner Is Flying Over Capital's Historic Citadel," *New York* Times, March 16, 1939

Nanchang
Wikipedia: Anti-Comintern Pact; Battle of Nanchang; Battle of Wuhan; Japanese invasion of Manchuria; Manchuria; Nanchang; Russo-Japanese War; Second Sino-Japanese War;
Other:
"First Sino-Japanese War 1894–1895," *Britannica*, October 12, 2023

The Arsenic Ring Murders
Books:
Cooper, George, *Poison Widows: A True Story of Witchcraft, Arsenic, and Murder* (St. Martin's Press, 1999)
Wikipedia: Philadelphia poison ring
Other:
"Carina DeLuca Favato," *Find a Grave*, September 20, 2015
"Carina Favato, Member of Philadelphia's 'Arsenic Incorporated'—1939," *Unknown Gender History*, September 22, 2011
Commonwealth vs. Petrillo, 12 A.2d 317, 338 Pa. 65 (1940) (Supreme Court of Pennsylvania)
Davies, Lawrence E., "Poison Death Plot Amazing To Police," *New York Times*, May 14, 1939
Foster, Fred, "The Chilling Story Of The Philadelphia Poison Ring," August 14, 2020
McCabe, Scott, "Crime History: Trial opens in Philly's Poison Ring murders," *Washington Examiner*, March 12, 2012
"Petrillo Again Doomed; Philadelphia Judges Sentence 'Insurance Murder' Prisoner," *New York Times*, October 3, 1940
"Petrillo Involved in 21 Ring Deaths, Detectives Say Convicted Agent of Poisoners 'Put the Finger' on 3 'Executioners'," *New York Times*, April 30, 1939
"Petrillo Loses Appeal For Life," *New York Times*, May 15, 1941
"Philadelphia Poison Ring," *Absolute Crime*
"Philadelphia Poison Ring," *Jabajabba*, 2019

"Ring Used 'Death Powders'; Woman Tells Philadelphia Jury That Cousin of Defendant Bragged of 'Magic Powders'," *New York Times,* March 19, 1939
Rowan, Tommy, "1938: S. Philly pasta peddler executed in prolific arsenic murder ring," *The Philadelphia Inquirer*, October 21, 2016
"The Philadelphia Poison Ring: 21 Incredible Mugshots of Criminals in the Late 1930s," *Yesterday Today*, February 24, 2017
"Twelve Indicted In Poison Deaths," *New York Times*, May 20, 1939
"Widow Gets Life in Poison Ring," *New York Times*, November 2, 1940

Chapter 7 (The Spanish Civil War and a Concert in Washington)

Spanish Civil War Ends

Books: See Books mentioned in Chapter 1
Wikipedia: Francisco Franco; Spanish Civil War; Spain During World War II; Claude Bowers; Italian invasion of Albania; Jewish volunteers in the Spanish Civil War.
Other:
"Regime of Franco Recognized by U.S.," *New York Times*, April 2, 1939

Marian Anderson

Wikipedia: Mariane Anderson; Marian Andrson: The Lincoln Memorial Concert.
Other:
"DAR Constitution Hall History: Past Performers," *dar.org*
"DAR History," *dar.org*
"DAR: Who We Are and What We Do...," *dar.org*
"Eleanor Roosevelt Resigns from the DAR," *Learning For Justice*
Hill, Alexis, "Marian Anderson and the Easter Sunday Concert, April 9, 1939," *National Archives: Rediscovering Black History*, May 20, 2014
Kozinn, Allan, "Marian Anderson Is Dead at 96; Singer Shattered Racial Barriers," *New York Times*, April 9, 1993
Roosevelt, Eleanor, "I regret exceedingly that Washington is to be deprived of hearing Marian Anderson, a great artist" [telegram], *National Archives and Records Administration*, archived March 1996
"The Concert That Stirred America's Conscience," *The Attic*

The Forgotten Castles

Wikipedia: Vernon and Irene Castle; The Story of Vernon and Irene Castle [movie]; Chicago Blackhawks; Elisabeth Marbury; Frederic McLaughlin; Irving Berlin; Orphans of the Storm"; *Watch Your Step* (musical).
Other:
"Orphans of the Storm," *orphansofthestorm.org*
"The Story of Vernon and Irene Castle," *IMDb*
"The Story of Vernon and Irene Castle, 1939 Biography," *Fandango*
"The Story of Vernon and Irene Castle," *Rotten Tomatoes*
"The Story of Vernon and Irene Castle," *Metacritic*

Chapter 8 (A World's Fair to End All World's Fairs)

Books:

Bussler, Mark, *1939 New York World's Fair: The World of Tomorrow in Photographs* (Classic Game Room Publishing Empire, 2019)

Cotter, Bill, *The 1939–1940 New York World's Fair: The World of Tomorrow* (Arcadia Publishing 2018)

Cotter, Bill, *San Francisco's 1939–1940 World's Fair: The Golden Gate International Exposition* (Arcadia Publishing, 2021)

Dawn of a New Day: The New York World's Fair, 1939/40 (New York University Press, 1980)

Gelernter, David, *1939: The Lost World of the Fair* (Avon Books, 1995)

Mauro, James, *Twilight at the World of Tomorrow: Genius, Madness, Murder, and the 1939 World's Fair on the Brink of War* (Ballantine Books, 2010)

Official Guide Book 1939 New York World's Fair (Exposition Publications, Inc., 1939)

Wikipedia: Billy Rose; Bronx-Whitestone Bridge; Dynamometer; Eleanor Holm; Fiorello LaGuardia; LaGuardia Airport; Fluorescent lamp; 1st World Science Fiction Convention (July 2–4, 1939); Grover Whalen; Johnny Weissmuller; Kennywood; Lupe Velez; Lupe Vélez filmography; 1939 New York's World's Fair; Nylon; Robert Moses; Tarzan Finds a Son!; The Girl from Mexico; Trapp Family; Virginia Union Panthers.

Other:

"1939: Building the World of Tomorrow At the New York World's Fair," 1996

"1939 World's Fair: What it would cost today," *1940 Census: Employment and Income*

"*1939: The Lost World of the Fair* by David Gelernter" [review], *Kirkus Reviews*, 1995

"Barco-Stevens Hall: 80 Years of History," *Virginia Union University Sports*, May 1, 2019, https://vuusports.com/news/2019/5/1/general-barco-stevens-hall-80-years-of-history

Bellis, Mary, "The History of Nylon Stockings: Strong As Silk," *ThoughtCo.*, January 21, 2019

Benz, Kate, "Thomas Town: Ride the Rails in Kennywood's New Spot," *Pittsburgh Magazine*, June 29, 2018

Berger, Meyer, "At The Fair," *New York Times*, May 1, 1939

Blakinger, Keri, "A look back at some of the coolest attractions at the 1939 World's Fair," *New York Daily News*, April 30, 2016

Cope, David, "1939 New York World's Fair: The Amphitheater," *World's Fair Historian*, 1939

Cope, David, "1939 New York World's Fair: King George & Queen Elizabeth's Visit to the Fair: The Government Zone," *World's Fair Historian*, 1939

"Crowds Awed by Fair's Vastness And Medley of Sound and Color," *New York Times*, May 1, 1939

Cutlip, Kimbra, "How Nylon Stockings Changed the World," *Smithsonian Magazine*, May 11, 2025

"Fiorello La Guardia, Mayor of New York City," *Britannica*, December 8, 2023

"Hot-Blooded Facts About Lupe Vélez, The Mexican Spitfire, *Factinate*

"Johnny Weissmuller—Lupe Velez," *FameChain*

McNearney, Allison, "A Smoking Robot Ruled the 1939 World's Fair" [last modified May 1, 2019], *History*, April 27, 2018

Porter, Russell B., "Reign At The Fair; Rulers Captivate Throng in Unique Spectacle of Tribute," *New York Times*, June 11, 1939
Schiff, Judith, "Robert Moses and the World's Fair: How the 'valley of ashes' became the 'World of Tomorrow'," *Yale Alumni Magazine*, March/April 2014
Schroeder, Barbara, "'Mexican Spitfire' Mystery Solved After 7 Decades!" [last modified December 6, 2017], *HuffPost*, May 24, 2013
Spellen, Suzanne, "The 1939 World's Fair: The World of Tomorrow in Flushing Meadows-Corona Park, Part 2," 2022
"The Exhibit Area," *New York Times*, September 30, 1939
"The Fair's Huge Exhibit Area," *New York Times*, April 30, 1939
"The Fair Today," *New York Times*, April 30, 1939
"The Fair Today," *New York Times*, May 1, 1939
"The Fair Today," *New York Times*, May 2, 1939
"The Fair Today," *New York Times*, September 30, 1939
"The Lagoon of Nations from the 1939 World's Fair and Epcot Center," *ImagiNERDing*,March 21, 2016
"This Day in History: New York World Fair opens" [last modified April 27, 2021], *History.com*, February 9, 2010
"Velez, Weissmuller Part; Film Couple Announce Trial Separation of Eight Days, *New York Times*, January 25, 1934
"World's Fair: Enter the World of Tomorrow," *Biblion*
Yuko, Elizabeth, "6 Everyday Inventions That Debuted at World's Fair" [last modified September 29, 2023, *History*, April 12, 2022

Chapter 9 (A Voyage to Nowhere)

THE SS *ST. LOUIS*

Books:
Thomas, Gordon and Max Morgan-Witts, *Voyage of the Damned: A Shocking True Story Of Hope, Betrayal, And Nazi Terror,"* (Skyhorse Publishing, 2010 [1974])
Wikipedia: Abwehr; Federico Laredo Bru; Final Solution; Gustav Schroder; MS. St. Louis; Ramón Grau.
Other:
"907 On Liner Radio Thanks For Refuge; Message Voices Gratitude to Joint Distribution Group and Host Countries," *New York Times*, June 16, 1939
Berger, Joseph, "Fleshing Out Stories of Ship Denied Refuge From Hitler," *New York Times*, March 21, 1999
Blakemore, Erin, "A Ship of Jewish Refugees Was Refused Landing in 1939: This Was Their Fate," *History Stories*, June 4, 2019
Breitman, Richard, and Allan J. Lichtman, "The Real Story of the MS St. Louis," *Columbian College of Arts & Sciences*, May 20, 2013
"Cuba Again Asked To Admit Emigres; $500,000 Bond Deposited for 907 on the St. Louis," *New York Times*, June 8, 1939
"Cuba May Relent on 907 Refugees; Possibility Rises After Talks That She Might Receive the Germans on the St. Louis," *New York Times*, June 4, 1939
"Fear Suicide Wave On Refugees" Ship; Officers See Mutiny if St. Louis Sails for Germany With 917 Barred From Cuba," *New York Times,* June 1, 1939

Feldberg, Michael, "The St. Louis: The German luxury ship, the St. Louis, sailed to Cuba with over 900 passengers on it, only to be turned away and sent back to Europe," *My Jewish Learning*, 2023
Froomkin, Dan, "Talking to survivors of the SS St. Louis" [last modified January 27, 2017], *Miami Herald*, June 5, 1989
"Gustav Schroder, Germany," *The World Holocaust Remembrance Center*
Lanchin, Mike, "SS St Louis: The ship of Jewish refugees nobody wanted," *BBC World Service*, May 13, 2014
"Netherlands to Take 194 of Liner's Refugees; Belgium and France May Admit Rest of 900," *New York Times*, June 13, 1939
Nucilli, Ryleigh, "The Saga Of The St. Louis Reveals How The US Sent Jewish Refugees To Their Demise," *Ranker*, April 1, 2019
Phillips, R. Hart, "907 Refugees Quit Cuba on Liner; Ship Reported Hovering Off Coast; Rumor The United States Will Permit Entry Is Spread to Avert Suicides," *New York Times*, June 3, 1939
Phillips, R. Hart, "Cuba Opens Doors to 907 on St. Louis; Offers Temporary Refuge" *New York Times*, June 6, 1939
Phillips, R. Hart, "Cuba Recloses Door to Refugees; 48-Hour Limit on Offer Expires," *New York Times*, June 7, 1939
Phillips, R. Hart, "Cuba Orders Liner And Refugees To Go; Navy to Escort St. Louis With 917 Aboard Unless She Obeys—Compromise Reported," *New York Times*, June 2, 1939
"Refuge Is Assured For All on Liner; Belgium, Britain, France and Netherlands to Admit 907 on a Temporary Basis," *New York Times*, June 14, 1939
"Refugee Ships Idles Off Florida Coast; Liner St. Louis is Watched by Coast Guard," *New York Times*, June 5, 1939
"Refugees Make New Plea; 907 on Liner Ask Chamberlain for Asylum in Britain," *New York Times*, June 12, 1939
"Ship Prefixes: Understanding SS and Other Common Uses," *J.D. Power*
"St. Louis Emigres Head For Antwerp; Those Who Are to Get Refuge on Continent Will Land There, Probably Tomorrow," *New York Times*, June 15, 1939
"The Story of the S.S. St. Louis (1939)," *JDC Archives*
"This Day in History: Ship Carrying 937 Jewish refugees, fleeing Nazi Germany, is turned away in Cuba," *History.com,* May 21, 2019
"'Voyage of the Damned…' by David Schoenbrun" [review], *New York Times*, June 30, 1974
"Voyage of the St. Louis," *United States Holocaust Memorial Museum*, July 12, 2021
"Yad Vashem," *The World Holocaust Remembrance Center*

The 5-year-old Mother

Wikipedia: Lina Medina; Precocious puberty.
Other:
Anglis, Jaclyn, "The Story of Lina Medina, The Youngest Mother In The World" [last modified February 18, 2022], *All That's Interesting*, November 6, 2021
Chao-Fong, Leonie, "Youngest mum, 5, on record forced to have C-section to give birth to son," *Mirror*, November 9, 2021
Mikkelson, David, "Was the World's Youngest Mother Only 5 Years Old?" *Snopes*, July 21, 2004
Roos, Dave, "The Shocking Story of Lina Medina, Who Gave Birth at Age 5," *howstuffworks.com*, July 25, 2022

THE PACT OF STEEL
Wikipedia: Benito Mussolini; Galeazzo Ciano; The Pact of Steel.
Other:
"Axis Powers Sign Ten-Year Alliance To Remake Europe," *New York Times*, May 23, 1939
Goldberg, Maren, "Pact of Steel: Italy–Germany [1939]," *Britannica*, May 15, 2023

THE USS *SQUALUS* SINKS
Wikipedia: Charles Momsen; HMS *Thetis* (N25); *Isles of Shoals*; USS *Sailfish* (SS-192)
Other:
"Behind the Scenes of the Film 'Submerged'," *SeacoastNH.com*
Newton, Marshall E., "Submarine That Sank Off The Coast Of New Hampshire: The Squalus, which is laying helpless 240 feet below the surface with fifty-nine men aboard," *New York Times*, May 24, 1939
Olds, Victor A., "USS Squalus And The First Submarine Rescue in U.S. History," *US Submarine*, August 3, 2021
"The Greatest Submarine Rescue Ever," *New England Historical Society*, 2023
"The Saved and the Dead," *New York Times*, May 25, 1939
"USS *Squalus* (SS-192): The Sinking, Rescue of Survivors, and Subsequent Salvage, 1939," *Naval History and Heritage Command*, August 15, 2016

Chapter 10 ("Pulling a Crater" and the Opening of Baseball's Hall of Fame)

JUDGE CRATER
Books:
Edmund, Elmaleh, *The Canary Sang But Couldn't Fly* (Union Square Press, 2009)
Riegel, Stephen J., *Finding Judge Crater: A Life and Phenomenal Disappearance in Jazz Age New York* (Syracuse University Press, 2022)
Wikipedia: Joseph Force Crater; List of people executed in New York; Tammany Hall.
Other:
Celona, Larry, "1930 Crater Vanish 'Solved'—Dead Woman's Note: My Hubby & Cop Pal Killed Judge," *New York Post*, August 19, 2005
"Confession Names Stein As Slayer of Vivian Gordon," *New York Times*, May 25, 1931
"Crater Will Case Up May 26," *New York Times*, April 28, 1939
"Crater Held Dead in Ruling By Foley; Surrogate Declares Vanished Justice Legally Deceased," *New York Times*, June 7, 1939
"Family Asks Hunt for Judge Crater; Wife, in Signed Statement, Says She Last Saw Him in Maine on Aug 3," *New York Times*, September 7, 1930
"Federal Men Scan Crater Bank Books; But They Have Found Nothing to Link Missing Judge to the Ewald Case," *New York Times*, September 6, 1930
Gendar, Alison, and Leo Standora, "Letter May Solve 1930 mystery of missing judge," *Seattle Times*, August 20, 2005
"Judge Crater Clues Sought In Yonkers," *New York Times*, June 26, 1964
"Judge Crater Vanished 30 Years Ago Today," *New York Times*, August 6, 1960

"Frederic Johnson, Aide To Judge Crater in '30' [obituary], *New York Times*, February 10, 1985
"Missing Since August 6, 1930: Honorable Joseph Force Crater," Police Department Poster, September 8, 1930
Rashbaum, William K. "Judge Crater Abruptly Appears, at Least in Public Consciousness," *New York Times*, August 20, 2005
"Search for Crater Near A Standstill; But Police Seek To Trace Report Missing Judge Is Voluntary Patient in a Sanitorium," *New York Times*, September 8, 1930
Shteir, Rachel, "The Dead Woman Who Brought Down the Mayor," *Smithsonian Magazine*, February 25, 2013
"The Missingest Man in New York," *Straus Media*, February 16, 2015
"Unexplained Mysteries—Judge Crater: The 'Missingest Man' in New York City," *Historic Mysteries*, June 7, 2010
"What Ever Happened To Judge Crater?" *Factinate*
"Wide Hunt is Begun For Justice Crater, Missing Four Weeks," *New York Times*, September 4, 1930

LITTLE LEAGUE:
Wikipedia: Carl Stotz.
Other:
"Carl Stotz, 82, Founder of Little League Baseball [obituary]," *New York Times*, June 5, 1992
"Historical Information," *LittleLeague.org*
"History of Little League," *LittleLeague.org*
"Little League International Remembers Jimmy Gehron, Nephew of Little League Founder Carl Stotz," *LittleLeague.org*, September 13, 2021
"Tribute Archive: James Gehron, Fort Lauderdale, Florida, September 15, 1931—August 26, 2021," *Aarons Low Cost Cremation & Funeral*

COOPERSTOWN:
Wikipedia: Abner Doubleday; History of Baseball; National Baseball Hall of Fame and Museum; Stephen Carlton Clark; Fort Sumter; The Explorers Club; The Otesaga Hotel
Other:
Cheney, Jim, "The Baseball Hall of Fame in Cooperstown: Everything You Need to know to Visit," *Uncovering New York,* November 23, 2022
Foster, Dave, "San Francisco cable cars," December 1, 2022
"Gen. Abner Doubleday" [obituary], *New York Times*, January 28 1893
Gramman, Brian, "Abner Doubleday: Why a Civil War General Received Credit for Inventing Baseball," June 27, 2012
"Hall of Fame inductions by year," *MLB.com,* January 25, 2022
Homer, Aaron, "The Tragic 1925 Death of Baseball Legend Christy Mathewson," *Grunge,* January 12, 2023
"Sterling & Francine Clark," *Clark Art Institute*
"This Day in History: U.S. Baseball Hall of Fame elects first members," *History.com*
"Tinker to Evers to Chance!," *Library of Congress* [collection: Baseball Cards]
Webster, Ian, "$30,000,000 in 1896 is worth $1,064,321,428.57 today"
"Who Invented Baseball?" [last modified July 1, 2021], *History*, March 27, 2013

"Why did Abner Doubleday Invent Baseball? (He didn't)," *IPL*

WEIDMANN:

Wikipedia: Eugen Weidman; French Revolution; Guillotine; Louis XVI; Marie Antoinette; Henri Desire Landru.

Other:

"80 Years ago the last public execution took place in France," *AFP*, June 15, 2019

"Eugen Weidmann: The last public execution by Guillotine, 1939," *Belfast Child*, March 26, 2018

"Eugene Weidmann: The Last Public Guillotine Execution" [documentary], *True Crime Documentary*, https://youtu.be/OK3Z_yIQbhk

"France Guillotines Head of Murder Ring; Weidmann Dies in Silence for Slaying Brooklyn Dancer," *New York Times*, June 17, 1939

"Louisett [definition]," *The Free Dictionary*

"The Last Public Execution in France: Eugen Weidmann" [documentary], *Death Row*, December 22, 2021

"What it was like to witness the Guillotine" [documentary], *Weird History*

Chapter 11 (Gehrig, Riggs, Marble, and Gandhi Writes Hitler)

LOU GEHRIG

Wikipedia: Lou Gehrig; Lou Gehrig Memorial Award; Murderers' Row; Wally Pipp.

Other:

Drebinger, John, "61,808 Fans Roar Tribute To Gehrig; Captain of Yankees Honored at Stadium," *New York Times*, July 5, 1939

Friend, Harold, "Lou Gehrig, Not Babe Ruth, Was Voted the American League's MVP in 1927," *Bleacher Report*, September 9, 2009

"Full text of Lou Gehrig's farewell speech," *Sports Illustrated*, July 4, 2009

Larkin, Kevin, "April 30, 1939: Lou Gehrig plays his final game with Yankees," *Society for American Baseball Research*

"Major Sports Yesterday: Baseball," *New York Times*, July 5, 1939

"New York Yankees Uniform Numbers," *Baseball Almanac*

Sandomir, Richard, "The Real Story Behind Lou Gehrig's Famous July 4th, 'Luckiest Man' Speech," *Gothamist*, July 4, 2014

Schlossberg, Dan, "Lou Gehrig, First To Have Number Retired, Launched A Major Tradition," *Forbes*

Snyder, Matt, "Happy 75th Anniversary: Lou Gehrig's 'luckiest man' speech," *CBS MLB*, July 4, 2014

"This Day in History: U.S. Baseball Hall of Fame elects first members," *History.com*

"When did baseball players start wearing numbers," *Microsoft Bing*

Whiteman, Mike, "May 2, 1939: Lou Gehrig's streak ends in Detroit," *Society for American Baseball Research*

BOBBY RIGGS

Wikipedia: Bobby Riggs; Battle of the Sexes (tennis); French Open; Gorgeous George; 1938 International Lawn Tennis Challenge; List of French Open men's singles champions; 1939 Wimbledon Championships—Men's singles.

Other:
"A History of the Colorado Tennis Championships," *USTA*
"Bobby Riggs: American tennis player," *Britannica*, July 27, 2017
"Bobby Riggs Biography" [last modified April 14, 2021], *Biography.com,* April 2, 2014
"Bobby Riggs's Son, 22, Found Dead in L.I. Room," *New York Times*, April 12, 1976
Finn, Robin, "Bobby Riggs, Brash Impresario of Tennis World, is Dead at 77," *New York Times,* October 27, 1995
Hamilton, T.J., "Riggs Downs Cooke in Five-Set Battle for Wimbledon Singles Championship," *New York Times*, July 8, 1939
"Major Sports Yesterday: Tennis," *New York Times*, July 9, 1939
"Riggs, Miss Marble Advance In Singles," *New York Times*, September 29, 1939
"Riggs Takes Senior Final," *New York Times,* June 23, 1969
"Tennis Grand Slam," *New York Times*, July 16, 1939

Alice Marble
Books:
Marble, Alice, with Dale Leatherman, *Courting Danger: My Adventures in World Class Tennis, Golden Age Hollowood and High-Stakes Spying* (St. Martin's Press, 2020 [1991])
Weintraub, Robert, *The Divine Miss Marble: A Life of Tennis, Fame, and Mystery* (Dutton, 2020)
Wikipedia: Alice Marble; Althea Gibson; Mary Browne; Rod Serling; William du Pont Jr.; 1939 U.S. National Championships (tennis); 1939 Wimbledon Championships – Women's singles.
Other:
"Alice Marble," *Britannica*, December 9, 2022
Brown, Ashley, "How Althea Gibson Faced Racial Barriers, Even as a Tennis Champion," *History.com*, August 21, 2023
Cutler, Jacqueline, "The mysterious Ms. Marble: Tennis and gender equality trailblazer," *Daily News*, July 24, 2020
Jaffe, Matt, "Review: Tennis legend Alice Marble's mysterious life traced in new biography," July 17, 2020
"Major Sports Yesterday: Tennis," *New York Times*, July 9, 1939
Maloney, Wendi, "Alice Marble: Wonder Woman of Tennis & More," *Library of Congress*, August 30, 2017
Rogers, Thomas, "Alice Marble, 77, Top U.S. Tennis Star of 1930's" [obituary]," *New York Times*, December 14, 1990
Weintraub, Robert, "The incredible mystery surrounding a tennis legend," *New York Post*, July 14, 2020

Mahatma Gandhi:
Wikipedia: Dear Friend Hitler.
Other:
Chang, Rachel, "Gandhi's Surprising Letters to Hitler Pleading for Peace," *Time*, October 1, 2020
Suhrud, Tridip, "'You Are Today the One Person in the World Who Can Prevent a War.' Read Gandhi's Letters to Hitler," *Time*, September 25, 2019

Chapter 12 (The Home Front)

Wikipedia: Alf Landon; Barbara Newhall Follet; Brenda Frazier; Lisa Fonssagrives; *Thanks for the Memory*; 1939 in comics; 1939 in radio: 1939 in the United States; Newport, Rhode Island; The year 1939 saw a number of significant events in radio broadcasting; *The War of the Worlds* (1938 radio drama); Winnie Ruth Judd.

Other:

Bell, Felicitie C., and Michael L. Miller, "Life Tables for the United States Social Security Area, 1900–2010, Actuarial Study No. 120"

Boyd, John, "Life in 1939: A time of transition," *Lifestyle*, February 24, 2015

Burns, Charles J., "The Age of the Debutante; Newport in the 1930s, Part II," *Social History*, October 6, 2020

"Dust, Debris, and Determination: Life in 1939," *History.com*, July 2022

"Electrifying Rural America," *Encyclopedia.com*

"Expectancy at Birth by Race and Sex, 1930-2010," *US Census Bureau*

Gallup, George, "What We, The People, Think About Europe: A Cross-Section of Opinion on Our World Role," *New York Times*, April 30, 1939

Halper, Donna L., "News While It Was News: Broadcast Journalism in Radio's Early Years," *The Old Radio Times,* No. 31, June 2009

"How Much Did Things Cost in 1939?" *Reference*, May 27, 2020

Hoyt, Jeff, "1800–1990: Changes in Urban/Rural U.S. Population," *Senior Living*, July 27, 2023

"Jim Ramsburg's Gold Time Radio: 1938–1939 Season"

Jordan, Karoline, "The Legacy of Harry's Boots is Part of a Greater American History," *Harry's Boots*

Nilsson, Jeff, and Herbert Hoover, "Everyday Life in 1939," *Saturday Evening Post*, October 30, 2014

"Old Time Radio Show Ratings by Year," *WorldRadioHistory.com*

Okwodu, Janelle, "Lessons in Style From Fashion's First Supermodel, Lisa Fonssagrives," *Vogue*, August 24, 2015

Pugh, Carl, "New Collection Documents the Infamous 1939 Carolina Buccaneer 'Sex Issue'," September 30, 2018

"Radio Listeners in Panic, Talking War Drama as Fact," *New York Times*, October 31, 1938

"Rural Electrification Administration 1934–1941," *Enclclopedia.com*

"TVA" [last modified June 13, 2023], *History.com,* August 3, 2017

"What Did It Cost? A Look Back," *David Manuel.com*

"What Happened in 1939 Important News and Events, Key Technology and Popular Culture," *The People History*, January 5, 2021

THANKSGIVING:

Barrett, Claire, "That Time FDR Changed The Date of Thanksgiving and alienated Half the Country," *HistoryNet*, October 20, 2019

Nilsson, Jeff, "The Year of Two Thanksgivings," *Saturday Evening Post*, November/December 2022

"October 3, 1863: President Lincoln proclaims official Thanksgiving holiday" [last modified October 1, 2020], *History.com*, November 16, 2009

"One Good Fact: Lengthening Christmas Shopping in 1939," *Britannica*, November 17, 2022

Chapter 13 (The World on the Brink and the Wicked Witch of the West)

EINSTEIN-SZILARD LETTER:

Wikipedia: Einstein-Szilard letter; Leo Szilard; File: Roosevelt-einstein-letter.png; Alexander Sachs; The World Set Free; Otto Hahn; John R. Dunning; Louis Brandeis.

Other:

"Albert Einstein," *Southold Historical Society*

"Albert Einstein, Leo Szilard and the letter that led to Manhattan Project," *Bulletin of the Atomic Scientists*

"Manhattan Project" [lasty modified July 21, 2023], *History.com*, July 26, 2017

Niderost, Eric, "First Sustained Nuclear Reaction," *WWII History*, April 2023

"The Manhattan Project, Part of the Einstein exhibition," *American Museum of Natural History*

"This Day in History: Albert Einstein born" [last modified March 10, 2021], *History.com*, November 24, 2009

"This Day in History: The first atomic bomb test is successfully exploded" [last modified July 13, 2021]," *History.com,* July 15, 2010

HOWARD HUGHES:

Wikipedia: Howard Hughes; *Hell's Angels* (film); 4th, Academy Awards; *Diamonds Are Forever* (film); Gene Tierney; *Iron Man* (2008 film); Jean Peters; Jane Russell; Oleg Cassini; *The Front Page* (1931 film); *The Outlaw*; William Marsh Rice.

Other:

"Howard Hughes: American manufacturer, aviator, and motion-picture producer," *Britannica*, December 20, 2022

"Howard Hughes Biography," *IMDb*

"Howard Hughes Biography," *TheFamousPeople.com*

"Howard Hughes Dies at 70 On Flight to Texas Hospital" [obituary]," *New York Times*, April 6, 1976

Obias, Rudie, "The Real People Who Inspired 5 Comic Book Characters, *Mental Floss*, May 27, 2016

HEDY LAMARR:

Wikipedia: Hedy Lamarr; *Lady of the Tropics*; *Ecstasy* (film); Barbara La Marr; Joseph Schildkraut; Ben Hecht; *Monkey Business* (1952 film); *Notorious* (1946 film); *Samson and Delilah* (1949 film); *Scarface* (1932 film); *Spellbound* (1945 film); *The Front Page* (1931 film)

Other:

"Bombshell: The Hedy Lamarr Story," dir. Alexandra Dean, *American Masters* (PBS, 2018)

DiMaria, Paola Macioci, "Hedy Lamarr and Prime Naked Integral Film (with Video)," *Cinema-Tv-Spettacolo*, September 27, 2014

"Hollywood Star Walk: Hedy Lamarr," *LATimes.com*

"Hollywood Walk of Fame—Hedy Lamarr—6247 Hollywood Boulevard"

"Lady of the Tropics Reviews," *TV Guide*

"Lady of the Tropics," *Rotten Tomatoes*

Nugent, Frank S., "The Screen; Four Films In Review: Metro-Goldwyn-Mayers' 'Lady of the Tropics'," *New York Times*, September 8, 1939
"User Reviews: Lady of the Tropics (1939)," *IMDb*

THE MOLOTOV-RIBBENTROP PACT:

Wikipedia: Molotov-Ribbentrop Pact; Battles of Khalkhin Gol; Finland in World War II; Gleiwitz incident; Molotov cocktail; Romania in World War II; Winter War.
Other:
Albertson, Mark, "Deal of the Devils: The Molotov-Ribbentrop Pact," *Warfare History*, June 2015
"Axis Powers Sign Ten-Year Alliance to Remake Europe," *New York Times*, May 23, 1939
Donovan, John, "7 Atrocities Soviet Dictator Joseph Committed," *HowStuffWorks*, April 1, 2021
"German-Soviet Nonaggression Pact [1939]," *Britannica*
"German-Soviet Pact," *United States Holocaust Memorial Museum, Washington, DC*, August 20, 2021
Kiger, Patrick J., "How Joseph Stalin Starved Millions in the Ukrainian Famine," *History*, April 16, 2019
Klein, Christopher, "How a Secret Hitler-Stalin Pact Set the Stage for WWII," *History*, June 17, 2020
Kuhn, Ferdinand Jr., "3-Power Military Talks To Begin In Moscow; Spur To Political Accord" *New York Times*, August 1, 1939
Kuhn, Ferdinand Jr., "British Discount New Difficulties; Expected to Meet Soviet Demands," *New York Times*, June 1, 1939
"Nazi-Soviet Pact Of 1939," *Encyclopedia.com*
Nye, Logan, "Khalkhin Gol: The battle that caused Pearl Harbor," *Mighty History*, November 21, 2022
Rosenberg, Jennifer, "The Nazi-Soviet Non-Aggression Pact: The 1939 Agreement Between Hitler and Stalin," *ThoughtCo*, March 30, 2020
Yegorov, Oleg, "Why didn't the USSR join Allies in 1939?" *History*, September 26, 2019
Yegorov, Oleg, "Why did the USSR do a pre-WWII deal with Hitler?" *History*, August 23, 2016

LEPKE:

Books:
Cipollini, Christian, *Murder Inc.: Mysteries of the Mob's Most Deadly Hit Squad* (Strategic Media Books, 2015)
Cohen, Rich, *Tough Jews: Fathers, Sons, and Gangster Dreams* (Simon and Schuster, 1998)
Kavieff, Paul R., *The Life and Times of Lepke Buchalter: America's Most Ruthless Racketeer* (Barricade Books, 2006)
Rabb, Selwyn, *Five Families: The Rise, Decline, and Resurgence of America's Most Powerful Mafia Empires* (St. Martin's Press, 2006)
Turkus, Burton B., and Sid Feder, *Murder, Inc.: The Story of the Syndicate* (Da Capo Press, 1992 [1951])
Wikipedia: Abe Reles; Dutch Schultz; Harry Greenberg; Jacob Shapiro; Lepke Buchalter; Lucky Luciano; Martin Goldstein; Murder, Inc.; Seymour Magoon.

Other:
"Harry Greenberg," *FamousFix*
Kantrowitz, R. Marc, "Kid Twist Goes Flying (1941)," from *Old Whiskey and Young Women: American True Crime Tales of Murder, Sex and Scandal* (Fonthill Media, 2015)
"Lepke Comes In," *New York Times*, August 26, 1939
"Lepke Surrenders to FBI; Racketeer Never Left City," *New York Times*, August 25, 1939
"Louis 'Lepke' Buchalter/Murder Inc. FBI Files," *BACM Research*
"Mobsters in America: Louis 'Lepke' Buchalter, The Only Mob Boss To Be Executed by the Government," October 1, 2021
May, Allan, "The Last Days of Lepke Buchalter," *Crime Magazine*, October 14, 2009
McFadden, Robert D., "Murder of Wrong Pair Recalls '39 Slaying in Bronx'," *New York Times*, August 15, 1972
"This Day in History: Louis 'Lepke' Buchalter, the head of Murder, Inc., is executed" [last modified March 2, 2021], *History.com*, November 13, 2009
"U.S. at War: Waiting for Lepke," *Time*, December 13, 1943

THE WIZARD OF OZ:
Books:
Marmetz, Aljean, *The Making of the Wizard of Oz* (Chicago Review Press, 2013[1977])
Woodhouse, Horace Martin, *The Essential Wizard of Oz: 101 Things You Didn't Know About the Most-Watched Movie in Film History* (History Company LLC, 2013)
Wikipedia: *The Wizard of Oz* (1939 film); *Bridal Suite*; Caren Marsh Doll; Judy Garland; Bert Lahr; Frank Morgan; Ray Bolger; Margaret Hamilton (actress); The Wonderful Wizard of Oz.
Other:
Anderson, Tim, "Judy Garland & the Munchkins: Sex, Scandals, and Secrets of the Stars of 'The Wizard of Oz'," *Reel Rundown*, October 5, 2019
Aravind, Ajay, "The Wizard Of Oz: 5 Things The Movie Changed From The Book (& 5 That Stayed The Same), *Screen Rant,* June 10, 2020
Bertram, Colin, "Judy Garland Was Put on a Strict Diet and Encouraged to Take 'Pep Pills' While Filming 'The Wizard of Oz'" [last modified December 10, 2020], *Biography*, June 4, 2019
Bertram, Colin, "Judy Garland's Life Was in a Downward Spiral Before Her 1969 Death," *Biography*, September 23, 2019
Carlton, Genevieve, "The Secret Political Symbolism You Never Knew Was Hidden Within The Wizard Of Oz," *Ranker*, July 1, 2019
Collins, Hannah, "This Fan Theory Proves Glinda Is Actually The Villain Of 'The Wizard Of Oz'," *Ranker*, December 11, 2018
Daly, Dana, "Co-Stars Made Filming 'The Wizard Of Oz' Nightmare For Judy Garland," *Do You Remember?*
Deutschmann, Jennifer, "Disturbing Things Judy Garland Had To Do For Her Role In The Wizard Of Oz," *Grunge*, January 13, 2022
Economou, Thane, "Old Hollywood Scandals That History Forgot," *Ranker*, December 30, 2021
"Every Song in The Wizard of Oz, Ranked by Singability," *Ranker Music*,July 10, 2019
"Frank Morgan, Veteran Actor, Local Property Owner, Dies," *Desert Sun*, Vol. XXIII, No 8, September 20, 1949

"Frank Morgan Funeral: 300 Friends of Actor at Rites in Beverly Hills Church" *New York Times*, September 21, 1949
Gibbons, Phil, "Strange Things You Definitely Didn't Know About 'The Wizard of Oz'," *Ranker*, March 12, 2020
Green, Kai, "Follow the Yellow Brick Road to These 50 Memorable Quotes From The Wizard of Oz," *Pinterest*, October 21, 2021
Hines, Sam, "Judy Garland Said She and Mickey Rooney Took So Many Drugs They 'Were Hanging From the Ceiling'," *Showbiz Cheat Sheet*, March 25, 2023
Marder, Hannah, "14 Actors Who Were Reportedly Excluded, Shunned, Or Just Disliked By Co-stars On Their Major TV Shows And Movies," *BuzzFeed*, March 24, 2022
"Margaret Hamilton Trivia," *IMDb*
McCann, Erin, "15 Nightmare Stories From Behind The Scenes Of 'The Wizard of Oz'," *Ranker*, October 15, 2020
McCann, Erin, "Behind The Scenes Of Munchkinland In 'The Wizard Of Oz'," *Ranker*, Semptember 23, 2021
McCann, Erin, "'The Wizard Of Oz' Stars: Where Did They Go?" *Ranker*, September 23, 2021
McCann, Erin, "These Old Hollywood Actresses Were Ruthlessly Bullied By Men On Classic Movie Sets," *Ranker*, June 14, 2019
Nucilli, Ivey, "What People Who Worked With Old Hollywood Stars Had To Say About Them," *Ranker*, December 28, 2021
Rogovoy, Seth, "The secret Jewish history of Judy Garland," *Forward*, June 10, 2021
Russell, Calum, "The most important film from every decade of cinema history," *Far Out*, January 26, 2022
Shrina, Iian, "Why 'The Wizard of Oz' Is the Most Popular Film of All Time, *Psychology Today*, June 4, 2010
"The Original 'Wizard of Oz' Books Are Shockingly Violent Compared To The Judy Garland Classic," *Ranker*, September 19, 2019
"The Wonderful Witches of Oz," *Remind Magazine*, Vol 15, No. 10, October 2023
"This Day in History: 'The Wizard of Oz' movie premieres in Oconomowoc, Wisconsin" [last modified August 11, 2020], *History.com,* November 16, 2009
Whitman, Alden, "Bert Lahr, Comic Actor, Dies; Played Burlesque and Beckett," December 5, 1967

THE GLEIWITZ INCIDENT

Books: See Chapter 1
Wikipedia: Gleiwitz Incident; Reinhard Heydrich.
Other:
Pope, Cassie, "How a False Flag Sparked World War Two: The Gleiwitz Incident Explained," *HistoryHit*, August 31, 2018

Chapter 14 (The War Starts, the Yankees Clinch the Pennant, and a Mobster Heads to Hollywood)

GERMANY INVADES POLAND

Taylor, Frederick, *1939: A People's History of the Coming of the Second World War* (W.W. Norton & Company, 2019)

Moorhouse, Roger, *Poland 1939: The Outbreak of World War II* (Basic Books, 2020)
Overy, Richard, *1939: Countdown to War* (Penguin Books, 2009)
Wikipedia: Invasion of Poland; Polish-Soviet War in 1920; World War II Casualties of Poland

Irving "Big Gangy" Cohen

Books: See Chapter 13
Wikipedia: Adolph Menjou; Barbara Stanwyck; Golden Boy (1939 film); Lee J. Cobb; Murder, Inc.; William Holden; Samuel Levine (mobster); Sullivan County, New York
Other:
"5 of the Deadliest Mafia Hitmen in History," *History Collection*, February 7, 2017
"Big Gangi Cohen Cleared Of Murder, Slaying Was One of 57 Laid To Syndicate In Brooklyn," *New York Times*, June 22, 1940
Cannel, Michael, "Irving 'Gangi' Cohen: The Man Who Escaped Murder, Inc. and Hid Out in the Movies," *Crime Reads*, January 6, 2021
"Cohen Brought Here As Contract Killer; Questioned Five Hours By O'Dwyer," *New York Times*, April 11, 1940
Conway, John, "Sullivan County: The Corpse In The Grey Suit," *New York Almanack*, July 24, 2014
"Jack Gordon," *IMDb*
Mogg, Diarmid, "The Unsung Joe: Irving Cohen," *Small Town Noir*, November 13, 2008
"Mug Shot of Abraham 'Pretty' Levine," *Lloyd Sealy Library*, John Jay College of Criminal Justice
"Murder Accusation Makes Cohen Weep, Breakdown Necessitates Recess at Monticello Trial," *New York Times*, June 18, 1940
"State Rests Cohen Case; Murder Defense Indicates It Will Not Call Any Witnesses," *New York Times*, June 20, 1940
"Whatever Happened to Pretty Levine?" *Ask MetaFilter*, May 22, 2008

Yankees Clinch Pennant

Wikipedia: 1927 New York Yankees season; 1939 New York Yankees season; 1939 in baseball; 1939 Major League Baseball season; 1961 New York Yankees season; 1998 New York Yankees season; Aaron Judge; Arch McDonald; Babe Ruth; Charlie Gehringer; Hank Greenberg; Jacob Ruppert; Joe DiMaggio; Joe McCarthy; List of New York Yankees in the Baseball Hall of Fame; Murderers' Row; Red Rolfe; Red Ruffing; Ted Williams.
Other:
"1939 All-Star Game," *Baseball Reference*
"1939 American League Standard Batting," *Baseball Reference*
"1939 New York Yankees," *Historic Baseball*
Baldassaro, Lawrence, "Joe DiMaggio," *Society for American Baseball Research*, SABR 51
"Charlie Gehringer," *Baseball Reference*
Kendrick, Scott, "Best New York Yankees Teams of All Time," *Time*, August 8, 2018
"Major League Baseball (MLB): 1939 MLB Leaders," *Retro Seasons*
"New York Yankees Hall of Famers," *Yankees.com*

Rimmer, Joe, "1939 Yankees: The most quietly dominant team in history," *Pinstripe Alley*, June 16, 2021

SIGMUND FREUD

Wikipedia: Anna Freud; Anschluss; Sigmund Freud; Freud family; Father complex; Ernst von Fleischl-Marxow; Oedipus complex; Psychoanalysis

Other:

Blumenthal, Ralph, "Hotel Log Hints at Illicit Desire That Dr. Freud Didn't Repress," *New York Times*, December 24, 2006

Coffey, Rebecca, "10 Things About Sigmund Freud You'll Wish You Hadn't Learned," *Psychology Today*, December 1, 2015

Jay, Martin Evan, "Sigmund Freud, Austrian psychoanalyst," *Britannica*, May 2, 2023

Kelmenson, Lawrence, MD., "Freud: The First Anti-Psychiatrist," *Science, Psychiatry and Social Justice,* December 15, 2017

"Sigmund Freud Facts," *Facts.net*, June 1, 2022

"Sigmund Freud, Psychoanalyst, Dies; Refugee in England at 83," *International Herald Tribune,* September 25, 1939

Chapter 15 (Germany Pummels Poland as Mr. Smith Goes to Washington)

OVERVIEW OF THE WAR IN OCTOBER

Books: see Chapter 1

Wikipedia: HMS *Courageous* (50); Karl Donitz; Phoney War; Robert Rice Reynolds; Saar Offensive; Siegfried Westphal; SS *Athenia* (1922); SS *City of Flint* (1919); Timeline of World War II (1939).

Other:

"Capt. Gainard Dies; City Of Flint hero," *New York Times*, December 24, 1943

"Cargo Is At Issue; Internment Suspected as Soviet Studies Nature of Vessel's Freight," *New York Times*, October 26, 1939

Catledge, Turner, "City Of Flint Ends 116-Day Sea Sage At Baltimore Pier," *New York Times*, January 28, 1940

Cowell, Alan, "Churchill's definition of Russia still rings true," *New York Times*, August 1, 2008

"Holocaust Chronology of 1939," *Holocaust Memorial Center, Farmington Hills, MI and Yad Vashem*

Kluckhorn, Frank L., "Hull Seeks Facts; Concerned Over City of Flint's Crew of 41," *New York Times*, October 25, 1939

Mawdsley, Even, "Sinking the SS Athenia," *Yale University Press*, August 4, 2020

"Nazis Seize U.S. Ship City of Flint, Sailing Her to Murmansk, Russia," *The Associated Press*, October 24, 1939

Schick, Joshua, "The Sinking of the SS Athenia," *The National WWII Museum*, September 3, 2020

"The U-Boat Commander Who Almost Killed Churchill," *Sky History*

"This Day in History: The U-505, a submarine from Hitler's deadly fleet, is captured" [last modified June 3, 2020], *History.com,* June 17, 2019

"U.S. Statement on Flint," *New York Times*, October 29, 1939

LaGuardia

Wikipedia: Fiorello La Guardia; Mayoralty of Fiorello La Guardia; LaGuardia Airport; Nathan D. Perlman; 64th, United States Congress; 65th, United States Congress; 66th, United States Congress; Steinway and Sons; Free State of Fiume.

Other:

"325,000 See Mayor Dedicate Airport to World Service," *New York Times*, October 16, 1939

Backes, Aaron D. "The History of New York's LaGuardia Airport," *Classic New York History.com*

"Fiorello H. La Guardia," *The Free Social Encyclopedia*, July 8, 2022

"Fiorello H. La Guardia Biography," *TheFamousPeople.com*

Hamlett, Roz, "LaGuardia Airport: Flashback to the Past," *PORTfolio*, June 17, 2016

"La Guardia, Fiorello," *Encyclopedia.com*, June 27, 2018

"La Guardia is Dead; City Pays Homage to 3-Term Mayor," *New York Times*, September 21, 1947

"Mrs. La Guardia Dies After Long Illness; Wife of President of Board of Aldermen Had Recently Returned from Saranac Lake," *New York Times*, November 30, 1921

Neves, Gabriel, "A Look at the Lost Amusement Park Where LaGuardia Airport Now Stands," *Untapped New York*

Parks, Brennan, "Fiorello!—A Study Guide," *Timeline Theatre Company*

"Thea Amerigotti LaGuardia," *Find a Grave*

"Thea LaGuardia," *Historic Saranac Lake Wiki*

Mr. Smith Goes to Washington

Wikipedia: Frank Capra; Mr. *Smith Goes to Washington*; October 1939; *A Song to Remember*; Academy Award for Best Story; Alben W. Barkley; *Arsenic and Old Lace*; *If You Could Only Cook*; *It Happened One Night*; *It's a Wonderful Life*; *Meet John Doe*; *Why We Fight*.

Books: see Chapter 2

Other:

"Barkley Assails Film; 'Silly and Stupid,' He Says of 'Mr. Smith Goes to Washington'," *New York Times*, October 24, 1939

"Box Office Hits By Decade and Year (Domestic Gross)," *filmsite*

Churchill, Douglas W., "Mr. Capra Girds (Mildly) At The Government," *New York Times,* May 14, 1939

Garrett, Victor, "10 Biggest Box Office Hits of the 1930s, Ranked," *Movieweb*, February 26, 2023

Langbart, David, "'Mr. Smith Goes to Washington': Ambassador Joseph P. Kennedy as Movie Critic," *Hollywood and Film*, October 14, 2014

"'Mr. Smith' Comes to Washington," *United States Senate*, October 17, 1939

"Mr. Smith Goes to Washington," *IMDb*

"Mr. Smith Goes to Washington," *Politics and Film Database, Honors 495*

"Mr. Smith Goes to Washington: Reviews," *Rotten Tomatoes, Fandango*

"'Mr. Smith Goes to Washington': THR's 1939 Review," *The Hollywood Reporter*, October 17, 1939

"Mr. Smith Goes to Washington," *Variety*, October 11, 1939

Nugent, Frank S., "Capra Cuts A Caper; And Offers a Passing Salute to Liberty in "Mr. Smith Goes to Washington," *New York Times*, October 22, 1939

Nugent, Frank S., "Frank Capra's "Mr. Smith Goes to Washington" at the Music Hall Sets a Seasonal High in Comedy," *New York Times*, October 20, 1939

Parker-Anderson, Scott, "Mr. Smith Goes to Washington (1939)," *Waldina*, October 18, 2021
Pfeiffer, Lee, "Mr. Smith Goes to Washington: film by Capra (1939)," by Lee Pfeiffer, *Britannica*, January 12, 2024
Ronald, Susan, "Joe Kennedy: A Complex And Shocking Ambassador," *The History Reader from the St. Martin's Publishing Group*, August 5, 2021
Shribman, David M., "'The Ambassador' Review: Joseph Kennedy's Diplomatic Disaster," *The Wall Street Journal*, July 16, 2021

Chapter 16 (Hitler Dodges a Bomb While Big Greenie Gets Clipped)

Hitler Dodges a Bomb

Wikipedia: Georg Elser.
Other:
"A Time Bomb Set; Goes Off at Shrine in Munich After Hitler Departs Early," *New York Times*, November 9, 1939
Andrews, Evan, "6 Assassination Attempts on Adolph Hitler" [last modified August 29, 2018], *History*, April 29, 2015
Gibbons, Phil, "14 Lesser-Known Stories From WWII That Should Be Made Into Movies," *Ranker*, December 22, 2021
Greenspan, Jesse, "The July Plot: When German Elites Tried to Kill Hitler," *History*, July 30, 2019
"This Day in History: Another plot to kill Hitler foiled" [last modified March 20, 2020], *History.com* November 5, 2009
Tolischus, Otto D., "Germany is Tense; Shocked By Munich Blast, People Now Feel Blow at Britain is Near," *New York Times*, November 10, 1939
Warde, Samuel, "Georg Elser Almost Assassinated Hitler Before Ending Up In A Concentration Camp," January 27, 2020

The Venlo Incident

Books: Best, Captain S. Payne, *The Venlo Incident* (Frontline Books/London/ Skyhorse Publishing, 1950)
Wikipedia: Venlo Incident; Sigismund Best; Richard Henry Stevens; The Hague; Arnhen.
Other:
"Gestapo Blamed for Venlo Clash; Witnesses Say German Secret Police Shot Netherlander and 'Kidnapped' 5 Men," *New York Times*, November 12, 1939
Jones, Nigel, "Unveiling Venlo," *HistoryNet*, March 2, 2018
Nambi, Karthick, "How one kidnap started World War II in the Netherlands," *Lessons from History*, June 7, 2020
"Nazis Charge Plot to Murder Hitler; Accuse Netherland Foreign Minister van Kleffens of Planning Killings in 1939," *New York Times*, February 18, 1942

Circular 14

Wikipedia: Aristides de Sousa Mendes; Antonio de Oliveira Salazar; Circular 14; H.A. Rey; List of countries by population in 1939; Madeleine Lebeau; Marcel Dalio; Margret Rey; Salvador Dali.

Other:
"Aristides De Sousa Mendes: His Life and Legacy," *Sousa Mendes Foundation*
Arshad, Fareeha, "The Man Who 'Almost' Saved Thousands of Innocent Lives From the Holocaust: Meet Aristides de Sousa Mendes," *Comments*
Lempkowicz, Yossi, "Holocaust Museum in Oporto, Portugal, opens, first in the Iberian peninsula," *European Jewish Press*, February 17, 2021
Reese, Catherine, "A little-known Holocaust hero saved thousands, including a boy who became a University of Utah professor," *The Salt Lake Tribune*, January 26, 2018
Tigay, Chanan, "The Untold Story of the Portuguese Diplomat Who Saved Thousands From the Nazis," *Smithsonian Magazine*, November 2021

BIG GREENIE
Books:
Cohen, Rich, *Tough Jews: Fathers, Sons, and Gangster Dreams* (Simon and Schuster, 1998)
Pasley, Fred D., *Not Guilty: The Story of Samuel S. Leibowitz* (G.P. Putnam's Sons, 1933)
Turkus, Burton B. and Feder, *Murder, Inc.: The Story of the Syndicate* (DaCapo Press, 1992 [1951])
Wikipedia: Bugsy Siegel; Frankie Carbo; Harry Greenberg; Whitey Krakow.
Other:
"Frankie Carbo, Underworld Figure Once Known as the 'Czar' of Boxing" [obituary], *New York Times*, November 11, 1976
"Greenberg Murder Laid to 'Syndicate'," *New York Times*, August 31, 1940
Harnisch, Larry, "Mob Slaying of "Big Greenie" Greenberg Retold in Bugsy Siegel Trial," *Larry Harnisch Reflects on L.A. History*, January 27, 2012

RUSSIA INVADES FINLAND
Books: Smithsonian, *A Short History of World War II* (DK London 2020 [2009])
Wikipedia: Continuation War; Finland; Finland-Russia Border; Finnish Civil War; Mannerheim Line; Winter War.
Other:
Andrews, Evan, "What Was the Winter War" [last modified September 3, 2018], *History*, November 30, 2016
"City 'Surrounded'; Rail Station and Point North of Port Claimed by Soviet Troops," *New York Times*, March 3, 1940
Eskelund, K.J., "Army of 100,000 Exiles on March As Sad Finns Leave Ceded Areas; Uprooted Families Plod to New Borders; Nation Tackles Task of Resettling 460,000 Left Without Homes," *New York Times*, March 15, 1940
"Finns Ask For Peace Negotiations; Say Mines Killed 1,000 Russians," *New York Times*, December 4, 1939
"Finns' Cabinet Resigns As Soviets Bomb Cities; New Government Expected To Seek A Truce" *New York Times*, December 1, 1939
"Finns Lay Peace To Lack Of Help; Plan Scandinavian Defense Bloc," *New York Times*, March 14, 1940
"Finns On Offensive, Raid Enemy Bases," *New York Times*, December 6, 1939
"Finns Report Soviet Drive Halted; Red 'State' Meets Moscow Terms," *New York Times*, December 3, 1939

"Russia Refuses Peace, Spurns League," *New York Times*, December 5, 1939
"Russians Start Their Invasion Of Finland; Planes Drop Bombs On Airfield At Helsinki," *New York Times*, November 30, 1939
"Soviets Set Up Red Regime On Finnish Border; Finns Rally," *New York Times*, December 2, 1939
"The International Situation," *New York Times*, December 1, 1939
"The International Situation," *New York Times*, December 2, 1939
"The International Situation," *New York Times*, March 13, 1940
"This Day in History: Stalin issues Order No. 227, outlawing cowards" [las modified July 24, 2020], *History.com*, November 5, 2009
"This Day in History: U.S.S.R. attacks Finland" [last modified November 24, 2020], *History.com*, November 5, 2009
"This Day in History: USSR expelled from the League of Nations" [last modified December 10, 2020], *History.com*, November 5, 2009

Chapter 17 ("Frankly my dear, I don't give a hoot.")

Nile Kinnick

Wikipedia: Nile Kinnick; Bob Feller; Croix de Guerre; Iowa Hawkeyes football; Phi Beta Kappa; Tom Harmon; Wendell Willkie.
Other:
Chapman, Mike, "Ironman: The Nile Kinnick Story," *Iowa History Journal*
Emmert, Mark, "Iowa's Nile Kinnick refused to 'stick to sports' and delivered a Heisman speech in 1939 that still resonates," *Gannett*, December 8, 2017
"Kinnick, Iowa Star, Calls on Boy Who Lost a Leg," *New York Times*, December 10, 1939
"Kinnick Killed in Plane At Sea; Former Iowa Football Star Loses His Life in Action," *New York Times*, June 5, 1943
Klein, Christopher, "The Surprising Stories of 7 Heisman Trophy Winners," *History*, December 6, 2021
Richardson, William D., "Kinnick, Iowa Ace, Gets Trophy Here; Sensational Back Receives Heisman Trophy at Dinner at the Downtown A.C.," *New York Times*, December 7, 1939
Rogers, Kevin, "Nile Kinnick Wins Heisman Trophy: Nile Kinnick is the Hawkeyes' greatest football player of all time," *World History Project*, 2018
"The Cornbelt Comet, Nile Kinnick, RB/Senior/University of Iowa," *Heisman.com*

The Battle of the River Plate

Books: Woodman, Richard, *The Battle Of The River Plate: A Grand Delusion* (Pen & Sword Military, 2015 [2008])
Movie: *The Battle of The River Plate*, dir. Powell, Michael, and Emeric Pressburger (Arcturus Productions, 1956)
Wikipedia: *Battle of the Heligoland Bight* (1939); *Battle of the River Plate*; Erich Raeder; German submarine U-36 (1936); Hans Langsdorff; Henry Harwood, HMS *Barham* (04); Patrick Dove (sea captain); Winston Churchill.
Other:
"Air Fleets Fight Off Helgoland; German Cruiser Sunk In The Elbe; British Submarine Hits 2 Others," *New York Times*, December 19, 1939

"Battle of the River Plate (December 13, 1939)," *Second World War History*
"British Defeat Nazi Raider in All-Day Fight," *New York Times*, December 14, 1939
"Captain, On Hitler's Order, Sinks Spee Off Montevideo After Debarking Crew," *New York Times*, December 18, 1939
"Spee Must Go By 6:30 P.M. Tomorrow; Finns Report Suomussalmi Retaken; British Planes Raid German Bases," *New York Times*, December 16, 1939
"Spee Still In Harbor At Daybreak Although Ready For Dash To Sea; Reinforced Allied Fleet Awaits Her," *New York Times*, December 17, 1939
"The International Situation," *New York Times*, December 21, 1939
"Troubling History: the controversy over a bronze eagle with swastika crest salvaged from the German battleship *Graf Spee*," *WWII History*, Volume 22, Number 6, Winter 2024
Trueman, C.N., "The Battle of the River Plate," *historylearningsite.co.uk*, May 18, 2015
"Uruguay Lets The Spee Stay For Repairs As British Mass Warships Off Montevideo," *New York Times*, December 15, 1939
"What You Need To Know About The Battle Of The River Plate," *Imperial War Museums*

GONE WITH THE WIND

Books:

Adams, Charles F., *1939: The Making of Six Great Films From Hollywood's Greatest Year* (Craven Street Books, 2014)
Harmetz, Aljean, *On The Road To Tara: The Making of Gone With The Wind* (Harry N. Abrams Publishers, 1996)
Mitchell, Margaret, *Gone With the Wind* (Macmillan Publishing Company, 1975 [1936])
Sennett, Ted, *Hollywood's Golden Year, 1939, A Fiftieth Anniversary Celebration* (St. Martin's Press, 1989)
Vieira, Mark A., *Majestic Hollywood: The Greatest Films of 1939* (Running Press, 2013)
Wikipedia: *Gone With the Wind* (film); *Gone With the Wind* (novel); Margaret Mitchell; Clark Gable; Vivien Leigh; Butterfly McQueen; Charlie Chaplin; Evelyn Keyes; Frankly, my dear, I don't give a damn; *Goodbye, Mr. Chips*; Hattie McDaniel; Myron Selznick; Paulette Goddard; Sidney Howard; 12th Academy Awards; Waterloo Bridge; William Cameron Menzies.

Other:

Berger, Meyer, "Atlanta is Won By Film of South, Rebel Yells for Miss Mitchell Mingle With Applause and Cheers of 2,000 at Premiere," *New York Times*, December 16, 1939
"Bette Davis Was 'Haunted' By Losing Out on Scarlett O'Hara in 'Gone With the Wind'," *Showbiz CheatSheet*, August 21, 2022
Chanda, Srija, "30 Best Scarlett O'Hara Quotes From 'Gone With The Wind'," *Kidadl*
Danao, Karen, "25 Scarlett O'Hara Quotes on Hope, Determination, and More," *Quote Ambition*
Dowson, Ernest Christopher, "*Cynara*" [poem], 1894
Ebert, Roger, "Gone With the Wind" [review], June 21, 1998
"Georgia Scenes," *New York Times*, December 16, 1939
"Gone With the Wind," *IMDb*

"Gone With the Wind, User Reviews," *IMDb*

Insdorf, Annette, "A Selznick Celebration," *New York Times*, February 24, 1980

Lambert, Gavin, "The Making of Gone With The Wind," *The Atlantic*, February 1973

Lindsey, Robert, "Reunion Recalls Those Gone With the Wind," *New York Times*, December 31, 1979

Mankiewicz, Ben, "Commentary on *Gone With the Wind*," *TCM*

Musto, Michael, "How Bette David Lost Out on Gone With The Wind," *The Village Voice*, August 15, 2011

"Red Paper Condemns 'Gone With The Wind,' Terms the Film a Glorification of the Ku Klux Klan," *New York Times*, December 24, 1939

Royle, Alan, "Evelyn Keyes," *Fascinating Holly wood Facts*, December 18, 2022

"This Day in History: Actress Carole Lombard killed in plane crash" [last modified January 13, 2021], *History.com*, November 13, 2009

"This Day in History: Audiences are shown a surprise preview of 'Gone With the Wind' [Last modified September 8, 2020]," *History.com* November 13, 2009

"This Day in History: Famous scene from 'Gone With the Wind' Filmed" [last modified June 26, 2020], *History.com,* November 13, 2009

"This Day in History: 'Gone With the Wind' [last modified June 29, 2020]," *History.com* November 24, 2009

`Books: Vieira, Mark A., *Majestic Hollywood: The Greatest Films of 1939* (Running Press, 2013)

Wikipedia: A Visit from St. Nicholas; Adolph Eichmann; *Hunchback of Notre Dame* (1939); Fluorescent lamp; Johnny Marks; 1939 Erzincan earthquake; Maureen O'Hara; Robert L. May; Rudolph the Red Nosed Reindeer; "Rudolph the Red-Nosed Reindeer" (song); Sonya Levien; William Dieterle.

Other:

Bracker, Milton, "1940 Born in Wild Revelry; Good Year for Nation Seen," *New York Times*, January 1, 1940

May, Robert L., "Rudolph, The Red-Nosed Reindeer" [poem], 1939

"This Day In History: Rudolph the Red-Nosed Reindeer is the #1 song on the U.S. pop charts" [last modified January 6, 2020], *History.com*, April 1, 2010

Index